TO CAP
IT ALL…
MY STORY

KENNY
SANSOM

TO CAP
IT ALL…
MY STORY
KENNY
SANSOM

WITH RITA WRIGHT

JOHN BLAKE

Published by John Blake Publishing Ltd,
3 Bramber Court, 2 Bramber Road,
London W14 9PB, England

www.johnblakepublishing.co.uk

First published in hardback in 2008
This edition published in paperback in 2010

ISBN: 978-1-84358-274-8

British Library Cataloguing-in-Publication Data:

A catalogue record for this book is available from the British Library.

Design by www.envydesign.co.uk

Printed in Great Britain by CPI Bookmarque, Croydon CR0 4TD

1 3 5 7 9 10 8 6 4 2

Papers used by John Blake Publishing are natural, recyclable products made
from wood grown in sustainable forests. The manufacturing processes conform
to the environmental regulations of the country of origin.

Every attempt has been made to contact the relevant copyright-holders,
but some were unobtainable. We would be grateful if the appropriate
people could contact us.

This book is dedicated to Elaine, Natalie, Katie, Harry, Mum and Lucky.

CONTENTS

ACKNOWLEDGEMENTS

First, going back to my terrific days at Crystal Palace, I'd like to thank the following: Peter Taylor for teaching me how to impersonate Norman Wisdom – there was so much laughter, so many jokes and wind-ups; Malcolm Allison for telling me I'd never make a left-back – you are pure class, Malcolm; Arnie Warren for spotting me – weren't *you* the lucky one, Arnie? Terry Venables – the main man.

Moving on to my Highbury days, I must give Don Howe a special mention – the man who followed me everywhere. Thanks for pushing me to run, run, run – seriously, you kept me going for a while.

Thanks, Terry Neill, you were brave to do that swap with Clive Allen; or was there more to it? George Graham – thank you for all your help, for teaching me so much, and I'm just sorry I didn't listen to you. I still remember the time when we were in Scotland for a pre-season match and after the first half you turned to Nigel Winterburn and said, 'That's how you play left-back.'

During my long England career I was managed by two of the best. I'd like to thank Ron Greenwood for welcoming me into the England squad and giving me my debut against Wales at Wembley when we drew 0–0. Bobby Robson – thanks for remembering my name sometimes, Bobby. Not all the time though – I was Charlie on more than one occasion. They were great times and I visited so many wonderful places with you and England.

But it all began back in south London when Joe Wilson, my very first manager, put so much work, time and dedication into us young lads. For me this was the start of something special.

I will be eternally grateful for all the PFA have done for me (and remain to do) over the years. They are a fantastic organisation.

To all my family – yes, all. We are a big family with lots of uncles, aunts, cousins and all of their children. My brothers and sisters Maureen, Midge, Peter and David and their partners. To Elaine's family – Alice and the late Bill. Sister Sheila and brother-in-law Gordon.

As for friends – they say if you have a handful of true friends you are lucky. Well, I am lucky. They know who they are: Kevin Carlier, Brian Wells, Ray Radmore, David Mendes, Tom Watt, Eamond, James Chitty, Duncan Jelley, Carmine, Linda, Alex Amuro, John Laws, Paul Weston, Perry Groves, Karl Howman, Steve Matthews, Tony Wilkins, Tony Hoskins, Danny and the staff at Thai Pan Chinese restaurant, Ray and Pat, Ray and Lyn from Barnett, Ron and Jackie, John and Jackie Leach (Harry's godparents), and Ian and Sophia Lasslett.

I can't leave out Tony De Silva at the Montechoro Hotel in Portugal as he has always looked after Elaine and I so well.

And finally – well not quite, not yet anyway – Sporting Chance Clinic and all involved in this unique setup, including Tony Adams, Peter Kay, James West and Julian. Thanks, you guys.

I'd like to thank Hy Money for the excellent personal photos she has taken of me and my family over the years – they are very special. Finally, a big thanks to the co-author of my life story, psychotherapist Rita Wright. As well as being my ghost writer she has been able to help me gain a clearer understanding of myself through these difficult times.

FOREWORD

Just like the legendary England left-back, Kenny Sansom, I love a song – and the one that comes to mind when I think of Kenny is, 'Thanks for the Memory'. That might sound a bit like an obituary, but I can assure you that one of the best left-backs the world has ever seen is still very much alive and kicking.

My first impression of young Kenny Sansom was, 'You might not be very tall, son, but you've got the body of a middleweight boxer with determination and guts to match.' He was 16 years old, short and stocky with tremendous upper-body power. But it was his lightning pace that made him one of the best left-backs of all time.

The combination of his natural talent and hard work ethic ensured his success; he was quite simply magnificent. It took only nine years for him to notch up an amazing eighty-six caps for England, and I make him one of the top three left-backs ever to grace this country – the other two being Kenny's successor, Stuart Pearce, and the terrific Ray Wilson.

I am very proud to have worked with Kenny. Thinking back to the seventies when I coached and managed him brings a smile to my face. He was warm and funny – a real character and joker. He took this easy manner onto the training ground where he added determination and hard work to his repertoire. Add a touch of genius and we have the package that has made him a football legend.

Kenny and I spent hours and hours practising skills and tactical moves – he opposite me, with us moving step for step as he copied my footwork. It was like looking in the mirror. Magical.

For almost a decade nobody could go by him. Passing Kenny Sansom was impossible. He created terrible problems for the opposition as he nicked the ball and made off with it down the left wing. Although a defender, he also loved to attack the game.

Those days at Crystal Place in the late seventies and early eighties were brilliant. Kenny is a true family man and therefore fitted in well with the 'family ethic' at Selhurst Park. I had just taken over from Malcolm Allison and we were floundering in the Third Division. I sensed the boys in the team were special and we were about to go to the top. I was proved right.

By the 1979–80 season, we were flying high in the First Division – today's Premiership; and we were widely referred to as 'the Team of the Eighties'

In the summer of 1980, I sold Kenny to Arsenal for more than a million. I was sorry he was leaving Selhurst Park, but also knew this was the right move for the young lad who was soon to become 'King Kenny' of the Arsenal.

Ron Greenwood rated Kenny highly. He knew he had all the qualities needed to be a part of the England squad. Everyone in the world of football has great affection for him.

But life is a funny old thing, as is the world of the footballer. Their career is a marathon – not a sprint. Staying power is an important ingredient in the psyche of a footballer. Yet throughout this long-distance run there are times when the player finds himself in a lonely place with time on his hands, and he can get lost in those moments.

FOREWORD

I know Kenny gave 110 per cent to his work. But off the pitch, away from the glare of centre-stage, he was struggling in silence with his addictions. I've seen it all before with greats like George Best and Gazza. George didn't make it, Gazza is trying, and now Kenny is going to tell you how his biggest battle is being won.

Now he's at a crossroads. If he is hungry enough and prepared to put in just a fraction of the hard work I've seen in the past, he has the world at his left foot. (The right one's not up to much!).

In the 1986 World Cup, Kenny was involved in one of the greatest football dramas of all time. When Diego Maradona scored his infamous illegal goal against England – allegedly with a little help from Him upstairs – Kenny was in the middle of the chaos. I think you'll enjoy reading his full and frank account of what really happened.

Kenny and his family have had a tough time of late, but he's a steely character. You don't get to be England's number one unless you're special. And Kenny Sansom is special all right.

I always advised him to keep something up his sleeve – to hold something in reserve. Thank God he listened!

Terry Venables
April 2008

INTRODUCTION

KNOWING ME, KNOWING KENNY

I was born lucky. I can't emphasise this fact enough. Although my dad left my mum and his children before I could even walk, I still consider my life to have been blessed. During the sixties my dad lived the life of Riley with the notorious gangsters in London's East End, and his sudden departure was a terrible blow to my mum. Although not big in stature, Louise Rose had a sturdy backbone and a cracking personality a mix that stood her in great stead, and in turn ensured her ability to raise happy and confident kids who would have the chance to reach their potential.

During my teenage years my boss and mentor at Crystal Palace, Terry Venables, gave me untold amounts of solid advice, but the biggest nugget of wisdom he passed on to me was, 'The harder you work, the luckier you become, Kenny.'

I kind of knew this already, so he simply confirmed my own beliefs. Mum had already taught me all about loyalty and trust. Loyalty was inbred in me, and I earned respect by giving my mum all her change back after going up the shop to buy her a loaf of bread. 'You can keep that sixpence, son,' she said, grinning. 'That's for being honest.' I learned to love that warm feeling you get from pleasing someone you care about.

Good fortune guided me along the winding road that has taken me to the far corners of the world representing my country in the beautiful game. I suppose, in a sense, I've kept my lucky star in my pocket, waiting for a rainy day – and thank God for that, because let me tell you: when it finally rained, it bucketed down.

I bided my time till I was ready to share my story, because I didn't want to pen a run-of-the-mill autobiography. It seemed as if suddenly anyone and everyone was writing their memoirs. Now I'm looking forward to telling you all about my life as a boy on the streets of London, close to where the Bow Bells chimed, and am excited about telling you previously unknown tales about legends I am proud to call friends – heroes, to name but a few, such as Kevin Keegan, Gary Lineker and Ray Wilkins. I can't wait to get stuck into stories about my time at Highbury, and tell you all about great characters like Charlie Nicholas and Frank Stapleton and, later on, Paul Merson, Perry Groves and the man who succeeded me in captaining the mighty Arsenal – the one and only Tony Adams.

Over the years the media have caught hold of snippets of information about my lifestyle off the pitch and attempted to magnify them, but with no success. I have to thank my wife Elaine for quite literally shooing the intrusive press down our pathway. I think the closest I've come to being linked with another woman was when some jerk asked Elaine if she knew I was having an affair with Fatima Whitbread. I know, I know, it's a long story – and I'll tell you about it later.

I'm a simple guy with simple needs, but somewhere along the glitzy path of fame simplicity became something in the past, and everything seemed complicated and a terrible struggle.

Gambling and drinking are insidious habits that grow slowly into addiction. Along the way the illness tricks you into believing it's your friend, and it's only later, when your power is stolen and you've spiralled out of control, that you realise it's your enemy. If you're lucky you catch the devil in time. You're damned if you don't.

But, hey, as I said, I'm a lucky bugger.

Nowadays, the man in the street who still recognises me asks brightly for my autograph. 'Hello, Kenny – how are you doing?'

I throw him a genuine smile and we have a brief chat. After I've written, 'Be Lucky, Regards, Kenny Sansom – No. 3', we go off in our different directions and he thinks he knows me. But he doesn't. Football fans know Kenny the footballer; a handful of close friends are acquainted with the joker in me who enjoys entertaining and doing impersonations; but no one as yet knows the private man – the real me.

Here's the story the tabloids once offered me a small fortune to tell. It's been a long wait, but I think you'll find it was worth it. I know I do.

Kenny Sansom – No. 3

CHAPTER ONE

BORN TO BE LUCKY

My teenage heroes were Frank Spencer, Norman Wisdom, Steptoe and Son, Del Boy and Rodney. The closest I ever got to a copper was putting on a dirty old coat and impersonating Detective Columbo. There was never any chance I'd go down the same road as some of my relatives.

How many books begin with, 'I was born and raised in a humble but happy environment'? Lots, thank goodness, and I'm glad to say I join the ranks of the lucky ones.

I came into the world on 26 September 1958 in my mum's bedroom at 55 Jardin Street. There I joined my three sisters and a big brother in a small south London prefab – and, for those of you too young to know what a prefab is, it's a kind of 'bitsa' home, made up of slabs of concrete. Home was small and crowded, but also warm and happy. In those days back doors were left wide open welcoming in neighbours for cups of tea and a slice of homemade cake, and all problems were shared and aired. We were of the fortunate generation, raised in an age of relative innocence where the worst local crime was to kick a ball through old Mrs

Smith's window and the most feared punishment of all was a clip round the ear.

The last child to be born into the family was my little brother David, and, shortly after that, my dad George left home to lead a more exciting life over in the East End, where he and his brothers chose to live on the wrong side of the law, rubbing shoulders with the Krays. It has been said that Ronnie and Reggie asked my dad to be their driver but that he turned them down. I find it hard to believe. Not that they asked him, but that he had the cheek to say, 'No, thanks,' and they didn't shoot his kneecaps off. Everyone knows that what the Twins wanted the Twins generally got.

My dad was one of the original 'spivs' – always ducking and diving – and I'm glad I wasn't around him to be influenced by his lifestyle. He never went to prison and I've heard it said he was too much of a coward to do anything really bad – unlike his brother Terry, who was, by association, involved in 'the crime of the century' – the Great Train Robbery, and is named in Mary Wisbey's bestseller, *A Gangster's Moll*. Mary was the daughter of Terry Wisbey, the girlfriend of 'Mad Frankie Fraser' for 10 years, and the godchild of Freddie Foreman. All three were notorious gangsters and all three were good friends with the Sansom brothers. There must have been something about that sinister world that fascinated the Sansom brothers and fed their edgy personalities.

If I am to believe family gossip, Dad inherited his ways from his father, and probably from his father before him. It's as though you just get set on a path and breaking strong patterns in families is difficult.

Dad couldn't stand being bored. So it should come as no surprise that he became addicted to anything that would give him an instant buzz. Needy kids like us didn't figure in his world. We didn't provide the instant 'hit' he craved. So off he went to find an atmosphere that did it for him.

I guess Dad was never going to hang round a decent woman like my mum for too long – not with all the tarts (his word, not mine) available in his chosen world, the underworld.

I have no memories of young fatherly love – *any* fatherly love, to be honest. But I can't say I missed him or felt I was lacking in care and affection, as my mum made up for his absence by making her children the centre of her universe. She couldn't be bothered with men after he left – well, he'd come and gone so many times and was such a womaniser that he ruined any trust she had in men.

Thankfully I was lucky enough to have my older brother Peter around. Being 10 years older than I was, he took on a paternal role and always looked out for me. He even chose my name. 'I like the name Kenny,' he told my mum and my mum said, 'Kenny it is, then.'

When I was about 2 years old we all moved to a small estate in Tulse Hill, which wasn't far from Crystal Palace, where I was much later to become one of the players dubbed the 'Team of the Eighties'.

Peter missed our dad something terrible, and went off to see him as much as he could. I remember his saying, 'I need my dad.' It was weird for me to hear that, and later very difficult to comprehend his loyalty. I guess being a decade older than I was, he got to know dad as a person, but for me he was no more than a man who'd left us.

If there was pain or anger inside, I never felt it and I guess friends and football filled the gap where grief might have otherwise festered.

My mum has often said I was sad whenever he went away. 'You had a broken heart, Kenny,' she would sigh. It all sounds a bit too far-fetched to me, but as they say, there's no smoke without fire, and it's for sure the fire ignited and raged within me as time went by.

All I can say with absolute honesty is that my mum more than made up for the loss of my dad. She was, and still is, in the words of the Barry White song, 'My first, my last, my everything'.

All of us adore her and are eternally grateful for the effort she put into bringing us up. She may have been small in stature, but she was a giant in every other way.

Off she'd trot in the late evening to do a night shift cleaning. But before she went she made sure we had everything we needed. Always determined to be around for us, she only ever worked while we were either asleep or at school. We were 'well turned out', as they say. Neat and tidy with shiny hair and scrubbed faces, we wore our Omo-white shirts with pride. I remember one kid asking, 'How come you and your David are always so clean?' I didn't have an answer – that's just how it was. But it set a precedent, because all through my career I kept my kit spotless while all around me were knee deep in mud with grass stains all over their bums.

There were no washing machines or modern-day gadgets to make life easier in our house. I tell you, the women of that era just soldiered on against any adversity, and my mum was one of them. She led the bloody parade.

Mum features heavily in my story and quite rightly so, as she has been with me every step of the way – following me all over the world. My number-one fan, she loved telling people, 'My son's the famous footballer you know. My son's Kenny Sansom.'

I suppose you could say she was bragging, but she did it in such an endearing manner that everyone who met her wanted to spend more time in her company. If she asked for a lift to a match people would almost fight each other to have the company of lively Louise in their car. She was pure entertainment.

Born Rose Louise Culwick, Mum had been one of twenty children. Twenty! Imagine that. By all accounts, my granddad was a bit of a character, and I'm told he enjoyed a pale ale – I'd say he enjoyed much more than that.

My Nanny Culwick gave him the responsibility of registering their children – she was probably too knackered to think about such trivia as what to name her latest baby. Granddad loved the names Rose and Louise so much that he gave two of his daughters the same name. He'd intended to call one Rose Louise and the other Louise Rose. But he got in a muddle and so they both got named Rose Louise. I'm guessing he'd downed a few pale ales beforehand

– and perhaps a Scotch or two in celebration. To end the confusion they referred to mum as Louise and her sister as Rose.

All the Culwicks were knee high to a grasshopper and Mum was probably the smallest of them all. Her brothers were stocky, though. At 5 foot 8, I have inherited the Culwick stature, with short legs and a solid frame.

One of Dad's brothers was a middleweight boxer, so it should have come as no surprise to me when Terry Venables pointed out how lucky I was to have a six-pack without trying. It was true. Other boys had to sweat their nuts off in the gym or on the training pitch to build muscles that didn't even come near mine. Thank God I wasn't scrawny. If I'd been born minus the muscles, I'd never have made it in football.

Mum's family were all full of life. My sister Maureen has this funny old black-and-white picture in her album of all the Culwicks waiting to board an old-fashioned bus, which was to take them to the seaside for a day out, courtesy of ITV.

My auntie Rose (who was by now Rose Welsh) had appeared on a new television programme called *Take Your Pick*, hosted by Michael Miles, and won the family an 'away day' to Margate. This show was hugely popular with the public. Up till 1955 viewers could receive only BBC, but the introduction of ITV was very exciting. Suddenly, television wasn't all serious news stories but had game shows, soaps and comedy.

In his show, which drew in massive audiences, Michael Miles invited audience members to go up onto the stage, where they would answer questions and were then given a key to a box. In the box was a prize. Smiley Michael Miles welcomed Auntie Rose onto stage and among the cheering of the lively audience he tried to buy the key back off her for £20. Good old Rose stood her ground and ended up winning the prize of a holiday for herself and her family.

The following weekend an old green bus pulled up outside No. 133 Kennington Lane, which was Nanny Culwick's home, fifty family members and friends climbed aboard and off they all went for a good old jolly-up down in Margate.

Whether they were cowboys or angels, both the Sansoms and the Culwicks were colourful characters. No one was academically bright, but from spivvy George Harry Sansom to his English Rose Louise, it was pure entertainment all the way.

Mum told me they'd met at a local dance hall close to Westminster Bridge. By all accounts he was not only very handsome but also a hardworking man – just the type my mum was looking for. Like his dad, he had worked the markets, and it wasn't until later when times got hard that he found he could earn large sums of money the easy way. Mum said they were happy together until his brothers 'turned his head'.

My brother Peter remembered Dad having very little cash in the early days, but that he always managed to get hold of money when things got desperate. It was a typical feast or famine lifestyle. Although Peter hated to admit it, he always knew deep down that Flash George destroyed Mum's trust in men, and, if you took away his good looks and seductive manner, he was really a dirty dog. But he was a dog in heavy disguise. He made Mum laugh and brightened her world. It's little wonder, then, that she took him back time and time again – until she really *had* had enough.

As for me, I knew nothing of this man called 'Dad'. He meant nothing to me or my life. I was happy that he was never around, but, unfortunately, he came into it with a loud bang when I became famous. You could say he chose to be with me when it suited him and being around me and my new world enhanced his life – not mine. My dad's wish to be around famous people, whether on the wrong or right side of the law, was to cause me untold trouble and chaos.

CHAPTER TWO

KIDS ON THE BLOCK

Like our fathers before us, we formed gangs as children. We had our small tribes and let off bangers and Jumping Jack fireworks to scare our enemies. Never in a million years would it have entered our heads to use knives and guns like the gangs roaming our streets today. Our tribal gangs would rather play football or cricket against each other than look for trouble. Revenge was not on our minds.

The Sansom kids were all wild and free, but I think my little brother David and I were the naughtiest. We took no end of risks. Nicking Mars bars from Woolworth's was a must for us. Although we never went short of essentials such as chops and chips, there wasn't much spare money left over for sweets. Anyway, if the truth be known, we'd rather enjoyed the thrill of grabbing the chocolate bars and running away.

Playing 'Knock Down Ginger' filled hours of potential boredom and by the age of 8 we had progressed to nicking lead from roofs.

The scrap-metal man must have heard us coming from streets away as we pushed a pram full of lead towards his yard. We must have looked a comical sight and, of course, he knew we'd been up to mischief, but he always paid up and we eagerly shared out our ill-gotten proceeds.

We never went out looking for trouble. Who does? But trouble always seemed to find us. It's funny how that happens. Nothing was our fault, you know. Like the afternoon we happened upon an old factory with a smashed window.

We had been entertaining ourselves by jumping across rooftops when we landed on the roof of what looked like a derelict warehouse. On closer inspection we were astonished to see loads of marbles inside. Well – this was like the Crown Jewels to us scallywags. Marbles! My God, finding a shedload of marbles was the luckiest thing ever. So we thought.

We scrambled through the broken glass and found ourselves gawping at Aladdin's cave. From the outside, the building had appeared to be abandoned; but it wasn't. It was a bloody chandelier factory, and the marbles were bloody crystals.

How could we possibly leave without pocketing some of the gems? Not a chance. We were going to take the jewels home to our mum and then we would be rich. Bingo! The lottery was won. But we didn't get far.

As we were boldly leaving with our stash, the police sirens screamed down the lane and flashing blue lights came into view, scaring the hell out of us. Being a nippy little bugger, I was off up the drainpipe and across the roof before David was even out of the window. But how could I leave him? I was supposed to be looking after him. Mum would kill me if I abandoned him.

As I peered over the drainpipe I could see a burly policeman dragging David by the scruff of his neck over to his panda car. Damn! We had so nearly got away.

I shimmied back down the drainpipe and slid into the panda car next to my terrified brother. We were both wearing grey shorts and long socks that had fallen down around our ankles – so his bony knees were visibly knocking. We had been nicked. I was 7 and he was 5. What in God's name was our mum going to say? We knew she loved us, but we also knew she would kill us for bringing trouble to her door.

Thankfully, the policemen took pity on our sobs and pleas for mercy and let us go with a clip behind the ear – but a great lesson was learned. We never nicked again. At the ripe old age of 7, I knew I didn't like getting into trouble.

Maybe this is why I've only been booked once and only once been given a red card (Crystal Palace v Coventry). I can't stand being *told* off, let alone be *sent* off. Being sent off meant being in someone's bad books and therefore unloved. I needed to be loved.

I remember clearly that, once, my mum gave me one and sixpence (7?p) and sent me up the shops to get her a loaf of bread and some potatoes (for chips). The items only came to a shilling (5p) and for some reason I forgot the sixpence (2?p) change was in my pocket. When I found it I gave it straight to mum and she said, 'For your honesty, Kenny, you can keep that sixpence.'

I was so chuffed and felt so good about myself that during my growing years I was never in danger of dishonesty. It was a bigger buzz to be trusted and loved, than naughty and always in trouble. Not that there wasn't temptation all around me. I was growing up in south London, after all, where being naughty was the norm.

One of my best mates, Duncan Jelley, was still nicking stuff and selling lead to buy sweets. Although I was envious of his stash of goodies, I vowed I was never going down that scary road again. They say you make your mind up about important things by the time you are 7 years old and I'd go along with that theory. But Duncan's done all right for himself, and he too has managed to stay on the right side of the law.

Running wild was what I loved the most. The thrill of jumping from one building to another and not knowing whether you'd actually make it to the other side in one piece was wicked.

I remember one day clearly. A group of us were scampering over the rooftops when we came to an extra-wide gap with a long drop to the ground. I calculated I could just about make it to the other side and as usual was the leader – so I went first.

One by one the others ran and jumped – hurling themselves to safety. Bringing up the rear was my mate Johnny Laws. Poor old Johnny didn't quite make it. Sorry to say this, but it was bloody hilarious – he hit the side of the brick wall and slid down the building. It was exactly like a scene from *Tom and Jerry*. He must have seen stars. Fortunately, we weren't too high up and he wasn't seriously hurt. Had we been higher, he would have been a goner. He's a black-cab driver now, and I haven't seen him in ages – but I haven't forgotten him. He fancied himself as a bit of a goalie, and, if I remember right, he *was* pretty handy.

Being a daredevil was highly enjoyable and, taking everything into consideration, I was lucky to survive without serious injury.

That said, I fell out of a tree once and got a painful poke in my right eye with a stick. Because I was 'Lucky Kenny', though, the stick just missed blinding me by a millimetre, and all I'm left with as proof of near devastation is a scar on my eyelid. If I had been blinded in one eye my football career would never have happened, and I might well have ended up getting into hot water like some of my schoolmates and learning the hard way: behind bars.

When I think back to the craziness of some of our antics I go cold. Take Bonfire Night, for example. We set rockets off in corridors, threw bangers through letterboxes, and Jumping Jacks found their way into enclosed spaces like phone boxes – while people were inside. Now I shudder at the lunacy of it all, but watching the mayhem was hilarious at the time.

One year we built the most humungous bonfire on the green in the centre of our neighbourhood square. When we lit it we were both excited and proud. But, as the flames licked high into the winter night sky, our excitement turned to panic and then horror as it flared up and went out of control.

The next thing we knew, three fire engines were clanging their way though the chaos and aiming their hose pipes at our magnificent bonfire. Once we knew it wasn't going to be a case of 'London's Burning' and that the firemen were going to save us, we began jumping on the hoses. Right little sods we were.

Another incident wasn't so funny. There was this old and abandoned Morris Minor parked up near to our flats, and one day David, Duncan Jelley and I decided to jump all over it. It really wasn't the most exciting of games, so David decided to light a match and throw it into the petrol tank. *Flash!* It blew back into his little face and he lit up like a Christmas tree. It was like a scene from a horror movie as he screamed in agony. Fortunately, a man was passing by and witnessed our stupidity. He turned into Action Man. He threw off his heavy sheepskin coat and wrapped it tightly around David's burning face before getting him to casualty in record-breaking time.

There is no doubt about it: that man saved my brother's life. Although David was in hospital for weeks and still bears the scars today, he is lucky to be alive.

I was 9 years old when I got into football. I was doing all sorts of crazy things and unwittingly building up skills that would one day ensure me worldwide success. One of my favourite pastimes was balancing on fences. The other kids would try in vain to copy me, but always wobbled and fell off after a few steps. But I could go round and round the fence surrounding our flats for miles and miles.

This was probably my first experience of showing off. It's no good saying I wasn't a show off. If playing football in front of the huge audiences the world over isn't a form of showing off, I don't know what is? But hey, that doesn't make me a bad person – just a go-getter.

Back indoors, life was calmer. My four older siblings, Peter, Maureen, Mary and Midge (we never had a Mungo, and Midge was short for Margaret, and I can't tell you the chaos when letters arrived for Miss M Sansom), and little David and I, had a brilliant home life. I was a Tarzan out of doors and I also resembled him at the dinner table. I really don't know why this happened, but I always ate with my fingers. The knives and forks were laid at the table, but I never used them.

We ate chops and chips a lot. First I'd pick up the chops and munch on them, and then I'd demolish the chips. Why on earth would I want to spoil the experience by using a knife and fork? This habit began at an early age and went on all through my teenage years, and I never saw anything wrong in enjoying my food in this way.

But I clearly remember when my first tour with the England Youth Squad caused my mum a bad headache. She was far more worried about my eating habits than how well I played. She *needed* to be worried – I didn't have a clue what to do with the knife and fork and so I picked up my meat just as I did indoors. It took a long time to drop the jungle way of eating, and I still like to chew on the odd bone.

I have always found eating a great pleasure. Our kitchen cupboards were always full of nuts, crisps, lemonade, cola and doughnuts – food that is scorned upon today. Hot crusty bread and dripping was another favourite. But I guess I was always active enough to work off the calories.

(By the time I was a teenager playing for the Crystal Palace youth team I was still munching on bread and dripping for breakfast, and devouring three pork chops before a match. I can't imagine the players of today eating such 'naughty' food. Arsène Wenger would blow a fuse if he ever caught players such as Cesc Fàbregas eating beef dripping on toast, but it was my staple diet.)

My sisters attended Brockwell primary school in Tulse Hill and close by was Brockwell Park. There was a great big outdoor pool that I believe is still there today but not used as much as it was back in the sixties. One of the lifeguards was a character I've never forgotten. We nicknamed him 'Dave the Whale'. He was this gentle giant who dived in the pool without making a splash and was the most elegant swimmer I've ever seen. I could watch him for ages as he glided through the water.

We kids spent endless hours swinging in trees and playing football in Brockwell Park. My finely tuned balancing skills ensured I never fell out of trees, but one day another incident occurred that could have put paid to my career. A boy called James threw a sliver of flint and it wedged in the artery behind my knee. Blood was squirting in great arcs from the back of my leg, and, if it hadn't been for the quick action of passers-by, I would have been in real trouble, which would have been tragic, as by now football was well and truly in my blood.

Every day after school David and I would rush out onto the square of grass by our flats and meet up with our friends – playing footie until the sun went down. Having so many mates to kick the ball around with made me very happy.

I have been told by the other boys that they knew David and I had something special – that we were always a pace ahead and would always win the ball. They said they would always choose us to be on their side, as it meant defeating our opponents by a huge goal difference.

In the early days I was always in goal and, despite my size, I was quick enough to save most of the shots. David was probably a better player than I was at that time, and although he never became a top-class footballer, I'm certain he could have if he'd had the same luck as I had, because he really was a classy player.

By the time I was secondary-school age we were on the move again. Home was now a flat on the Brandon council estate, close to the Elephant and Castle, and not far from the local pie-and-mash shop. (I know, I know, I ate too many pies in the end, but that was to come much later.) My older siblings had by now found places of their own, so there were just David, Mum and I now – a solid little unit.

The two-mile journey to school, which was in Lambeth Walk, kept me on my toes. But I never walked on the pavement. Instead I balanced on fences again. Don't ask me why I chose not to walk on the pavement like normal people, because I don't know. Perhaps it was the challenge of not falling off. Or maybe I wanted to be different. Whatever. The reason is not important. The main thing was it gave me the most wonderful sense of balance that was to help to take me into the world of top-flight football.

There was this fantastic fish-and-chip shop up the Elephant. At lunchtime my mates and I rushed out for chips, free crackling and cola, before going back for afternoon lessons. Then at home time I'd hurry back so I could play football till the sun went down. I was never, ever still.

My best friends at Brandon became my very first teammates.

Joining me and my brother David was Johnnie 'Awight' Laws – the boy who'd flattened his face *Tom and Jerry* style. Then there was Tony Morris who was great at right-back – a really good footballer who might have gone far. Barry Fulbrook and Arthur Duncan joined us to complete our five-a-side team. I clearly remember our winning a five-a-side tournament, which fuelled my passion for winning.

All that swinging through trees and jumping over rooftops was starting to pay off, and my eye-to-foot coordination became finely tuned during these years. My reactions were getting sharper and sharper by the day, and by now I found I was moving in the right direction before being fully aware of which way I was going.

This was in the swinging sixties, when London, like the rest of the country, was living life to the full and 'anything goes' was the theme. For those of us too young to be enjoying 'free sex', we got our kicks by playing football, anywhere and everywhere. We were lucky. The grown-ups welcomed our free spirits and high jinx.

Today there are miserable 'No Ball Games Allowed' signs every-where – but for us that wonderful sense of freedom and wildness just went on and on.

Our natural curiosity was nourished and we learned from experience rather than being told what we could or couldn't do. There are no lessons greater than falling down and having to get up again.

Next I played for a team called Spring Park Wolves. Our greatest moment was when we won the Dewar Trophy. The match was played in Shirley, near Croydon, and it was the most exciting experience of my very young football career.

By now I was as athletic as I was agile and capable of playing in any position, which was just as well, because our left-back, Terry Eames, got injured and there was no one waiting in the wings to step into his boots, so I got the job.

Being switched from goalie to left-back was the beginning of my journey to the top of my profession. My guardian angel must have been sitting on my shoulder, because I wasn't growing at the same rate as the other boys and therefore goalkeeping was never going to be my forte. Being a Peter Shilton or Ray Clemence would have been impossible. So a lad called Terry Bruna became goalkeeper and I moved over to the position I was to make my own for many, many years.

We had raw talent and from Monday to Saturday were rarely away from the local parks. But, without a doubt, Sunday was the best day of the week.

Sunday morning was all about playing football and the afternoon was spent in front of the television watching *The Big Match*, which started at two o'clock and coincided with a roast dinner. Then afterwards at least fourteen of us would congregate on the green and have the time of our lives.

Every spare minute of every day was spent with a ball balancing on the end of my foot. And, despite my terrible diet, I was as fit as a fiddle. I guess chips just worked for me.

KENNY SANSOM

DOING THE LAMBETH WALK

I went to an all-boys school called Beaufoy Secondary School, which was situated in the Lambeth Walk, south London, and it was during my time here that I won my first England schoolboys' cap. The Chelsea legend John Hollins presented me with it in a big elaborate ceremony in the main hall we used for assembly. John gave a great big speech to all the boys about sport and education. He told us that football was great, but that our schoolwork must come first. Later, when we were alone, he whispered to me, 'Just do what you want, Kenny. If it's football that's in your blood, then go for it.' I willingly took his advice.

Our sports teacher was Mr Bond. My name is Bond – James Bond. Oh, he was so smooth and fit. He was also excellent at his job. I can't say he actually produced top-class athletes, but he was enthusiastic and encouraging, which was good enough.

When I was playing football for England schoolboys while at Beaufoy, there was another pupil playing basketball for the country. Mr Bond nurtured any boy who demonstrated talent, so I guess that, as well as being a smoothie, he was also a great motivator. Later I was to be managed by another smoothie, George 'Stroller' Graham, but that was way down the line.

This was the late sixties in London and there were lots of black lads living in our area. Attitudes to racism, which had been born out of ignorance more than anything else, were rapidly changing. My parents had been raised in the heart of postwar London at a time when close-knit communities resented what they perceived to be an intrusion in their 'manor', but I'm glad to say this was never an issue for us. A generation down the line made a big difference. Later on I was to become great pals with Viv Anderson (the first black player to represent England) and Vince Hillier (my big buddy at Crystal Palace), so, even if I had taken any of these small-minded prejudices on board, it would have been wiped out when I met these true gentlemen.

I was in Tudor House, and there is no way on earth you could describe our housemaster as smooth. He was a big black man who stood for no nonsense whatsoever. If you misbehaved you got the slipper and there was no escaping it. I'd like to say I was smart enough never to get caught, but I was driven by fear more than by brains. Having some old boy whack me over the backside with anything at all filled me with terror.

At least my fear made me sharp and my little legs run faster than the wind. I'm a bit embarrassed to confess that sometimes I would get a mate of mine to carry out a prank on my behalf. I'd think up something wicked and then pass the dirty deed on. I'd feel guilty for a while, but then my sense of humour, which was always waiting in the wings, used to click in and, even though I say it myself, we would all end up roaring with laughter.

Some of the boys may have had a sore arse, but not Sansom. My arse stayed a slipper-free zone. I'm talking about daft stuff here – never anything serious. School meant sport, lessons and hopping the wag – normal schooling for most of us.

One of my best mates, Tony Morris, lived in a flat not too far from our school and his parents were out at work all day, so naturally it was his home we invaded on a regular basis. We'd sit there chatting about football and girls while scoffing choc-ices and lollies out of his freezer.

I wasn't a rough, tough, kid – far from it. I only ever had one fight, and that was a reaction to catching some rotten kid banging my brother David's head on the ground. I didn't have a violent bone in my body, and still haven't, but I saw red that day. David and I, like most brothers, often argued, but if outsiders threatened us we would defend our own.

Defending has always been a bit of a theme in my life. I find it quite ironic that I could defend for my country for almost a decade, but that I often found myself too afraid to defend those close to me. Take Elaine, my childhood sweetheart and wife of 27 years, for example...

CHAPTER THREE

ELAINE, FAMILY LINKS AND LOVE

The day my mother went into labour with me dawned a fine autumn day. I had a home birth and Bill Sansom's wife, Auntie Margaret, who was known to the whole neighbourhood on the Old Kent Road as Maggie, helped ease my tiny body into the world. Listening to stories of my birth and all my siblings running around the house reads like a Martina Cole novel, and I never tire of listening to the nostalgia my big sister Maureen likes to tell.

My cousin Elaine has also told me the whole story about the kettle boiling in the kitchen, endless cups of tea poured for the anxiously waiting family and friends, and my mum as calm as you like. When my healthy lungs were filled with enough London air, I yelled the place down, which made everyone very happy. Cousin Elaine was the first to enter my life. Soon there would be another Elaine.

THE TWO E'S

First, as we've seen, there were Rose Louise and Rose Louise – just to confuse everyone. Then, when I was a young teenager, my cousin Elaine introduced me to another Elaine – who was to become *my* Elaine. They were such good friends that everyone referred to them as 'The two E's'.

Both Elaines were lookers. They just *had it* – they had that special magic you can't put your finger on and identify with clarity. It's a feeling – an instinct – and all you know for sure is you can't walk away from it. I suppose you could say she was a 'bloke magnet', but she never bothered with anyone but yours truly.

I was shorter than most of the boys, so it was very handy that my gal was 5 foot nothing. My cousin wasn't any taller, either – so I guess we were all short arses together. Nice arses, though – theirs, that is. (Mine was a good arse as well, until it became a bit lardy and the boys on the terraces began to sing, 'He's fat, he's round, he bounces on the ground – Kenny Sansom!')

They were fabulous dancers and would spend hours indoors practising and perfecting their routines so they could wow the crowds at local discos – and wow them they did. While the girls were strutting their stuff on the dance floor, I was strutting around the football clubs and pitches of every corner of London – everywhere south of Watford. I was loving my life. I was doing what I was born to do and had all the support in the world.

Terry Venables used to have this nickname for me. He called me Miguel and said it was because every time I left training I'd say, 'I'm off to see "me gal" now'. And Elaine *was* my gal, right from the very first day I set eyes on her pretty blue eyes. It took a little while until we announced we were girlfriend and boyfriend, but when it happened it came as no surprise to anyone.

We'd first met at a local youth club when I was 10 and she was a whole 9 months older than I was. But it was later, when we were both holidaying on Canvey Island at a caravan park that was practically the Sansoms' second home, that we became an item.

I remember the day I knew I loved Elaine. She was sitting on a horse, patting his head and smiling at me. Her horse wouldn't budge, so I told her squeeze her legs tight to the horse, and then nudge him (well, kick, really, but that sounds awful) and then he'd move on. Off she went with a jolt and a shriek, leaving me standing there smitten.

My brother David fancied her as well and he actually asked her out first, but she turned him down. I thought this left the coast clear for me, but I was wrong. She was seeing someone else, so I had to wait a while longer before she would say yes. Some years later, she would walk down the aisle and say 'I do' – but for now it was a case of courting and getting to know each other.

Elaine has always had more balls, as it were, than I have. I was a terrible wimp when it came to keeping her safe. Boys have always been expected to walk their girls home and ensure their safety, but it didn't quite work out that way for us.

I would hold her hand as we walked down East Lane and Camberwell New Road, and everything was hunky-dory until we came to the last part of her journey, which involved her walking down a dark alleyway. I was scared of dark alleyways, but full of wonderful advice.

'Now, Elaine, you make sure you walk down the middle of the alley. Keep away from the fence and gateways on your right and the brick wall on your left – you don't want someone to jump out and attack you.'

Elaine the Brave didn't bat an eyelid. Off she went – all 5 foot nothing of her, and I would wait at the mouth of this scary black tunnel until she made it to the other end and yelled, 'It's all right, Kenny, I'm safe.' And off my lovely would go on the final leg of her journey. It's funny how you can convince yourself you've been a brave soldier. 'Watch your back, Elaine,' I'd yell from underneath a brightly lit lamppost.

On our first *real* date, Elaine took me to the Wimpy Bar and bought me – guess what. Yes, a Wimpy. Well, she was older than me, had more money than I did – and I loved Wimpys.

By the time we were 16, we were dining in the Steak House at the Elephant and Castle. It was close to the cinema, so we didn't have to walk far for dinner after we'd watched Bruce Lee as he kung-fu'd all over the screen. I took Elaine to see *The Texas Chain Saw Massacre* as well. No romantic films for us, but she didn't seem to mind. It was all about being together. With hindsight, I guess it was all about me. But if she was happy doing what I wanted to do I wasn't going to complain, was I?

We'd scoff down a three-course meal before heading off up the road to the Tin Pan Alley. Afterwards, I'd see her back to *her* alleyway again – and all the time I was thinking about getting up for training the next day. But I'd always ring her up when I got home to let her know I was all right.

Our young love was not without a hitch or two, though. I was dead jealous of any boy who dared to get close enough to breathe in her air. It was a terrible thing for me to be surrounded only by boys all day long at school while I knew she was in a mixed school and some boy might try to take her away from me. I complained all the time and it caused lots of rows.

We were forever breaking up and making up. Sometimes after a quarrel she would stand outside my home and throw stones at my window. My mum would call up the stairs, 'Kenny, that little girl's outside again.'

I'd try to act cool (I couldn't quite pull it off, mind you) and wait a respectable amount of time before slipping outside to give her a kiss and make up. From day one we promised each other we'd always be together.

When we were 17 and had left school I was training hard and she got a job in some offices. I hated her being at work while I had free time, so I'd go to meet her whenever I could. I always got there early and waited outside on the corner of the street hoping she'd catch sight of me and leave early.

Apparently, I caused a bit of a stir, as her boss thought I was some scallywag casing the joint. 'I think we've got a burglar outside,' he said one day and was just about to call the Old Bill when Elaine jumped up to the window to try to look out. In the end she stood on a box and then she declared excitedly, 'Oh, that's only my Kenny. He's not come for the money: he's come for me.'

'Go on, get off home,' he'd say exasperated.

MY MUM

Everything that happened during my childhood paved the way for my glory days in top-flight football. I was the lucky boy born with a gift that I enjoyed working hard to improve on. It was no hardship to train all the hours the sun was up, and at night I'd dream of being the best footballer in England. They say you need to have a dream to make a dream come true – and I certainly had a dream. So did my mum. She was getting so excited about my budding talent and, like most mums, all she wanted was the best for me. No problem was so big that it couldn't be sorted out. She knew this from harsh life experience.

Six of her siblings had died in childbirth or childhood, so she knew all about loss and grief. When my dad left home she knew he'd come back, and he did, many times. But, when she reached the point where 'enough was enough', she switched off and focused on keeping the home fires burning, and her family became her life.

The scenes in our front room could have come straight out of *The Waltons*. We always had 'goodies' to devour in front of the television, especially at weekends, when crisps, nuts and other snacks and tasty bites were laid out on the table. We washed this down with Coke or some other pop that wasn't exactly good for our health but made us feel all lovely and warm inside.

Outside in the parks my little brother David and I played and played until our skills were finely honed. We were both perfecting every aspect of our game and hoping and praying to make it to the top. We'd continually head balloons to each other over washing lines. Later we progressed to a proper football, which wasn't exactly an easy swap because the footballs back then were very hard with laces you had to avoid if you didn't want a black eye.

David couldn't balance on fences or climb trees as well as I could, and, although he joined me in leaping across rooftops, I believe I was the instigator of these dangerous activities. I know David was as good as I was on the pitch, and it has always saddened me that we didn't both make it like the Neville brothers, but I think I was hungrier and more willing to work and work till I dropped. I was very competitive and hated losing and I'm certain that it was this passion for the game that made all the difference.

As my ability grew, my mum was quick to realise both my potential to become a professional footballer and what opportunities it would give me – such as travelling and a good income on the right side of the law. She had aspirations that went way beyond what other parents wished for their kids. She was determined to do everything in her power to ensure I led a different life from the one I was in danger of falling into – a life in the underbelly of London's gangland. Not because I was the type to fall prey to a life of crime, but purely because of the environment and association I had with boys who had a less fortunate upbringing than I had.

Many of my peers found themselves detained at Her Majesty's pleasure, and Mum had the foresight to steer me clear of danger.

Later she was to hold my face and say to me, 'You built my life, son.'

The fact of the matter is, she built mine. If my mum hadn't been on the ball and known how I ticked, my career would have been over before it had even begun. Way back then she understood the lonely and insecure part of me and acted on an instinct – had it not been for her actions on one particular winter's night, the chances of my going on to play professional football would have been slight. Like my brother David, I would have been lost in the shadows of fortune and fame.

'I'VE COME TO COLLECT YOU, KENNY'

I was at that tricky pubescent stage of development when hormones are flying around and mood swings take you from laughing your head off at some funny joke one minute to becoming angry or miserable the next without really knowing why.

I was still football crazy and loved training as much as ever, but I was beginning to hate the long, laborious, one-hour-long Tube ride across London to Ruislip. I was never good at sitting alone with my own company and, as the draughty, smelly train rattled through the tunnels, I'd be sitting there wondering what everyone else was doing, thinking of all the things I imagined I was missing out on, such as going to the pictures with Elaine, or hanging out at youth clubs with my mates.

I was used to being surrounded by familiar faces, noise and often madness and mayhem. Being alone for hours on public transport faced with nothing but my thoughts for company makes me think about Alan Sillitoe's story, *The Loneliness of the Long Distance Runner* (and the film of the same name). Two hours a night may not seem much, but it got me down.

I know it sounds a bit daft, but it really disturbed me and I didn't want to do it any more. So, one night, when my hump was notably bigger than usual, I announced to my mum that I was giving up football.

Mum didn't seem particularly fazed, which was strange really, as she was my biggest fan and always told me how brilliant I was. All she said that night was, 'All right, Kenny, if that's what you want, it's your life.' And then she casually added, 'But why don't you go one more time, just to make sure you're not making a mistake you might regret.'

The next day I picked up my pork chop (call me Homer Simpson) and munched on it for a while before heading off for the Tube station to begin the tedious trip to training. It was a freezing-cold night and I entertained myself by blowing hot breath into the cold night air. It relieved my boredom of having no one to talk to.

After training I sauntered out of the makeshift dressing room feeling down about my earlier decision. I didn't really want to give up on my dream.

Then I heard a familiar voice me calling, 'Hello, Kenny, I've come to take you home.' I swung round to see my mum standing there in her red headscarf. She was shrugging her shoulders and wearing a woolly coat and a wide grin.

I still get a lump in my throat talking about it. At first I thought she had planned to collect me right from the moment she'd suggested I give it one last shot, but to this day she insists it was a spur-of-the-moment decision. According to her, she'd been standing by the kitchen sink when in a flash it popped into her head that it would be a good idea to jump on a train and come and meet me. How about that?

The very next week Arnie Warren came to our training ground and spotted me. Arnie was chief scout at Queens Park Rangers and was about to move to Crystal Palace. It seemed he wanted to take me with him and put me into the academy. As it turned out, Kenny Sansom was just the type of rough diamond they were looking to sign.

Scouts in those days really put themselves out to seek raw talent in the parks of England. They would tirelessly travel from John o' Groats to Land's End and were usually rewarded by finding talent. There were no ridiculous restrictions on how far a scout could travel outside his area in search of a new David Beckham.

The scouts knew (or used to know) how to keep an eye out for any boy who shone during his school years and, if I say so myself, I had definitely shone in the Dewar Shield tournament, where I played out of my skin. I can almost remember that important match, minute for minute. We beat a team called Hitchin by two goals to one. They scored first, but then we came back to level with them. The icing on the cake was that I scored the winner with a header. What an intoxicating feeling that was.

So, in a nutshell, I think it's fair to say that if my mum hadn't handled my teenage sulk and childlike insecurity like the trouper she was, it's highly likely I would have missed out on my professional football career. You could say I got lucky again. It was a bloody good job I was at training that night when the scout turned up, and not hanging out on street corners with my mates.

But was I too young to be thrown into the pressurised world of competitive football? Or would it be a breeze?

CHAPTER FOUR

THE EAGLES

Arnie Warren was the sharpest knife in the drawer and had the reputation for being one step ahead of other scouts when it came to snapping up a good young apprentice. Apparently, Spurs, QPR and the team I was later to captain, the mighty Arsenal, were all interested in signing me, but I'm glad my destiny was Crystal Palace, as they provided the perfect environment for a homely boy like me.

I was blissfully unaware of what was going on behind the scenes – all I was interested in was playing football.

My state of ignorant bliss was a blessing, because had I known what my dad was up to I would have been even more pissed off with him than I was already. A deal was about to take place between my dad and the Crystal Palace manager – one of football's most charismatic figures – Malcolm Allison.

Malcolm was an iconic man with a larger-than-life character very similar to my dad, who was also tall, dark and handsome. Malcolm became almost as famous for wearing his Fedora hat and smoking expensive cigars as he did for his football prowess. Once a player with lots of potential, he unfortunately contracted tuberculosis in the mid-fifties and had to have a lung removed, which, of course, ended his playing career. Miraculously, even after all the cigars he puffed on, he's still alive today and in his eighties.

As the story goes, Malcolm would often go to the chairman of Palace, Ray Bloye, and ask for a thousand pounds to secure a deal or sign someone. One day Malcolm went rushing up to him and out of breath told him, 'I need five hundred in readies. I've got to have the cash as soon as possible.'

'Steady on, Malcolm,' says Ray. 'What's the hurry?'

'I want to sign this kid. He's outstanding and another club will get to him first if we don't move quickly. His dad wants five hundred notes tonight to seal the deal and then we can sign him tomorrow.'

'Who is the kid?' asked Joe.

'His name's Kenny Sansom and he's a nippy little left-back. Terry Venables rates him and so do I, so we've got to get the cash for his old man.'

Ray, who owned butchers' shops all over south London, thought for a moment and then the two of them piled into Malcolm's snazzy car and went all round these shops raiding the tills of five-pound notes until they came up with the full amount needed to secure my dad's signature on the dotted line.

How true this story is, I don't know. It was news to me when I heard it from my old agent Richard Coomber some years later, but I have a hunch, given what I know about my old dad, that it's the truth. How about that? My mum champions me and gets me the break and my dad pockets five hundred smackers. Life can be a bitch.

So I became a Palace player while still at school, and I was the youngest ever to play in the first team. Until this day, I remain the third youngest debutant at Palace.

When I say things like this I still have to pinch myself – there's still an element of disbelief about my achievements. Sometimes it feels as if I were talking about someone else.

When I marched into the magnificent world of football at Selhurst Park in southeast London Terry Venables was second in charge to Malcolm Allison. He was a young and ambitious coach who was destined for a terrific career in management, one day moving on to manage the England team as well as other top-flight clubs both domestically and in Europe. I was now breathing in the same air as two of the most influential giants in the world of football. It was bloody great.

Malcolm was a great motivator and was brave enough to insist on some changes. He traded in the Crystal Palace nickname of 'the Glaziers' for 'the Eagles', and the sixties hit, 'Glad All Over', by the Dave Clark Five, became our anthem. In fact, it would be fair to say that Allison used his flair to reinvent the club.

'Big Mal' rebranded the Palace crest and chose the club's new colours, which were copies of *big* European teams such as Benfica and Barcelona. So, gone now were the old claret and blue shirts and in came the red and darker blue.

Dagenham-born Terry Venables had worked his apprenticeship at Chelsea FC and had enjoyed a great England career. He was the first player to represent England at all levels – schoolboy, youth, amateur, Under-23 and the full team – and came to Palace from QPR as a player in 1974 and was appointed the new and dynamic manager after just fourteen games.

There is no doubt in my mind at all that Terry Venables is the best manager *ever*. Crystal Palace knew it, I knew it, and I like to think he knew it as well. He always told me that knowing how good you are is important. The Sansom luck was holding firm.

'GLAD ALL OVER'

My mornings would still begin with bread and dripping and two jam doughnuts. Mum put this fandabydozy grub on the table to ensure I had a contented belly and my tank was full for the day. There was none of that 'go to work on an egg' nonsense in the

Sansom household. And forget the 'apple a day keeps the doctor away' – that wasn't me. Just take a look at the photographs of me during my young adulthood – do I look like a boy who's just eaten all the pies? I was bloody gorgeous – Handsome Sansom.

In my early days at Palace I trained with the youth team at Langley Park. My mum and I would catch the double-decker bus home together and more often than not we'd sit opposite each other on the long seats downstairs. She was so proud and so funny. In her loud cockney voice she'd call over, 'Kenny, who are you playing on Saturday?'

Blushing like mad I would try to ignore her, which was ridiculous – you couldn't ignore Louise Sansom.

'Kenny, who's Crystal Palace playing on Saturday? I suppose you'll be at left-back as usual.' She'd be shouting by now.

Still blushing like mad, I'd nod a silent response, but she wasn't having any of it. Mum was never content until I answered – for the whole of the Old Kent Road to hear me – words such as, 'We're playing Liverpool in the third round of the FA Cup.'

Now that really would make her happy. Don't get me wrong, she wasn't one to brag. Well, she loved every minute of it – and good on her!

TERRY AND KENNY

Terry Venables and I clicked straightaway and I think this was as much to do with our similar personalities and sense of humour as our passion for football. I had always been a joker and loved the old comedians – as did Terry. We both found the old-school types such as Tommy Cooper hilarious. He had a bar called the Laurel and Hardy, and once we did a fine rendition of these two old comedians, but we rarely got into 'a fine mess' the way they did. On the contrary, we rarely messed up. These were golden days – days of hard work, laughter and innocence.

Being an apprentice in a big club in the seventies was bloody hard work – but, as Terry was telling me often, 'The harder you work, the luckier you become, Kenny.' So I got stuck in. Some days the other boys and I would be pushed so hard running around the track that we'd fall in a heap afterwards. Some of the others were actually vomiting, and the sweat would be pouring off us.

I was a young member of the team and very fit, so I coped better than most. (In fact the photograph on the front cover of my book was taken just after one of these runs.) I remember watching George Graham, who was a senior player, gasping for air as he slumped on the ground. Life for us could be quite gruelling and much harsher than the lads today have to contend with. It would be commonplace for us to clean out the referee's room (and, trust me, the ref's room could be a right old smelly place – it was a good job Robbie Savage wasn't around then).

During preseason training we'd paint the stadium. Imagine that happening today.

Can you see John Terry and Frank Lampard getting busy with a paintbrush during the hot month of July? I don't think so.

I wouldn't have had it any other way, though – and I really mean that. I honestly think that, had I been a part of this football world today, when wages and temptation are ridiculously high, I would have totally, *totally*, self-destructed. The discipline and positive mentorship I received was worth its weight in gold and saved me just in time from that self-destruction.

You know something? There's hard work that is exhilarating, and then there's hard work that is a bloody drag. Fortunately, my kind of work fell into the former category. At the end of the day I'd literally collapse into the chair with exhaustion. The day had been a great big ball of fun and, as the evening turned into night, I fell asleep with a great sense of satisfaction at a job done well.

In my early days at Palace I took great pride in shining the boots of some of the big names of the day, like Jim Cannon – a rarity who chose to spend his entire 16-year career with one club. I also polished Nicky Chatterton's boots. He was a highly industrious midfielder and I was later to play alongside him in the 'Team of the Eighties'. Another teammate was the legendary Dave Swindlehurst. It really was quite something for a youngster like me to be surrounded by such talent.

We *all* ate hearty food such as pies, pasties, sausage rolls and chips. We also played our hearts out in our quest to take our team to promotion.

My mind still held onto a childlike quality and it rarely crossed my mind that I had been signed by a famous club, that I was being coached by a man destined to become a legend, and that I was in a prime position to realise many a schoolboy's dream. I didn't think about 'being a pro'. I was simply having fun. Being coached by Terry Venables and Don Howe was quite something.

I wasn't sure about our 'kit man', though – he troubled me somewhat. At 6 foot 2 inches, he towered above me, and his name was David Horne. He wasn't sinister, but I couldn't understand how his mind ticked. I was used to kindness and consideration and I felt he was less than gracious when he declined to give me a lift home, even though he drove past the end of my road.

I'd look into his mustachioed face and gingerly ask him, 'Are you going to be long, Mr Horne?' This was a subtle way of saying, 'Give us a lift, mate. I hate doing this bloody bus journey on my own!' But I wasn't brave (or cheeky) enough to say, 'I hate travelling alone, Dave.'

But I have a hunch he looked upon me as an annoying little bugger he wanted to avoid. He'd say, 'Sorry, Kenny, I've got masses to do here yet.'

So, off I'd trot to the bus stop and then, as I stood in all kinds of weather, he'd sail past me in his comfy car without as much as a backwards glance. How can you do that to an eager kid who would give his last Rolo away? I suppose it takes all sorts to make the world go round.

RED-CARDED

The one and only sending-off of my career came during the 1976–7 season when we were playing away at Coventry City. I can't remember the score, but that's not important – what *is* important is that I acted like an idiot. I was marking Scottish forward Ian Wallace, and it wasn't too long into the match before he started kicking the shit out of me. I think my attacking game took him a bit by surprise and rattled him. I guess I got pissed off as well because, after one kick too many, I shoved him in the chest and sent the pair of us flying.

The whistle blew and I was shown the red card. But that wasn't the worst of it: I was given a one-match ban and missed playing against Liverpool at home. I was devastated – and promised myself I would never be shown a red card again.

I was still that boy who didn't like to get into trouble; still the kid who needed to be liked and loved – getting a red card meant I was naughty and therefore needed to be punished. Phew! Being ejected from the game hit me hard. It felt like rejection. It felt bloody awful.

To balance out these difficult early experiences at Palace, in 1977 I captained the Palace Junior team to the FA Youth Cup. It was another of those very proud moments.

At the same time I was skippering the England Juniors. Even as I write, it sounds quite phenomenal. If I pinch myself any more I'll be bruised. Yet I guess the fact that I won the first nine of my full England caps while in this fertile atmosphere at Palace, should come as no surprise. I was receiving great coaching, even greater mentorship, and was playing out on the pitch with a terrific bunch of lads.

THE TEAM OF THE EIGHTIES

Looking back over my long career, I have come to realise that my years with the Eagles were the best days of my life. If I could be transported back in time to anywhere it would here to Crystal Palace. It was safe, it was fun and it was magic.

I was a naïve young man, very down-to-earth, and called a spade a spade. To be surrounded by other people with similar life values was truly magnificent. If I could get just 75 per cent of that happiness and contentment back I would be a happy man. Everybody felt it. Players and teammates like Billy Gilbert – who was a tough nut – were fabulous characters to have around. Then there were the likes of Peter Nicholas, Ian Walsh and Steve Leahy. They were all the salt of the earth with not a pretentious bone in their bodies. In lots of ways we were very childlike – kids playing a game of 'being big boys'. There was a kind of innocence and purity about us. I know that might sound a bit soft, but that's the truth of it.

We were a football family, and that suited me right down to the ground. What a great bunch of lads I was blessed to be among!

How could I exclude the names of the Palace team of the eighties from my book? The boys who played in the years when Allison handed over to Terry Venables, who then ignited us and spurred us on to great things and great times? Not a chance.

First there was George 'Mr Smoothie' Graham, whom I was to be managed by later at Arsenal. Then there was Nick Chatterton – Nicky, who was so quick in the shower that he was in and out and off on his way home to Eastbourne before the rest of us were even wet.

Rachid Harkouk was a larger-than-life character. I remember once when we were all on a jolly boys outing to Jersey, some idiot in Bonapartes nightclub spilled a drink all down him and didn't apologise. Rachid was fuming, so a few of us went down to the underground car park and all I can say is that, if Ernie Walley (our first-team coach under Venables and a tough old Welshman who stood no nonsense) hadn't intervened, there would have been a nasty scene. Rachid hadn't realised just how big the other bloke was. Later he said, 'Thank fuck Ernie showed up – that bloke never stopped coming out of his jacket.'

Vince Hillarie was the worst dresser ever. He wore brown socks with black shoes. His excuse was that he got dressed in the dark, but over the years this wore thin.

John Burridge was highly professional and believed firmly in good preparation. He used to take sleeping pills on a Friday night so he'd be nice and fresh in the morning. One of our centre-forwards, Mike Elwiss, used to room with him and once, as a joke, he swapped the sleeping pill for a paracetamol. After about 20 minutes John was saying, 'Oh yes, the pill's working now. Yes, they're definitely kicking in' and began to slur. Then the phone rang and he sparked into life. Mike was laughing so hard when he was telling us the story later. 'You should have seen him. He was all dozy one minute and full of life the next.'

David Kemp, who is now the number two at Stoke, struck lucky when he went to Champneys for a weekend and was mistaken for the *EastEnders* actor Ross Kemp and given a luxury suite of rooms.

Then there was Phil Holder, who was canny enough to put money on Burnley to beat us in our promotion game so that he'd get the bonus from the club if we won the match and the League title, or a payout from the bookies if we lost.

The stories could go on and on for ever: these Eagles were the salt of the earth. Other squad members were Martin Hinshelwood, Neil Smillie, Tony Burn, Ian Walsh, Ian Evans, Peter Caswell, Steve Perrin, Peter Nicholas, Jerry Murphy, Billy Gilbert, Dave Swindlehurst (who used to room with me and colluded with Peter Taylor to frighten the life out of me on the night before my Palace debut) and Paul Hinshelwood. Apart from me, Jim Cannon was the best player, and as for Peter Taylor – well, I'll tell you all about him in a minute.

I'm inclined to say you don't get this kind of family atmosphere in big clubs today, but I could be wrong. I think Ryan Giggs, the

Neville brothers, David Beckham and some of the other Manchester United players were a similar outfit. But, unfortunately, the general attitude of scouts versus agents has taken this young 'family' focus away – maybe for good. This is a travesty.

We had great team spirit and shared each other's secrets. I remember Phil Holder, who was small and stocky, going for his weekly weigh-in and putting his own weight down as 11 stone 2 pounds, and our trainer, Charlie Simpson, believing him.

Then the astute Terry Venables sauntered into the room wearing a slightly crooked smile. He took a quick look at the recorded weights and turned to Charlie, saying, 'Did you see Phil on the scales?'

Well, Charlie couldn't lie. 'No, not exactly.'

'Get your kit off, Holder,' he yelled.

Poor old Phil had to strip to his bare essentials and step on the scales for the gaffer in front of the rest of us – who were sniggering of course.

'You weigh five pounds more than you've put down here. What's the point in trying to cheat? You're only cheating yourself.' He said more, but I don't intend to repeat the finer details now, as it was embarrassing enough for Phil at the time, and I'm sure he wouldn't want it dredged up now.

The weigh-ins were farcical. We were healthy young lads with appetites to match and enjoyed our grub to the full – especially the bacon rolls John and Babs dished up at Selhurst Park – and we just couldn't stop munching.

It was like being at the tuck shop at school and was all part of the Palace experience.

We were weighed on a Friday, so to keep our weight down we might not eat on the Thursday. All sorts of tricks were used to reduce our weight before we stepped on the scales. Our super-goalie Pat Jennings was very conscientious about keeping his weight at acceptable levels and would often sweat it out in a hot bath to achieve the required results.

THE EAGLES

You would have thought that my terrible diet would do me no favours and that I'd get teenage spots and become very fat. But this was far from the truth. My body remained lean, fit and strong and my hair and skin shiny and healthy. I was a hunk whom the *Sun* newspaper dubbed, 'Handsome Sansom'. And this fact led me into a sticky scenario with one of my teammates – one Peter Taylor.

<a> Peter Taylor loves me

Winger Peter John Taylor (not to be mistaken for Brian Clough's managerial partner at Derby and Nottingham Forest) had a 3-year spell at Palace in the seventies. He tried to throw a spell over me, too – and terrified the life out of me. I'm not talking about on the pitch, either. This was much more of a personal matter.

I knew him to be a bit of a joker, as he was always impersonating Norman Wisdom. In fact it was Peter who taught me to do the impersonations I have since become famous for with some of the England fans.

He seemed harmless enough. In fact at first I thought he was shy – but I underestimated how far he would go on a wind up.

Peter was 3 years older than I was, which, as you know, when you're a teenager seems like a wide gap. An established player with kudos, he too was at the front of the queue when good looks were dished out, and although a bit reserved when he first meets you he soon shows his confident side. I don't mind saying that I was slightly in awe of his achievements. He had been voted Crystal Palace Player of the Year in 1974 and was to repeat this feat in 1976.

As I said, I'm a home boy at heart and whenever I used to play away (and I mean at football!) my mum and wife would always be at my side. That was, until the day arrived when I had to go on away with my teammates minus my chaperones.

It was my Crystal Palace debut and little did I know that 16-year-old Kenny Sansom was in danger of being initiated into much more than a football match. I was on my own – a fact that wasn't lost on the astute Peter Taylor.

While my mum was worrying about my table manners and my long-established penchant for eating with my fingers, Peter seemed interested in my eating something else – him.

We were on the train to play Tranmere Rovers when I realised I was the focus of his attention. There were several of us travelling. David Kemp was there, as was Alan 'White Rat' Whittle. They all seemed to be oblivious of Peter's apparent affections towards me, which I found a bit weird. I thought his attentions were blatantly clear.

The first time he mouthed, 'I love you', I didn't quite know where to put my face, so I suddenly found the view out of the window very interesting – I never realised tenement blocks could be so fascinating. But when we were in a dark tunnel I could see his face reflected clearly in the window – and he hadn't gone away. Instead, he was still mouthing terms of endearment.

In panic I threw a glance in the direction of the other lads desperately hoping for I don't know what. Help? But they seemed to be engrossed in their own business of card playing and continued to be unaware of my dilemma.

Blushing furiously, I braved an eye-to-eye with Peter and immediately wished I hadn't, because he started blowing me kisses. Oh, my God! Where the hell were my mum and Elaine when I needed them the most?

I found a newspaper I had no interest in and hid behind it for the remainder of the long and painful journey, and was mightily relieved when it was time to alight. With internal dialogue like 'Just keep yourself to yourself, Kenny boy,' I checked into my room. But Peter was there again. 'Who are you rooming with?' he asked with that special glint he gets in his eye when he's up to mischief.

'Dave Swindlehurst,' I gulped.

'Lucky Dave,' smiled Peter. 'You know he's gay, don't you?'

I nearly fainted with shock and, as I didn't drink in those days, there was no comfort or Dutch courage to be found in the bottom of a beer bottle. Then Dave 'Swindles' Swindlehurst came over to me and said chirpily, 'Hi, Kenny. See you upstairs in a little while.'

I was waiting for them to laugh and tell me it was a wind-up, but it never happened. I wished I'd been able to be angry and say, 'Hey! What the fuck's going on?' But the words got stuck in my throat.

Fortunately 'words' were the only thing to be caught in my throat that night, which is nothing short of a miracle, as, when I sheepishly peered around the door, I noticed the two single beds had been pushed together and Swindles was sitting up in bed reading a porno magazine. I didn't sleep a bloody wink. It was not a good start to my Crystal Palace debut.

The next day Peter laughed and said I was gullible. Me? Gullible? I was mortified. I thought 'gullible' meant I ate too much. Was I letting my mum down by eating too much? This anxiety stayed with me for the whole weekend as I tried my hardest to conquer a knife and fork. Only later was it pointed out that 'gullible' meant I was young and daft, whereas 'gluttony' was the right word for being a pig.

I was about to play my first match as a professional footballer and here I was being tortured by a man who was better known for terrorising opposing defenders. Damn it, Peter – you were supposed to be on *my* side. As it happened, neither Peter nor Swindles batted for the other side. Bastards!

OH! WHAT A NIGHT! CRYSTAL PALACE V BURNLEY (1978–9 SEASON)

It was a very special night indeed at Selhurst Park. A massive crowd of 52,000 were anticipating a match where both sides' prize for victory was top-flight football – something the Palace fans had been dreaming of for years. The noise on the terraces was as loud as I'd ever heard, and there is no doubt in my mind that anyone there that night still treasures the memory.

A goalless draw would have seen us promoted to the First

Division after 6 years of exile to the lower ranks. But that wouldn't have been good enough for us – we wanted to go up in style. We wanted a spectacular win.

We attacked without success during the first half. Then Vince Hillarie found the head of Ian Walsh from the wing and suddenly we were one up. The crowd went wild. You could smell victory in the air.

We attacked straightaway and almost scored another, but it floated just wide of the goal mouth. Burnley's defenders were unable to clear the ball and then Jerry Murphy shot a cracking ball that flew agonisingly across the goal mouth. That bloody ball just didn't want to go in.

Eventually, the winning goal came from a midfield break and seconds later Dave Swindlehurst had notched up yet another goal to his already brilliant tally.

Terry Venables was standing proudly in the wings, holding his arms aloft in triumph. My God, it was brilliant. I threw my shin pads into the crowd and other players stripped off their shirts and threw them.

Elaine and the rest of my family, who were in the stands, said they had never experienced anything like it. Fans rushed onto the pitch, but this was one invasion everyone welcomed; we were all in terrific spirits. As far as the fans were concerned, Terry Venables had brought success to their club and financially it had cost next to nothing.

We had won the Second Division championship in style and we were very happy. The Burnley players made a quick exit, just in time to escape the south London revellers.

We were going up, and were getting a bonus – we were glad all over.

I just have one more thing to say about this fantastic and historical night. I walked into a shop in Bromley many years later and the shop owner's eyes nearly popped out of his head when he saw me standing there. 'Kenny? It *is* you, isn't it? My God, it only *is* you. I'm a big Crystal Palace fan and I've got your shin pads at home.'

Now, even more years later, I'd like to know if he's still got them. So if anyone reading this knows the bloke in Bromley who has got my shin pads, can you tell him I want them back now to sell on eBay, 'cos I'm a bit broke.

ELAINE AND TERRY

It was the award ceremony for Crystal Palace Player of the Year and Elaine was looking stunning in a beautiful cream dress. She didn't *feel* stunning, though. She felt like a fish out of water and this made her temporarily lose her confidence.

We were both still very young and naïve and not yet used to being in the limelight at social functions. Elaine passed a programme round asking everyone to sign it so she could have a keepsake of this important night. When it came to Terry Venables's turn he wrote 'To Elaine, the belle of the ball. You are what you are. Never forget that you are as good as anyone else.'

Terry had offered her a word of advice in a fatherly way that meant a hell of a lot to a young girl in a world where you are mixing with people from all walks of life, and she still has the programme tucked safely away.

You see, Terry's a very perceptive and intuitive man, and these are just two of the skills that make him an exceptional person as well as manager. If he comes across to the public like a lovable rogue – that's because he is.

I remember that he was a great prankster, and poor old Ken Shellito (a great player but of the shy and retiring type) often bore the brunt of Terry's wicked sense of humour.

Terry and Ken had been apprentices together at Chelsea and often travelled to and from training sessions on busy rush-hour trains. Terry used to get off the train two stops before Ken, and just as the train was pulling into his station he would stand up before bending down and planting a kiss full on Ken's lips. Then, as camp as he could manage, he'd tell him he couldn't wait to see him the next day, before leaping from the carriage and leaving a red-faced Ken sitting among the shocked commuters.

Remember, being openly gay today is accepted, but way back in the sixties, when Terry and Ken were apprentices, homosexuals had a tough time coming out.

It got so bad for Ken that he took to getting off at the same station as Terry just to avoid the embarrassment and then standing and waiting for the next train. Poor bugger.

CAR TROUBLE

By now Elaine and I were married and living in a lovely house in Epsom, Surrey. I was not a drinker yet and only had the occasional flutter on the horses; but these two insidious enemies were lurking in the shadows, ready to pretend to be my friend. But, for now, it was still orange juice and lemonade in the club bar, and bacon rolls and cups of tea in the wooden shed. After training we would head off to Solly's café for, um, well, pork chops and chips!

There was this kid, an apprentice at Palace who used to eat at Solly's, who was a bright little spark. I think he used to hero-worship me a bit – in a similar way to my hero-worshipping Peter Taylor.

I had been sponsored by Mitsubishi to drive a beautiful silver Colt, and this kid said to me, 'If I beat you at pinball tomorrow will you let me drive your car?' Cheeky bugger!

Anyway, I agreed to the deal, thinking he wouldn't show up and that if he did he wouldn't have a hope in hell of beating me – but I was wrong on both counts.

The little whippersnapper raced into the café and finished off the deal by beating me fair and square. My luck had abandoned me that day.

So I let this little underage and uninsured lad drive my prized

Colt out of the car park. Moments later he came flying back down the shingle driveway and skidded straight into Vince Hillaire's sponsored car and took the side clean out.

Vince wasn't too happy and, to be honest, neither was I, but we both saw the funny side of it – I guess everything was funny in those days. We told the sponsors that a hit-and-run driver had been the culprit and thankfully they repaired both cars without question. It's amazing what you can get away with when you're afforded celebrity status. I suppose I was beginning to feel like a celebrity and it wasn't all to the good. Occasionally it made me feel and think in stupid ways.

Now on the up and up, I'd become the proud owner of a flashy Triumph Stag. Oh, did Elaine and I ever think we were the bee's knees!

Elaine hadn't learned to drive yet, but she had the bright idea to get her brother-in-law to drive her to Gatwick Airport to pick me up from a holiday in Corfu with the lads. As I walked out of the terminal there she was sitting in our pride and joy waiting to greet me.

It was a pig of a night, with torrential rain and the wind blowing a gale as we made our way back to Epsom. We were happy to see each other again, but the tension in the car was palpable, as we weren't familiar with the area and the roads were not well lit. Suddenly the car chugged to a halt. We looked at each other in horror.

'We've run out of petrol,' I cried.

Elaine, who always had all the answers, was struck dumb.

'Why didn't you fill it up with petrol before you left?' I asked. But, not being a driver, she hadn't thought about this necessity. I jumped out and flagged down the first car to come our way and lucky old me again – it was only Paul Hinshelwood. Now, what were the chances of that?

A decision was made in a split second. Paul and I would go and find the nearest 24-hour petrol station while Elaine waited in the warmth and safety of our car. 'Wait here, Elaine. We won't be long.'

Off we went in search of fuel and, as luck would have it, there was a garage nearby. But it was shut. So we continued along on our journey. And, although we passed a couple more garages, none were open. Didn't anyone do night duty in Surrey?

We finally found a little garage in Tooting Broadway. How did we manage to get that far away from Epsom? The fact was – mystery or not – that was where we were.

'Can I buy a can, please? I've run out of petrol.'

'It's an emergency,' added Paul.

'I ain't got no cans,' mouthed the cashier from behind a bulletproof glass window.

That was it. My usual moderate temper was lost. 'What do you mean, you've got no cans? This is a bloody garage. Lots of people run out of petrol.'

'I ain't got no cans,' he insisted.

'What *have* you got?' Paul chirped in again.

'I only got cans of oil,' he growled menacingly. This guy was almost as wild as the night.

'Give us a can of oil, then.' I was really panicking now as I thought about my wife, who I had abandoned alone on a dark scary night. What on earth had possessed me?

I was that mad I poured all the oil from the can over the garage forecourt and then, having filled the can with petrol, we drove as fast as we could back to Elaine, with me beating myself up all the way back for leaving her in danger. I'd like to think that those days were safer than today, and in some ways they were. There wasn't quite so much road rage going on, but that didn't take away the fact that some other car could have crashed into the back of her on a poorly lit country road.

I wasn't in the slightest bit surprised when she screamed, 'Where the hell have you been?' But at least we had enough petrol to get us out of trouble.

THE BETTING SHOP – THE SANSOM BROTHERS BECOME BOOKIES

My dad was a gambler, a drinker and a womaniser. That, I'm afraid, is the harsh truth of the matter, and I still wanted nothing to do with him.

As I said before, my older brother Peter, who had built up a strong father–son bond with our dad, spent lots of time in his company over in the East End, and that was his choice and none of my business.

One day Peter had the idea that we should open up a betting shop. 'We'll be millionaires by this time next year, Roddy... I mean... Kenny,' he told me with all the conviction of Del Boy.

I'll tell you something. A success it was not. My brother and I must be the only bookies in the land to have *lost* money – *my* money.

Why didn't anyone warn me the last person who should run a bookie's is a gambler – a bloody expensive lesson that turned out to be!

LEAVING THE EAGLES

We were a great bunch of mates who had bonded together so well that I have to wonder how far we would have gone as a team had we all stayed together longer – we were that good.

It had been Malcolm Allison who'd transformed the club in the seventies and who had laid the foundations for El Tel to take over and guide us back to the First Division in 1979. We were the team of the eighties and all of us had an absolutely fantastic time. Unfortunately, the promise of a decade of brilliance was dashed and, by 1981, Palace were relegated. Terry was vilified in the media, but of course, in true Venables style, he took all the controversy in his stride.

As for me, I was about to fly the nest, off to pastures new.

In the summer of 1980, when I was 21 years old, a bizarre week took place that saw my popularity soar to an all-time high and life change for ever.

It was a sunny summer's day (a Monday, as I recall) when Terry Venables called me to his office and offered me a 5-year contract to stay at Crystal Palace. I was delighted about this, as I was really happy there, but then he called me back into his office the following day and said he'd had Arsenal on the phone and did I want to go over to Highbury and have a word with them? I was curious, but didn't think too much about going over to Highbury other than that it would be good to have a look around the historical ground.

I was ushered quickly through the door leading into the East Stand before being taken to see Ken Friar over in the West Stand. It was all very impressive for a young impressionable lad like me, and I was flattered when I was asked if I wanted to play for the Arsenal.

Did I want to play for the Arsenal? Was he having a laugh?

'That would be terrific,' I gulped.

And that was that. Canny old Friar signed me up on the spot before any other deals could be struck up with other clubs.

I telephoned home to let my mum know I'd signed for the Arsenal and my brother Peter answered. 'Don't tell me you just went there and signed up just like that.' He was aghast. 'But I've had Bob Paisley on the phone and Liverpool want you – you could get a better deal and they'll even give you accommodation.'

But it was too late. I was going to Arsenal. I was staying in London and that was what I wanted more than anything in the world.

Later, when I sat across the table watching the now-familiar Terry Venables grin spread across his face, we talked about the deal in more detail.

He was just about to sign a deal with Ken Friar that astonished many – not least of all the Arsenal fans. Some were asking if the board of directors and management at Highbury had gone off their rockers. Arsenal fanzines were full of questions. 'Why on earth would the Arsenal swap the great striker Clive Allen, who he'd only recently signed and had yet to play a game, for a young left-back from Crystal Palace? And in a bizarre million-pound-plus deal to boot.'

The newspapers went crazy, as did the Gooners (the Gunners' fans). Would these fanatical fans accept me into the Highbury fold or did I have a tough time ahead of me? Only time would tell.

But, before we move on to Highbury, let's have a taste of England in the seventies.

CHAPTER FIVE

LAND OF HOPE
AND GLORY

My very first game for my country saw the Sansom clan in full swing as they hurried down Wembley Way towards the twin towers. Heading the way was my mum, closely followed by lots of other Sansoms and Culwicks.

I was 15 years old and our opponents were none other than Germany. The newspaper headlines read, ENGLAND SCHOOLBOY GOES TO WEMBLEY. Oh boy, were these ever brilliant times! It was 7 August 1975 and the prolific broadcaster Brian Moore was commentating on ITV. I could barely contain my excitement.

Mum led her family onto the terraces of glory like a mother duck followed by her offspring. My sister Maureen was clutching a mini-television because she wanted to watch the match on TV as well as live. My brother Peter was tuning his radio into the sports channel for some decent commentary. Many years later he was to tell me how he had cried buckets that day. 'Seeing you standing out there on that pitch with the national anthem playing was too much. I melted. You looked so little – a dot in the distance. I have never been so proud of anyone – not before that day, nor since.'

Before the match we were all led out onto the Wembley turf to get the feel of the place. I felt something all right. I had never seen Wembley in real life, and the sheer size of it frightened the out life out of me. Most kids get scared about the big things in life – and flipping hell! – this pitch was very big.

I am trying hard to remember everything about that day, but some of it is a blur – like a dream. I *do* remember a boy called Peter Coyne. He played up front and scored three goals. Imagine that. Imagine scoring a hat-trick at Wembley as a schoolboy. It doesn't get much better than that.

Mark Higgins was our centre-half, and he went on to play for Everton. I think I'm right in saying he played for England Schoolboys 2 years on the trot. He was a giant of a boy at over 6 foot (he certainly towered me), and in all honesty he was way ahead of his 15 years.

Germany had a winger who was also very tall and as quick as lightning. Whoosh, and he was gone. There was one horrible moment when he knocked the ball past me as if I weren't there.

That was pretty devastating, especially knowing the whole nation was watching from its living room. 'I can't do any worse,' I told myself. 'I might as well just get on with it and hope for the best.' I wish I could remember that winger's name.

As soon as I relaxed I began to play well. I had a good game, and you could never begin to imagine the buzz I got when Jack Charlton singled me out and praised me, saying he predicted I would have a long and successful England football career.

After the match we celebrated with a smashing meal of fillet steak, mash and vegetables (sorry, no vegetables for me); I can still taste it now – it tasted of sweet success.

My sister and I sat down a little while ago to recall that extra-special day. She reminded me that our Nanna Culwick (who is no longer with us) was led out onto the pitch for a treat and was completely overwhelmed by the occasion. We had a good old cry at that memory, I can tell you.

RON GREENWOOD

Ron Greenwood prepared me well for the 1980 European Championships by playing me as much as he could. I found myself at the core of a team that included Glenn Hoddle, Gary Lineker, Peter Shilton and others of that calibre.

Once again, I was blessed with being taught by a brilliant coach. First I had Terry Venables and then Ron Greenwood. It's bloody marvellous when I think about it.

Ron had been West Ham's gaffer from 1961 to 1974, and I'm not the only one who thinks he's been one of the best England coaches ever – lots would agree. At club level (with the Hammers), he won both the FA Cup and European Cup Winners' Cup. During his illustrious managerial career he developed the two 1966 World Cup heroes, Bobby Moore and Martin Peters. And, to cap it all, he then he took over the England job in 1977 – just in time to nurture me and jump-start me towards a record-breaking eighty-six caps.

I believe the reason I slotted in well with the legends that played for England in the late seventies and eighties was because we were similar characters. Like the above, I was well respected by peers and management alike. I played with strength and courage, but was also calm and had leadership qualities that were perfect to skipper teams. But I wouldn't say I was fearless.

The reason why I'd worked so hard perfecting my skills with the ball was so I wouldn't need to go in hard for a tackle. I didn't like getting my shorts dirty any more than I liked to play dirty.

I guess I didn't like getting into trouble with authority, either. Being told off still made me feel like a 5-year-old boy. So I played my heart out and did everything I possibly could to be the very best. Only then could I feel good.

IF THE CAP FITS: ENGLAND V WALES (23 MAY 1979)

My very first England match in the full squad was a home game at Wembley Stadium.

West Bromwich Albion's Laurie Cunningham and I were the new faces in the squad that day for what was to be a difficult Home Championship match against the Welsh that ended in a nil–nil draw.

At the age of 23, Laurie was a couple of years older than I was, and a really nice guy. He had already gone into the record books as first ever black player to represent England when he gained Under-21 recognition in a match against Scotland, and now the winger who was born in Holloway was making his full England debut alongside me.

We began brightly. Kevin Keegan was, as usual, right on the ball. He really worked hard – always. Laurie had a fabulous start as well, demonstrating great flair. He was a flamboyant character and is probably remembered as much for being a member of West Bromwich Albion's very own 'Three Degrees' as for his football skills. (the other 'band' members were Cyrille Regis and Brendon Batson – hilarious.)

Critics of the match said Wales deserved their point, but I beg to differ. Apparently, we didn't finish terribly well, but I think luck went against us. Don't forget I was a young and eager 21-year-old and always thought we were better than the other side.

During the first half Kevin almost scored twice, and when Terry McDermott shaved the outside of the Welsh goalpost the whole crowd gasped. Laurie hit a blistering shot that almost saw him score his first, but that too was tantalisingly close – unlucky or what?

We were solid at the back and really and, truthfully, I don't think goalie Joe Corrigan was ever in danger of letting one in, and showed his usual confidence in saving a powerful long-range shot from John Toshack.

I learned a valuable lesson about how to behave in England matches compared with club games. I was getting a bit hot under the collar and at one point, when there was a throw-in in their half, I yelled over to Tony Currie, 'Close them in. Don't let them out.'

Well, he must have glared across at me for at least a full 10 seconds before he chose to turn his back and ignore me. I was astute enough to know that was not proper behaviour in the England setup.

With 20 minutes to go, Ron made a couple of inspired substitutes when he brought on Trevor Brooking and Steve Coppell. Their fresh legs made all the difference – fresh legs always make all the difference – and Steve also almost scored.

But we all know how useless it is to 'almost score' and that 'winning is everything', so we had to make do with a draw. Laurie had shown he had potential to enjoy a long career, but unfortunately he was dogged by injury for years before a tragedy in a car crash in Madrid, where he played for Real, robbed him of his life.

In June 1979 I was picked to play away for the England B team against Austria. These were exciting and educational times. The first team were due to play on the Wednesday night, but the game was abandoned in the first half due to a terrible storm with lightning that was frightening to watch at such close hand.

I roomed with Cyrille Regis – one of the 'Three Degrees', who was in no way, shape or form a woman. He was a giant of a man. The first time I met him I stood in awe as he removed his jacket. He just never stopped coming out of it. It was quite something.

Next we had to catch a train to where the first team were playing and most of the lads were drinking alcohol. Being teetotal, I stuck to my orange juice, and therefore remained sober while all around me were getting off their faces.

Russell Osmond had this joke pen with invisible ink and squirted it all over Big Joe Corrigan's shirt. 'What have you done?' An over-the-top Joe ripped it off and threw it off the train. 'Take your socks off everyone and throw them off the train.' Everyone did it. Everyone did what Joe asked – I mean, demanded. He was far from being aggressive, though. Joe was known as the Gentle Giant. We referred to him as 'Gentle Joe with a heart to show'. Mind you, if you chipped a ball over his head and scored during training, he'd run and give you a punch on the arm. It didn't half bloody hurt. He could take it back, though – and in very good humour.

I remember another funny incident concerning Joe. We were at a PFA Awards dinner at the Hilton Hotel in London and everyone was having a good drink, when Steve Foster turned to him and asked him if wanted a small aperitif. Joe looked across menacingly and howled, 'Now why would I want a small aperitif when I've got a bottle of champagne?' So Steve throws back, 'Not a small aperitif as in a drink Joe – I was wondering whether you'd like a smaller pair of teeth.'

Joe had little pearly teeth, you see. Funny bastards – funny times.

ENGLAND V BULGARIA

It was late November before I was selected to play my next match for my country, and again it was a home match.

For the first time ever, the game had to be postponed because of terrible dense fog and, although more than seventy thousand fans managed to make it for the match, the following day, poor old Kevin Keegan had to fly back to his Hamburg team for commitments over there. Norwich City's Kevin Reeves was very happy though (one man's misery is another man's delight), since he got to win *his* first cap.

Ron revelled in giving new blood a chance, and his other choice that day was the man who was to become my 'away' roommate, Glenn Hoddle.

We were awesome from the first whistle – even if I say so myself. It took us 9 minutes to score. It came from a Tony Woodcock corner that was only half cleared from the edge of the box. Glenn curled the ball across to Dave Watson, who headed the ball home. Ray Clemence only had to make one save in the second half, whereas we kept the pressure on until our second, long-awaited goal came in the 70th minute when Glenn Hoddle side-footed the ball into the top corner from a 20-yard shot.

It had been a wonderful experience, and it was reported that all the other nations were taking note of our good form.

With the seventies coming to a close I had no doubt in my mind that I was going to win many more caps.

The seventies had been brilliant. Now what were the eighties going to bring?

CHAPTER SIX

A BAD NIGHT
IN BASLE

All of a sudden, my dad was back in my life, and I didn't see it coming. I should have run a mile and then kept running some more. He wanted to know me now I was famous.

'My Kenny plays for England, you know.' 'My Kenny' this that and the other! 'He's a Crystal Palace player who has a dazzling career ahead of him.' He'd been spewing all this bigheaded chatter all over London for months. He mixed with his type and I mixed with mine. But he was my dad and I'm a sentimental old fool.

When I was growing up I hated him. That's what little boys do when someone hurts their mum. My mum was my life and he'd messed her about too much. My older brother Peter, who had always stayed in contact with our dad, had told me everything about the other women – of how he'd go off with one for a while and then wander back into our house, where Mum would eagerly take him back for a while, until he got bored or found another bird. Peter said most of them were dogs. The worst one, he said, was a great big woman who weighed 15 stone and who had a facial wart he couldn't take his eyes off. I couldn't believe I was hearing this kind of talk.

'Surely you're exaggerating,' I laughed out loud. But Peter was adamant that she was uglier than a bumble bee chewing a wasp. 'Kenny, you were ten years younger than me. I saw it all. And you and David were so much more protected compared to us older kids.'

'Protected?'

'Yes, protected, Kenny. Too right. Mum protected you. The truth is when it came to any of us kids she'd punch as hard as any man.'

Punch? My little mum?

'Don't exaggerate, Pete,' I said.

'I'm not exaggerating. She saw red if anyone dared to hurt any of us – or even suggest we'd done wrong – she let them have it.'

I shook my head in wonderment. 'What was the worst thrashing she ever gave anyone?'

'Oh, that's easy. It was the white woman with the big lips and nose that spread across her face. When she found out dad was giving her one, she punched the life out of her.'

I couldn't believe it. Not little Louise, who had pandered to me and my little brother and always made sure we had the whitest shorts on the park pitch. It just shows you the passion in the woman. God love her.

Now here I was, standing in the line-up in the tunnel as we waited to run out onto the pitch at the St Jakob Stadium in Basle for an important World Cup qualifier against Switzerland, knowing my dad was out there in the stands. Yes, my dad and his mate 'Black Ray' had decided to fly out to watch me play for England. I was the hero son now. It was odd. I didn't know how I felt. Fortunately, I entered my favourite world as soon as the whistle blew and got to work on defending my country.

It turned out to be a terrible match. It was as if my dad had brought some very bad vibes from the East End.

We started off well, which was usual for us. We were always pretty quick off the mark and in no time we'd settled down playing neatly and constructively. But in the 28th minute the Swiss player Gian

A BAD NIGHT IN BASLE

Pietro Zappa found Alfred Scheiwiler with a great pass. He played a fabulous one-two with Claudio Sulser, before smashing a brilliant shot past poor old Ray Clemence, who didn't stand a chance.

Sulser was a tricky little livewire and when he sped towards me I did all the usual defensive things I was now famous for, but as I lunged at him he swerved and put the ball in back of the sodding net – two goals in a short space of time. I should have recognised the bad omen.

Suddenly it all kicked off on the terraces as horrendous violence and disgraceful scenes were picked up by television cameras. It was alleged the match was inadequately policed. As a player you are never sure what's going on up in the stands, but the sight of teargas is usually a giveaway. I was told it all got very ugly and the press said afterwards that something had to be done about the rising hooliganism among the English fans.

But we just kept on playing – badly. Dave Watson was having a crap game and even the brilliance of Bryan Robson and Ray Wilkins was ineffective against their opponents, René Botteron and Umberto Barberis. Paul Mariner was having a tough time up front, finding the well-organised Swiss defence too strong. As for me, I did my best, but by my usual standards my performance was well off.

I don't know if my dad in the stands had affected my play, but I doubt it. Mind you, when the trouble began among the English hooligans, the thought that good old George was somewhere up there with his mate Black Ray did fleetingly cross my mind. Was he all right? Of course he was all right – he was in the bar.

After the match I joined him. I was reeling from the dodgy game and deeply disappointed as I knew this defeat had almost fatally damaged our chances of qualifying for the World Cup. We would have to beat Hungary in our next match and then face Norway after that. We'd need all our prayers answered if we were to go to the World Cup finals in Spain.

When I arrived back at the hotel my dad was standing there larger than life with his dark hair flowing, and was holding up a bottle of champagne. He'd already poured out loads of glasses of champagne and orange juice. He thrust a flute of buck's fizz in my hand and said, 'Here you are – get that down you, son.' I took it and drank it. It was lovely and not much different from my normal juice. So I had another one. Had Elaine been there I would have stopped right there and then. She would have made sure of that. But instead I just joined in, while all the time reflecting on our poor performance.

Before I knew it I was drunk. It took no time at all to get that heady euphoric feeling the first buzz of booze gives you. I had no idea alcohol could taste so innocent.

Suddenly the misery of the game was forgotten and I was enjoying myself so much I kept on drinking.

We eventually wound up in a nightclub. Was I supposed to dance in this condition? It was looking that way. I started to have a little bop, but soon realised I needed to hold onto a bar on the dance floor. I thought I must look really good. I was certain I was dancing better than usual. However, the next minute I was sliding to the floor – and the next I was under the table groaning, 'I don't feel very well. I want go to bed.'

Dad and Ray just left me there and got on with their drinking and dancing. I haven't a clue how long I was slipping in and out of oblivion, but I suspect it was most of the long, boozy night.

I was still reeling from the revelation that my dad had acknowledged my existence. It was as simple and as devastating as that. Not only had he travelled to Switzerland to watch me play, he was also armed with gifts. He had bought me shiny shoes, a snazzy herringbone overcoat, and other such flamboyant clothing. I'm not exaggerating when I say I was blown away.

I was surrounded by family and friends and having the best time. I looked over at my tall dad and something inside felt right.

A BAD NIGHT IN BASLE

Suddenly I was as happy as a sand boy and thoroughly enjoying unleashing my inhibitions.

I was telling myself, 'Why *not* have a drink? Everyone else around you is letting their hair down. Your dad's here – just lighten up and enjoy the moment.'

I had heard these words before from outside forces. When you play football and are surrounded by blokes who like to down pints of lager and laugh louder than their sober counterparts, it seems the right thing to do to join in the fun. It stops the feeling of being an outsider.

'Come on, Ken, what you havin', mate? Pint?' This was a familiar echo, and there's only so long you can keep asking for an orange juice in this environment. I didn't like lager, though. In fact beer didn't do it for me at all. Champagne did, though. Champagne and orange juice went down a treat. And that night in the bar in Switzerland was my initiation ceremony into the world of alcohol.

I drank more champagne than enough. I drank so much of the stuff that when I staggered out of the club in the early hours of the morning and the cold air hit my brain I had to grab hold of some railings to try to steady myself. But my head was spinning and the nausea sweeping over me finished me off. I slid to the cold pavement before unceremoniously throwing up.

By now I was only with Dad and Ray. (Everyone else had disappeared when I was hibernating under the table.) Dad managed to hail a cabbie who was willing to take us back to the hotel, but I bet he wished he'd driven on like the other cabs who had refused our custom, as we hadn't gone far when I was sick again. No cabbie in his right mind would have taken us home that night. We were rotten.

The cabbie went mental, so Dad gave him twenty quid to clean his cab. I wonder how many times he had to do *that* in his lifetime.

The following morning I woke in my own bed with a monster hangover. I didn't know what the bloody hell had hit me and now I had to fly home. Ugh!

The way I felt physically you would have thought I'd never touch a drop again. But I clearly remember the train of thought that sliced through the fog in my brain. 'Oh, well, I've had my drink experience now. I might as well carry on.'

I could just as well have told myself, 'You have experimented, Kenny. You've got sick and are now suffering from a hangover from hell. Now just drop it and go back to the orange juice and lemonade.'

Had my thoughts, and subsequent behaviour, swung in that direction, life would have turned out to be very, very, different. But I had chosen to join the ranks of the hard drinkers. My mind was made up. My dad drank to get drunk – so did his brothers and my older brother, Peter. Why not me?

I already knew how to work hard, now I was about to play hard. I thought to myself, 'I can afford it.' But it was to turn out to be far too expensive a price to pay.

On the plane back to Heathrow my dad handed me a Malibu and pineapple. It was bloody gorgeous and, just like the buck's fizz, tasted like nectar. My one-man show of jokes and impersonations on the way home went even better than usual. I was so funny – I think.

Back in London I met up with my brother Peter in a pub in Peckham. 'What you having, Kenny – the usual?'

'No, I think I'll have a Malibu and pineapple, please Pete.'

He looked genuinely aghast. 'But you don't drink.'

'Oh, I had a drop of Malibu on the plane back from Switzerland – with Dad.'

'Kenny, are you sure? What about your football?'

'Hey, I'll be fine. Everyone else drinks.'

Peter told me many years later how that was a turning point in my life. He said there was a dramatic change in my personality when I was in drink. But apparently I was still fun, still warm, and still lovable.

Maybe I was being forgiven for everything because I was Kenny

– lovable Kenny Sansom – one of the best footballers in the land and a funny bloke to boot. Brilliant. Tragic.

After our dire efforts in Switzerland, England eventually managed to scrape through to the World Cup finals. Phew, that was a close call – and only a win against Hungary in 1981 ensured our qualification. I was a young man with a bright future, just as Jack Charlton had predicted.

My dad continued with his dubious lifestyle in gangland and I don't know what happened to Ray – I can only wonder. As for me, I stayed focused on my football career, the only difference being I was now a drinker. The eighties turned out to be phenomenal years on the pitch. Off-pitch, however, my addictions would threaten to destroy all that was dear to me.

I wasn't flash about my new status. Anyone who knows me will confirm that. I hadn't been raised to think I was any better or any worse than the next guy. I was a south London boy from a working-class family who had got lucky. But to say I didn't feel different would not be honest. I felt different because I was treated differently and my life was not the same as that of someone with a regular nine-to-five job who had the weekends off.

Life in the eighties was about to begin in earnest. Weekday mornings we would slog it out in training at London Colney, the afternoons most of us were in the pub, drinking and playing snooker, or down the bookie's. Weekends it was all about the match, but by night we'd hit Langhams, Tramp or Stringfellow's.

'Come on, Arsenal!'

CHAPTER SEVEN
JOINING ARSENAL

One day I was at Crystal Palace happily playing football in my comfort zone, and the next I had signed a 3-year contract with the Gunners. It was nuts. Everything happened at such lightning speed that I was left reeling.

When something monumental like that happens, you travel through a numb period when nothing seems real. I have always gone along with the flow of life and that's exactly what I was doing now. Instead of getting up every morning and driving to Selhurst Park, I aimed my car towards Arsenal's training ground at London Colney, where I would train with legends like Willy Young, David O'Leary, Frank Stapleton and Graham Rix. How bloody marvellous is that?

The press had a field day speculating as to why Arsenal would want to get rid of the prolific goalscorer Clive Allen, who had been at Highbury for only a matter of weeks. They dubbed it a 'Mystery Transfer' and were buzzing around wanting to take photographs of Clive and me wearing top hat and tails and celebrating with champagne in front of a Rolls-Royce. The hype of 'the big time' had now begun.

Terry Venables had made no secret of the fact he wanted Clive Allen in his side at Palace. Arsenal had bought him into their squad but, on a rethink, Terry Neill decided he didn't need him as much as he needed a new left-back – and it would appear I was their man.

My new club had been observing me closely at the European Championships in Italy, and I'm certain it was my performances for the national side that clinched my move to such a huge club.

I could have chosen other paths, but I was a London boy. I wanted to go to Highbury. I wanted to be a part of the whole setup at the Arsenal. It was straight out of a *Roy of the Rovers* comic, where a young hopeful's dreams are realised.

The Arsenal fans weren't as ecstatic as I was about my arrival, as they were still reeling from events the previous season when Liam Brady had chosen to go abroad to Juventus. It had unnerved them – they feared their much-loved team of the seventies was breaking up. 'Will Frank Stapleton follow?' were the rumbles in the club magazines such as *When Saturday Comes*.

The answer was a miserable 'yes' as Frank eventually went to Manchester United – and the fans' hearts were broken all over again.

An Arsenal fan and author of *Highbury – The Story of Arsenal*, Jon Spurling, told me many years later, 'We all wondered what Terry Neill was playing at. To be honest, we couldn't understand why he'd bought Clive in the first place. We had so many strikers it was like a traffic jam up front. There was talk both in the seats and on the terraces of a crisis enveloping Highbury. Tragically, the rumblings became a reality.'

So it was into this tricky era that I entered my new club. I was nervous, but most of all, honoured.

THE BRADY BUNCH

The Arsenal couldn't have been more welcoming. Having played for Palace and already being well established in the England side, I wasn't exactly in awe of the Arsenal team, but I certainly looked up to them.

Graham Rix was the main man. We just hit it off on the pitch from the start. This may sound a bit odd, but we had similar football brains and therefore understood each other and communicated well instinctively. It was as if we were telepathic. The kind of partnership we had is rare and to be treasured.

Away from the ground it was one of those friendships that are, as the song says, 'easy as Sunday morning'. We often enjoyed a pint and a game of snooker together. He was a terrific man and a terrific player, so it came as a great relief to the fans that he stayed on after the exit of Brady and Stapleton.

I can't emphasise enough how bad it had been for the club when legendary Liam Brady insisted on leaving, and for me it was a great disappointment to miss out on playing alongside him. Personally, it was the one single thing that dampened my arrival at Arsenal. Brady was a huge loss to the club. He was a Highbury legend, and the fans as well as the players missed him badly. It was as if the North Bank were mourning a terrible death.

Liam 'Irish' Brady, the lad whose roots were firmly in Dublin, had football running through his veins. His uncle and two brothers (Ray and Pat) had played with QPR and were living in the huge Irish community in north London. Hundreds of thousands of Irishmen had had no choice but to seek employment in London after the Second World War as there were few jobs in Dublin, Cork and Belfast.

Liam was only 15 when he moved from the Emerald Isle to join the Arsenal youth squad. He was outgoing and fun to be around, and had great spirit.

The previous manager, Bertie Mee, had set up Liam's career by handling the young Irishman wisely – using him sparingly and therefore allowing him to grow into his skin and mature before making him a first-team regular. Now that's what I call good management.

It must have been easy for Liam to feel at home at Highbury. It was *so* Irish. Terry Neill was an Ulsterman and during Liam's playing career in north London his teammates were Irish legends David O'Leary, Frank Stapleton, Pat Jennings, Pat Rice, John Devine and Sammy Nelson. With his fellow countrymen on the pitch with him, and the London Irish cheering from the North Bank, it was no wonder Liam felt at home at Arsenal.

Contrary to what many had to say about the Irish players being cliquey, Englishman Graham Rix blew that myth right out of the water by being Liam's best mate.

So you can see why the fans were so devastated when he left. But go he did. Liam Brady was as confident off the pitch as he was on it – he knew what he wanted and what was right for him and no one was going to sway him from his decision.

But, before he'd flown away to pastures new, he had been a key player in the 1979 FA Cup final, when Arsenal beat Manchester United 3–2 in a thrilling Wembley encounter. As far as the fans were concerned Liam Brady was top of the London Irish – top of the Brady Bunch.

But being an Arsenal player was no longer enough for Liam or Frank. Although the club had been enjoying great Cup runs, they weren't showing enough form to be contenders to win the League. Both wanted new challenges and who can blame them. But it was a bastard for Arsenal and a bugger for me.

Jon Spurling also made the following astute observation: 'The fact that Frank Stapleton followed Liam Brady out the door didn't help our mood, and some people think their exits hailed a dark age that coincided with Britain's economic recession.' That's a heavy statement, but it's also the truth.

Closer to home, as far as *I* was concerned, to miss the opportunity of playing in a back three of Brady, Rixy and me was a tragedy. We would have been fabulous combination – I just know it. We had the same potential to be in the same league as the later combination of Tony Adams, Nigel Winterburn, Lee Dixon and Stevie Bould.

It wasn't too long until I became one of the lads. David O'Leary and Pat Jennings were special people, but I can honestly say there was no one I didn't get along with, which was great. But you will see as my story unfolds that being one of the lads became part of my personal problem.

Graham Rix had been a regular on the left wing for 5 years when I was positioned beside him. He had replaced George Armstrong in the mid-seventies and had enjoyed being a part of the attacking midfield line-up that took Arsenal to three successive Cup finals, all of which I had just missed out on. Thank God he didn't decide to go as well. But even so, the barren spell of not winning silverware was to continue for some considerable time.

But I took my hardworking ethos to Highbury and worked as hard as I had at Crystal Palace. This was to be my time in a great club and I was going to give it my all.

DARK DAYS

I was in my early twenties and at the peak of my fitness. Although it was fabulous being an Arsenal player, the early eighties weren't exactly wonderful years for the club, Jon Spurling had been right: we were entering the 'Dark Ages'.

I had always been used to a strict routine. To make it to the top you need to be dedicated and disciplined and know where your priorities lie. In my early days at Arsenal I adhered closely to these strict regimes. It wasn't difficult, as it was all I knew. I was playing for both Arsenal and England, and loving it.

Being the kind of man I am, I rarely had cross words with anyone. I'm not a passive wimp, but I *am* pretty easygoing. I look for the best in people and trust them till they do something to make me backtrack and keep my distance. This meant I rubbed along with everyone. I was lucky Kenny Sansom, whose career was just getting better and better.

I have to admit, my teammates were a different kind of 'family' from the Crystal Palace lads. In a sense I had moved overnight from a safe, middle-working-class environment to the upper classes. That might sound weird and I don't mean to be derogatory to anyone, but that was the way it felt.

I was a boy from south London whose mum had gone out to clean to put food on our table and I am damn proud of my background. But when I became a player for the Arsenal I gained all the privileges and kudos afforded to a top-flight footballer. It was phenomenal. Arsenal were up there with Liverpool and Manchester United – the cream of British football; and it felt amazing to have made such a major step forward with my career.

Back at Selhurst Park I had played in 156 games for Palace – missing just one match. I had loved being at the heart of the defence in the Team of the Eighties as we surged forward until we reached the top of the old First Division at the end of 1979. They had been in the Third Division when I'd joined, so this was quite some achievement. However, just as I had progressed through the schoolboy ranks and youth teams to playing for England's full team, so I had moved from my teenage club to a senior establishment. It was one hell of a leap.

THE TERRY NEILL YEARS

I spent the first three of my 8 years at Highbury under Terry Neill's guidance. He talked a good talk, did Terry. But often everything seemed to fall flat on the pitch. I didn't sense a hunger in the club and that rubbed off on the players and, therefore, our performance. I was as ambitious as ever, as were the others. We were all winners longing to win something, but when I look back I can see we weren't knitting together as a team as well as we should have, and that's why the silverware kept eluding us.

Terry Neill had been a part of the Arsenal establishment for so long that he'd virtually become a fixture and fitting. He'd already enjoyed a long career as a player there, clocking up 270 games, and had been the youngest captain in club's history. He had originally managed Spurs, before crossing the north London divide in 1976 to join fellow his Irishmen at Arsenal.

At first things went well for Terry and the Brady Bunch. The new signings of Malcolm McDonald and Pat Jennings brought an added strength and a period of relative success to Highbury, and a trio of FA Cup finals between 1978 and 1980 had lifted the spirits of all who loved the club. It was a shame they converted only their 1979 final into a winning event but, as we all know, to get to Wembley in an FA Cup final is a fantastic day to look forward to, take part in and remember – so just getting there gave a lot of people at the club a boost.

When you consider we had players of the calibre of Sammy Nelson, Willie Young and Pat Jennings in our team, we should have been clearing up – but we weren't.

Some people think the 'boring boring Arsenal' years began after the arrival of George Graham, but we were in dire straits long before. Lots of our games under Terry were awful, and only brief touches of brilliance gave us short reprieves and kept the diehard fans coming to support us.

My first FA Cup run with the club was a personal disaster for me. We lost in the third round away at Everton by two goals to nil, and I scored a goal – at the wrong end – to put us one goal down. I nearly died on the spot. My heart was in my mouth. Pat Jennings couldn't believe what was happening as my shot flew past him. The look on his face mirrored the agony on mine as the one and only time I beat him contributed to the end of our FA Cup challenge.

My intention had been to clear the ball with my weaker right foot, but suddenly I changed my mind and decided to control the ball with my stronger left. Unfortunately, the ball hit the inside of my foot and slipped past the near post. Gutted or what? I had to close my ears to the abuse directed at me from the Gooners who had travelled 'oop North' with high hopes.

In the dressing room I put my hands up and prepared to take it on the chin. I stood there apologising profusely to Terry Neill's number two, Don Howe, but he held up his hand and said quietly, 'Don't worry, Kenny. It's one of those things.'

It came as little comfort, but I was grateful for his understanding. Just as I turned towards the shower he added, 'You should have cleared it with your right foot.' Thanks, Don.

It was a long journey home on the coach, and although I was feeling down it didn't take me long to get into the swing of the jollity on board. The lads were fine with me and my howler was quickly forgotten. Soon I was encouraged to do a few impersonations. So I threw myself all over the coach calling to 'Mr Grimshaw' in a silly Norman Wisdom voice, and then falling about in Frank Spencer fashion.

We shouldn't have been that happy. We should have cared more. With hindsight the speed of how quickly we'd all managed to get over this FA Cup disappointment was a travesty. After all, this competition is one hell of a big deal. Did we, the Arsenal players, care enough about winning? I couldn't possibly have asked myself all these questions then. I was young, impressionable and doing what I've sadly done for much of my life – going with the flow.

We were all playing well as individuals. But as for knitting together and going out there as a unit who could deliver enough to be winners, it just wasn't happening. We were way off the mark and so the silverware eluded us.

We knew where we were going for our Saturday night out, and we were quick to make arrangements for a Sunday lunch outing to the pub. We also loved a drink after training during the week. But had we lost our edge on the pitch? Were we taking things for granted where the football was concerned? I think if the answers to these questions are to be answered honestly, we all have to own up to a certain amount of complacency that ran from the top down to the grass roots.

JOINING ARSENAL

After a disastrous defeat to Walsall on 29 December 1983, the Arsenal board acted quickly: just over 2 weeks later Terry was sacked.

A TALE OF TWO CLUBS

At Crystal Palace the ethos had all been about the football. Our social life was a bacon roll in the wooden hut during training and going home to the family for your tea. I drank orange juice in the club house and was very content with my lot. I didn't need booze in those days – my football and my family were enough. Every day finished with a feeling of satisfaction and it was only when I reflected on these terrific days while scouring through my wonderful catalogue of photographs in preparation for this book that it struck me just how beautiful life had been over in SE25.

Elaine had found her feet as the wife of a footballer at Crystal Palace but now, at Arsenal, she had been promoted to a fully fledged wag (for the uninitiated, 'WAGs' is the acronym for 'wives and girlfriends'). She remembered Terry's words and remained true to herself. Once when I was away playing for England she was invited to a function and in my absence she took the lady from the tea hut as her companion. When one of the WAGs pointed out to her that it wasn't really the done thing to take the tea lady to a posh do, she turned on the woman and told her to mind her own business. 'I'll bring who I like,' she bounced back.

She was already friendly with Ann Hoddle because of my association with Glenn, who was often my roommate on England away trips. But soon she also became firm friends with Jill Rix. There was no one she didn't get along with, so she was growing into her own skin pretty well and enjoyed every aspect of being a footballer's wife – well, most of them, anyway.

Arsenal in the Terry Neill years was as much about the social life as the football. Even before Saturday's match we would be planning our night out on the town. There was rarely a weekend when we weren't frequenting some celebrity haunt or another.

By now I had acquired the nickname 'Mr Chablis', as I loved a bottle of cold, crisp, white wine. The drinking that had begun in Switzerland with my dad and Ray had now well and truly become a habit. And I have to say, it was a habit I enjoyed to the full during the eighties.

Elaine and I had hit the big time. We had well and truly arrived on Planet Celebrity. People were referring to me as a 'Face' – how crazy is that? My dad must have been so proud.

I traded in my yellow Datsun for a white Jaguar XJS and just loved swerving into our smart driveway and parking up my new motor.

By now Elaine would think nothing of spending a thousand pounds on a dress she would wear only once. She'd confidently moved from being the south London 'It Girl' to a north London wag. We were caught up in a whole new world far away from sobriety and bacon rolls served up in a wooden hut. But was that really a good thing? It seemed so at the time.

THE DON HOWE YEARS

Arsenal handed Don Howe the chalice after sacking Terry Neill. He had been a terrific full-back in his playing days spending most of his career at West Bromwich Albion. He joined them as an apprentice in 1952, made his debut in 1955 and over the 12 years with the club played more than three hundred games. He had an impressive England career as well, winning twenty-three caps and playing a part in the 1958 World Cup finals.

The late great Billy Wright signed him at Arsenal in 1964 and made him his captain. It was there his luck ran out. Playing away against Stanley Matthews's Blackpool team, he broke his leg and that, as they say, was the end of that. He never played again.

His managerial career had also been prolific. Bertie Mee took him on as youth coach at Highbury, but it wasn't long before he had been promoted to the role of first-team coach, taking over from Dave Sexton, who went off to Stamford Bridge in 1968.

JOINING ARSENAL

Arsenal won the Double in 1971 – it was a fantastic high for the club – and Don was right at the centre of the celebrations.

After another short spell at his old home of West Brom he returned to north London yet again – this time as head coach to Terry Neill. I guess it was only a matter of time until he took on the management challenge.

Don Howe was at Arsenal with me in the eighties. He was part of the England setup some of the time during my England career, and then later on we worked together at Queens Park Rangers and Coventry. So you could say we got to know each other pretty well over the years. We had good times and bad times – bright lights and dark days. Let me share two examples of the extremes.

London Colney

The first happened in training at London Colney in 1985 and I was the skipper. Don Howe said to me, 'Get the first team squad together. I want a chat.'

We all stood there in front of him as he went on to say, 'I've not been happy about how you have been playing together as a team in the last few matches. You need to do better. I also think your fitness levels are poor – you're just not fit enough. Today I want to train without a ball.'

Our hearts sank. Training without a ball meant running, more running, and even more running. 'Kenny,' they *all* groaned. 'This is shit. Have a word. Talk to him, Kenny.'

I tried to talk Don out of such a harsh session, but anyone who knows Don Howe knows it's like talking to him while he's wearing earmuffs. It was a nonstarter. So we started running what we call 'box to box' – which involves running from one penalty box to the other and then back again, and then your partner runs off – a kind of relay. Even in the warm-up everyone was moaning and going on at me to do something.

Anyway, I decided to walk instead of run.

When Don Howe noticed me sauntering along he went mad. 'If you don't start running, Kenny, you'll do twice as much as a punishment.'

So I started walking off towards the changing rooms, all the while looking furtively over my shoulder to see who was following me. But they were all bloody running. No one followed. I thought that if one walked the rest would follow – like in the coalmines when they all stuck together. But no – they were going from box to box and doing what they were told. I couldn't believe it. Where was the loyalty? So much for team spirit!

Angry words reached my ears as Don Howe shouted, 'You prima donna bastard, Sansom.'

In turn, I simply raised my arm and waved. Even as I drove my car out of the car park I had the cheek to blow my horn and wave yet again. But that wasn't all I was going to be blowing: I was about to blow £1,000 on a fine for my bad behaviour. Now that wasn't very clever of me, was it?

Rotterdam

Another Arsenal story from the Don Howe days happened in Rotterdam when we were in Holland for a pre-season training tournament. Well, we played terribly.

After one particular match, which we lost by six goals to one and where our performance had been even worse than the scoreline suggested, a big tall guy who turned out to be one of the directors of Arsenal came into the dressing room and gave us a dressing down. 'You have let the name of Arsenal Football Club down. I am very, very upset.'

He didn't need to say any more – those few chosen words were enough to shock us. Don Howe hadn't finished with us, though. 'You are all cunts.' Now, Don Howe never, ever swore like that, so it just goes to show that this was probably one of his most miserable moments in football.

I went over to him and said, 'It was poor and we let the club down. But I'm not a cunt – none of us are that.'

Like a true gentleman he apologised for using that word, but with that great thing called hindsight I can see just how mortified he was with our play and what a dreadful time the press must have given him.

ARSENAL AND A *SUN* REPORTER GET NAKED AND TOMMY CATON GETS TWO DOGS

It was during the Don Howe and Terry Burton years that we all booked into a naturist hotel and got naked. We were in Holland again – this time for a pre-season tour of both Holland and Germany. The hotel we booked into, unbeknown to us, was a naturist resort. At least, I don't think anyone else knew, but some funny bastard might have been having a laugh at our expense.

The rules were that you could walk around with your clothes on, but if you wanted to use the pool or the sauna you had to be naked. We were all a bit shy at first. Some were embarrassed and others nervous and not sure they wanted a swim after all. But after a while we all relaxed into it, so to speak.

There was this *Sun* reporter with us – I'm damned if I can remember his name, but he joined in all the fun. However, it nearly went horribly wrong on the last night when the reporter, Tommy Caton and I stayed up very late and got very drunk and disorderly.

After everyone else had gone to bed the three of us got behind the bar and started to serve each other drinks (as far as I can remember we *were* fully clothed at this point). We managed to get into the fridge that housed the bottles of Don Perignon, so you can imagine how out of it we were. We drank from the best crystal glasses and I reckon we drank a whole bottle each – at least.

On the way back to our rooms we had to pass three German Shepherd guard dogs housed in their kennels and, thankfully for us, chained up. But Tommy decided he wanted to fight the damn dogs. He danced around like a boxer and started to rattle their chains, which, of course, set the dogs off barking like mad. It was a scary few minutes and it would have been far scarier if we'd been sober and seen the danger Tommy had got himself into. Thank God he had his trousers on or the *Sun* reporter would have had a front-page headline all right. But the reporter was hardly able to stand up, let alone write a juicy story.

In fact none of us could stand in the morning – which was only a couple of hours after Tommy nearly got eaten by the guard dogs.

Terry Burton came marching over to where I was staggering and told me, 'You are a disgrace.' As I was drunk I arrogantly told him I would only talk to the boss. My God, how the drink can change you!

During his reign as manager at Arsenal, Don bought in three fantastic players who all became very good friends of mine – Tony Adams, Niall Quinn and David 'Rocky' Rocastle. But there was still no sign of any silverware and he resigned in 1986, making a vacant space for George Graham to stroll through the doors of Highbury.

BOYS WE'VE LOST

Paul Vaessen retired from football at the age of 21 after being plagued by recurring injuries. His glory moment came in the 1978 UEFA Cup tie in Turin, when he came on as a substitute, scored and became an instant north London hero. Unfortunately, he went from hero to zero overnight and had to retire from football with a terrible knee injury. Right from the moment I met him I felt he was a fragile boy. His confidence levels weren't great, although he had terrific passion and enthusiasm about his play. I feel saddened that his career didn't flourish in the way it should have, and I often tried to help him out all I could.

Way back during his heyday when he played thirty-odd games for Arsenal there were rumours circulating that one of the Highbury boys had attempted suicide and Paul's name had been linked to the drama. How true these rumours were I still don't know, but what I *do* know is he's dead now. He died far too young and in such tragic circumstances that, given my own addiction problems, I'm mightily relieved I am still here to tell my story. Paul's addiction to drugs led him into a world none of us would wish on our own worst enemies. When I think back to his joy at scoring in Europe, it saddens me deeply to think he died so young.

Tommy Caton died from a heart attack at the age of 30. He was a Highbury legend who thrilled the crowds and was also a great friend of mine. He came to us from Manchester City in 1993 and was a regular player during his first 2 years at the club. He had been retired only a matter of months before his heart stopped beating. RIP, Tommy.

Rocky Rocastle was very popular with the fans – probably because he was such a showman. Don't get me wrong, he worked as hard as the rest of us, but there was a quirky side to his nature. He was like a playful puppy at times. He was down to earth as well, though – a 'what you see is what you get' kind of man – and I loved him to bits. He would do anything for his team and in turn we all respected him hugely. His death from cancer came too suddenly and, like Paul and Tommy, he was too young to die – too good to leave all those who adored him.

Three great guys. Three terrific football players. Three men gone. A trio resting in peace.

CHAPTER EIGHT

INHABITING AN EMOTIONAL WASTELAND

I gave 100 per cent in training – as did the other Arsenal lads. I also enjoyed our weekend play time in London's hotspots.

On the pitch we'd run, defend, attack, and work on skills ready for Saturday and midweek matches. That we were united as a team was not in question. But for me, the time between one o'clock when training ended and five o'clock when I'd finally reach home, I would just slip away.

Some of the other hard-core drinkers went off to the pub together – united and happy to chat about everything from women to football to gambling (and not necessarily in that order), before going home to their wives and girlfriends for dinner.

I, on the other hand, would be desperate for solitude. Depleted after giving 100 per cent to my job, I craved my own company. So I'd slide into the shiny new car that was now well within my budget and begin the long journey back to Epsom. (These were my early days at Arsenal, so we were still in Surrey and we were yet to move to north London.)

A few miles down the road I'd pull into one of my many pit stops as I travelled through Muswell Hill, Crouch End, on towards Highbury and Islington and then finally over the water.

Once in the safety of known territory, I'd stop at the Elephant and Castle, before resuming my journey onwards through Brixton, Tooting and Streatham, until I reached the leafy suburbs guiding me home to Epsom. It was one hell of a long journey.

Every so often I'd find somewhere to park legally, usually a car park of some kind, since I didn't want to park on a meter, where there was a time limit and I'd be in danger of getting a parking ticket or clamped. I knew that once I entered my twilight zone in a betting office or pub I'd lose all sense of time.

Once in the bookie's I'd study the form and place my first bet of the long afternoon that lay ahead. I'd nod a polite 'hello' to the other punters before retreating into my much-needed personal space. This atmosphere was strangely comforting and it was a comfort I craved.

After placing my bets I would climb back into the car and drive towards home with my music playing. There were no mobile phones as such then, so I didn't have to worry about having to switch off the outside world.

When I reached my next regular betting office, I'd check to see if my horse or dog had won and then place another bet. Thus was my staggered ride home – making time, playing for time, but never *on* time.

Before I reached my home, the pub and fruit machine would call to me, and the chances of my ignoring the opportunity of disappearing into oblivion were nil. I think Pink Floyd called it, 'comfortably numb'.

With one hand holding a glass of wine and the other tapping buttons in the hope of hitting the jackpot, I blanked out the world around me. Don't get me wrong, I loved everything about my world, I just couldn't live without this pocket of escapism.

In one sense you could say I was entering an emotional

wasteland, a place that was detrimental to my wellbeing – and, of course, it was. But, in another sense, by taking some time out for just me (not Kenny Sansom the Arsenal hero or the loyal husband and attentive father), I managed to remain intact as an individual.

I used to ask myself over and over, 'Who am I?' And I continued to ask myself this question most of my life. A feeling of 'being misunderstood' niggled away at me, but I had no way of communicating this troubled part of me to anyone. Years before I began to understand myself better, I had to find other ways of feeling good – and gambling and drinking made me feel good. It was as simple as that. The buzz was instantly gratifying – and it was all mine.

This might seem selfish, and I guess in a sense it was, but it was so unbelievably powerful and it really didn't feel as if I had an option but to carry on gambling and drinking. Addicts reading this will know exactly what I mean – but I guess those of you who do not fall into the label of 'addict' are likely to be less sympathetic. So be it.

At first the gambling was far and away more important to me than drinking. But as time went on throughout my Arsenal years I fell further and further into alcoholism. I never knew I was becoming an alcoholic. I wasn't drinking any more than my teammates.

At around this time I went back to Selhurst Park to watch Palace play. In the bar afterwards one of the old boys there asked what I'd like to drink. 'Champagne, please,' I said. The guy raised an inquisitive eyebrow and said, 'Hmm, times have changed, Kenny.'

And he was right – they had. The kid who used to drink orange juice had grown into the kid who downed copious amounts of champagne and pints of Chablis. I don't know what to say about that, really, other than the memory has stuck with me and therefore on some level I must have known I was falling into a dangerous habit.

The gambling had been part of my makeup. I took risks as a kid by jumping across rooftops, and risk-taking is part of the makeup of a gambler. I strove for perfection and that put me at risk of pushing my luck too far. My gambling addiction was part of my journey into my alcoholism.

One instant stands out clearly. Elaine had been to bingo with her mum, Alice, and won £800. This was in the seventies, so a grand was a lot of money then – even to a professional footballer. Well, Elaine and I have always been of the belief that says, 'What's mine is yours and what's yours is mine' – it was simply the old-school way of thinking. But I think I abused this theory when I took the money to the bookie's and blew it on a dead cert that wasn't so certain after all.

I went home with a heavy heart and, just like a child, locked myself in the bathroom and hid. When Elaine realised I had gone walkabout inside the house she came looking for me. I don't remember how long she banged on that door, or how many times she pleaded with me to come out. All I have lodged in my memory bank is that terrible sinking feeling of dread. I'd let my wife – and myself – down.

When I finally unlocked the door to face the music, Elaine looked at me with such an expression of fear that my heart went out to her. But as I explained the error of my ways that look on her face changed and some colour came back to her cheeks. During her wait outside the bathroom door, she had managed to convince herself I was having an affair. The knowledge that all I had done was gamble her winnings away came as a huge relief.

I swore to her and to myself that I would never gamble again and I meant it – but the addiction was bigger than I was. And it would be a very long time until I hit the point of crisis when I would have no choice but to change.

However, the dive into the ditch of despair was still a long way off then. I may have been battling with two progressive addictions, but I was still in control of my football career. I was a functioning alcoholic, and I didn't ever want to stop drinking. I enjoyed it far too much.

The consequences of how I was feeling, thinking and ultimately behaving were lost on me. My loved ones were out of reach. I was unable to glimpse outside my bubble, because the fog was too dense. But that was OK – or at least I kidded myself it was. The comfort zone that was my sanctuary was also my prison. I was locked into a self-depreciating world – hating being lonely, but at the same time choosing this existence.

I was in free fall, but my safety net was still in place. I was young, fit and still very much into my career, which was just as well, as now the time had come around for me to go off to the 1982 World Cup finals in Spain. Pretty bloody amazing, really.

CHAPTER NINE
1982 WORLD CUP, SPAIN

I don't regret anything in my football career, except for the
summer of 1982 when I made a couple of howlers and
nearly scored – but missed.

Losing Kevin Keegan and Trevor Brooking to injury was a
terrible blow. I'm going to stick my neck out and say, 'If they
had been fit and we'd had that special ingredient of good luck that
helps everything to click into place perfectly, we could have won
the World Cup in Spain.'

But anyone who knows and loves their football will remember
we came back home out of the tournament without even losing a
game. Had it been a knockout competition instead of those bloody
group scenarios it would definitely been a different story. Oh, the
ifs and buts! I know, they sound like sour grapes. But, you know,
when you're young and playing for your country in the World Cup,
losing and going home early makes you naturally ask yourself,
'Why?' When you know you are part of a team that is as good as
any other and better than most, but have still 'failed' to make it
through to the end, it's a bitter pill to swallow.

Ideals of fate or destiny soften the blow: 'It was rotten luck, and not meant to be' or 'It was in God's hands.' But ultimately it wasn't anything to do with God (unlike the 1986 Mexico World Cup when that rogue Maradona spun his wizardry and then cheated us with his 'Hand of God' – but more about that later). It was all about us.

The Spanish sun was savage and I remember losing 10 pounds in weight in the game against the French. At half time we were given frozen towels that soon melted on our hot bodies. Chocolate bars and salt tablets were handed out, and we drank gallons of water thirstily.

Ron Greenwood was a special manager with a quiet demeanour, but he had firm ideas about how to coach and how to play the game. 'Let the ball do the work' was his constant message. 'Knock the ball in front of your teammate; let him run onto a pass instead of having to control it.'

Simple but effective, rather like Ron himself. Not simple as in 'not quite the full shilling', but, simple as in 'calm and easy'. He really hated to hurt any of his players' feelings and he found telling a player that he was dropped very difficult indeed.

I'm surprised he didn't begin to get a complex, because, whenever he singled out a player in training and started to walk towards him with a pained expression on his face, the player would run away, quite literally. Glenn Hoddle was, without any shadow of a doubt, the player who turned on his heels the quickest.

'Oh, no, I'm not playing,' he'd grimace before legging it to the other end of the pitch. It was an amusing sight. What wasn't funny was Ron having to tell Alvin Martin he wasn't even *coming* to Spain. What a blow for Alvin, and what a rotten part of Ron's job!

Ron thought seriously of quitting halfway through that hot steamy summer, when nothing seemed to go right. But we were having none of it. As far as we were concerned he was going nowhere. We loved him. The press could slaughter him all they liked but we were firmly in his camp, totally convinced he was the best man for the job.

Anyway, the last thing we wanted was more disruption. We'd lost Kevin Keegan and Trevor Brooking and we were not about to stand by and let our gaffer walk out because of the dastardly press piling on the pressure.

I can't say that I felt under pressure personally. I was young, fresh and eager to play football. I wasn't watching *The Big Match* with my mates on a Sunday afternoon now – I was *on* it. I was the professional footballer kicking, throwing and heading for England – and relishing every minute of it.

There was no longer a Sunday roast cooked by Mum while watching Brian Moore introduce the programme that had become a must in so many households, followed by a game of footie up the park with my mates. Instead I was there, playing in magnificent stadiums like the Bernabéu. I had to pinch myself at times.

Regularly wearing my England shirt with No. 3 stamped on the back was a dream come true. I wasn't a nervous player. I was far too confident in my abilities. My game was solid and, therefore, my place secured. I had been playing for my country in the full team for 2 years now. If someone had told me then that I was to be England's number-one choice for almost a decade I would not have been surprised. It was what I expected of myself, and I knew my personal goals were achievable.

ENGLAND V FRANCE (WE WON 3–1)

The England v France game was the first of our matches. It was stifling in the San Mamés Stadium in Bilbao, but the real heat was on when, after just 27 seconds, Bryan Robson hooked a high, waist-bouncing ball down and beyond their goalie, Jean-Luc Ettori. *Yesss!* It was pure magic.

Bryan's record-breaking goal began right from the kick-off really. The French put the ball out and then Steve Coppell threw a long ball into the penalty area, where good old Terry Butcher flicked the ball across the goal mouth. In sped Bryan, all on his own, and put it away. We had been practising these throw-ins in training, but on my side of the pitch, so it came instinctively to Steve. What a terrific start – but sadly it was just a case of beginner's luck in what was to be a disappointing tournament.

We slaughtered the French by three goals to one, which was quite something given that Kevin and Trevor weren't part of the action. After that first goal we were able to contain rather than attack. Don't forget, the thermometer was nudging 100 degrees F and we felt we needed to conserve as much energy as possible. But, as it happened, this wasn't wise, because we actually gave France a chance to come back at us.

Michel Platini, who in my opinion is up there in a league with Maradona, Bestie, Pelé, and Johann Cruyff, had a relatively ineffective game, and that was down to the tremendous efforts of Ray Wilkins and Bryan Robson.

For 25 minutes we played a chesslike game. Then they scored. Damn! Unfortunately, Trevor Francis lost possession and this allowed Jean-François Larios (which is also the name of nice drop of Spanish gin) to pass to Gérard Soler, who sped with the speed of light towards goal, leaving the relatively inexperienced Terry Butcher way behind. There was nothing Peter Shilton could do to save a cracking shot.

At half time we were level. I could imagine viewers at home groaning, 'Here we go again – we've thrown away another lead' as they downed their beer. God, how I would have loved a long, cool pint. Actually, the sun began to go down after our first 45 minutes, and the air instantly became cooler. I can't tell you what a relief that was. Our heavy feet had wings again and in the 66th minute we gained a much-deserved lead, once again with a goal from Bryan Robson. The goal seemed to come from nowhere. He just snapped up the ball crisply and put it away.

We were defending really well and the French were getting hot and bothered. So you can imagine my delight when Paul Mariner half-volleyed a terrific shot past a well-and-truly-beaten Ettori.

After this stunning performance against the French we genuinely believed we could go on to repeat the 1966 triumph. But, alas, it was not to be, even though we went on to beat Czechoslovakia and Kuwait.

I played in the Czechoslovakia game and it was very different from playing the flamboyant French. In contrast the Czechs were all over the place and very undisciplined in their play. We should have beaten them by a bigger margin, but shots by Steve Coppell, Paul Mariner and Ray Wilkins missed the target by the tiniest of whispers. I was rested for the Kuwait game, as were Bryan Robson and Terry Butcher, and, even though we won 1–0, it was a poor game, scrappy and undisciplined. We couldn't seem to find the motivation we needed. But we weren't worried, as we assumed we would get through these group rounds and go on to win the World Cup. I've learned since that it's a dangerous thing to make assumptions.

THE FABULOUS BERNABÉU

In our next match we drew 0–0 with West Germany at the fabulous Bernabéu Stadium – the home of Real Madrid. What a place! It's a very special and unique stadium. The high tiers bring the fans closer to you and make for an already highly charged atmosphere even more spectacular. Unfortunately, the play didn't match the splendour of the arena. The Germans were determined not to lose against us and played boring, defensive football. We weren't much better – our usual flair had abandoned us and we simply couldn't find a way through to score. Steve Coppell nearly scored but didn't, and we all know how that feels when a World Cup prize is at stake. Mind you, he must have put the fear of God into the German goalie, Harald Schumacher, because he was taken full stretch and only just got his fingertips to the ball. Ray Wilkins kept up the pressure by striking a powerful shot from 25 yards out, but again it was saved. Their sweeper system, however, was awesome and they were lightning quick on the break – but their breaks were few and the game ended leaving us with everything to do against the hosts, Spain.

West Germany had beaten Spain by 2–1, which was another blow for us, as we now had to win by two clear goals if we were to reach the semifinals. Ron chose to play Tony Woodcock instead of Steve Coppell.

Even though they weren't fully fit, Kevin Keegan and Trevor Brooking came onto the bench as subs. We were to go out with all guns blazing.

However, my guns weren't firing from all barrels in this important match – and this is where my rare and very personal regret comes in.

I made some errors I shouldn't have made. I was marking Miguel Alonso and twice he squandered chances I'd stupidly given him. They could have gone 2–0 up.

From there on in the game went slowly downhill for us and despite Ron's sending on Kevin Keegan and Trevor Brooking and Kevin's sparking of some brilliant action into our side, we just couldn't pull it off. Desperate to make amends for my earlier mistakes, I almost scored myself. Ray Wilkins took a free kick and I pounced on it at went for goal. If only it had gone in. If only.

If we were guilty of any one thing during these championships it was probably that we became too timid as we progressed through our group games. A little more courage might have seen us through.

We returned home with our heads held high, though. We stood tall (well, some of us), proud, but disappointed. And it's as the years roll by that I glance back over my shoulder and, although my regrets have been too few to remember, I *do* regret that things did not turn out differently. To have lifted the World Cup would have been brilliant.

Our exit from this tournament wasn't the only goodbye. Ron Greenwood retired and, although we had failed to qualify, he could leave the England setup with his head high. But I don't suppose he saw it that way.

He might well have stayed had we made it through. But instead he left after this match against Spain without finishing on a high. There was no fairytale ending – this is football, remember, not 'Cinderella'.

So I came back from Spain and got down to work back at Highbury. These were barren years at the club. Terry Neill and the Brady Bunch came and went. No silverware and no glory meant the fans were disgruntled and worried as to where their club was going to next – the dogs? We had the potential to achieve great things, but it wasn't happening for us. Charlie George had left Highbury, but thankfully David O'Leary stayed on a while longer – as did Charlie Nicholas. Willy Young remained a star and I remained strong in defence, still playing really well alongside Rixy. It was strange – we gelled so well it sometimes felt as though we were telepathic.

I was still gambling and my drinking was on the increase. It's really strange how well I was still able to play. In fact it was a bloody marvel most of us were able to play as well as we did, given the drinking culture that was growing at an alarming rate.

Thank goodness I still loved the game and was still as fit as a fiddle, as there was much work to be done for my country.

CHAPTER TEN

ENGLAND MATCHES

I have listed my eighty-six caps at the back of this book. They are caps I am immensely proud of and at times I still have to pinch myself to make sure it's true. My gift for being able to play football is not something I have ever taken for granted. Instead, I worked solidly and was paid back handsomely.

There have been so many special matches. One of the most spectacular is the one we all know about – the controversial 'Hand of God' game when Maradona scored *that* illegal but allowed goal that sent us reeling out of the 1986 World Cup. I'll tell you more about that bloody disaster in a bit, and you can look forward to finding out the real reason why we lost – never before told.

In this chapter I thought I'd give you a little taster of a collection of my most memorable games. I couldn't possibly remember details of all eighty-six games, but the following give an overall flavour of the best.

On 23 May 1979, at the age of 21, I made my full-team debut. We played Wales and drew a disappointing 0–0. But nothing could have taken away my immense pride. I was on the first step of a majestic journey and realising dreams only very few boys manage.

KENNY SANSOM

My next game was away for the England B in Austria, and a decade of travelling had begun.

In November, England played against Bulgaria in a European Championship qualifier. The weather was horrendous and for the very first time in history a Wembley international had to be postponed. Everyone was disappointed but Kevin Keegan more than most, as he had to fly back to his Hamburg team to play in a match for them.

In my first match of the eighties, England played the Republic of Ireland in a European Championship qualifier at Wembley and we won 2–0. The goal-scoring power of Kevin Keegan was fantastic, and an excited Bryan Robson made his debut. Playing against David O'Leary, Liam Brady and Frank Stapleton, two of my soon-to-be teammates, and one whom I'd have loved to play against, was very special.

In May 1980 I came face to face with a young new phenomenon – the one and only Diego Maradona. The Argentines came to Wembley and the stage was set for a classic match. Maradona was still a teenager and I was just 21.

I think it would be fair to say that he had a marginally better game than I did, as I managed to give a penalty away against him. He was so clever and amazing and did not make a single mistake. Despite my slip-up, I never gave up. I ran myself ragged and we had a real battle that must have been quite something to watch.

Later that month we travelled up to Hampden Park in Glasgow for a battle of monumental proportions. It was always something special to go to Scotland and take on our arch-rivals – especially when we won, which we did by two goals to nil – and extra special when we were involved in a goal, which I was.

Going to Hampden is like going into a cage full of lions without a whip – but we too were lions and, thankfully, we came out on top. I marked a brilliant Gordon Strachan, and other great Scottish legends playing were George Burley, Joe Jordan and Kenny

Dalglish. The fact that Sky's Andy Gray could only get on the bench spoke volumes about the calibre of their side.

I could have gone across the world to Australia to play some friendly matches, but I was nursing an injury, so Frank Lampard Sr went in my place. As there was still much to do for England that summer and because I was about to move to Highbury in the autumn it was probably just as well, anyway.

The following spring Brazil came to Wembley and lit up the stadium like a beacon. It was only a friendly, but you wouldn't have known it. Brazil are such a wonderful team to play against, as the incredible flair on the pitch and carnival atmosphere of their fans make the whole event seem like one big festival. The Brazilian fans play loud samba music and, win or lose, it's a fabulous, one-off experience – which is just as well, because we lost 1–0.

If my memory serves me right West Brom's Peter Barnes was the victim of a vicious tackle, which didn't seem fair at all, because he was playing like lightning down the wing and leaving the Brazilians standing.

To be fair (and this isn't making excuses) we had a depleted team, as lots of our players were injured. But we battled and battled and never gave in, which wasn't easy: they were so wonderfully skilful and seemed to play in tune to the beat of the samba music.

We were already down by half time but came out firing on all cylinders for the second half. To be honest, our adrenalin levels were so high it would have been nigh on impossible not to play at a high level. I think our fans really appreciated the fast-moving tussle as the noise in the crowd reached a crescendo towards the end of the match. We may not have won, but our efforts had not gone unnoticed or unappreciated, since the fans gave us a standing ovation.

The next match worth a mention is the one I've already told you about – the one against Switzerland in Basle, when good old dad introduced me to the world of booze. Who is to say I wouldn't have gone that way anyway, but we won't go there, eh? At the end of the day it was my responsibility.

Then there was a Home Championship match against Northern Ireland, which we won by a wicked 4–0. We had the best start ever when, after just 44 seconds, Bryan Robson zoomed past Sammy Nelson and scored. We'd got a quick free kick and the next thing the ball was in the back of net.

The Irish had Pat 'God' Jennings in goal. What a star! Simply the best. I'm not sure what happened to him that day – or am I? Of course I am: *we* happened. Kevin Keegan got the next goal, and then we just kept the pressure on. Ron Greenwood had decided to try a new formation and played Ray Wilkins as an extra defender and, although I'm not convinced it was the right decision, it didn't affect the end result. I think I nearly scored in that match, but Pat Jennings got the better of me and it was not to be.

Although our match against Holland at Wembley in May 1982 was just a friendly, it's worthy of a mention because we beat them 2–0, which was quite something given that they were one of the best teams in the world at that time. It began with our eyeing each other up, wondering what was going to happen. I had a sense they were nervous of us, and why not? England are anything but predictable.

It was a special game for Peter Shilton, as he captained us for the first time. We filled the midfield with as many players as possible. Bryan Robson and Wilkins worked so hard – they were all over the pitch; awesome. We found and created so much space. Their goalie was on form, but so was Shilts. My buddy Graham Rix came on in the second half and from that moment on we took a hold on the game.

Tony Woodcock scored and then Rixy provided a brilliant cross to Paul 'Marrers' Mariner, and the Ipswich player also found the back of the net. The match was effectively won and lost in that 5 minutes. Rixy and Wilkins kept their cool and remained in control right up till the final whistle blew. That was definitely a reason to celebrate.

ENGLAND MATCHES

We went to Hampden Park needing only a point from the Scots to win the Home Championship. This was the hundredth official international between England and Scotland, so we were led out by English legend Tom Finney and the Scots had George Young. Finney would certainly have been happy with the outcome, but he was always going to be a good omen for us, since England never lost an international at Hampden when Finney, the Preston North End wizard, was in the team.

With the World Cup just around the corner, the game took on an even greater significance than usual, but, despite the great Hampden roar from the 80,500 people present, it was England who started the better. Trevor Brooking, who was at his most elegant throughout, hit a volley that was well saved by their goalie, Alan Rough. Terry Butcher just missed from close range and then Paul Mariner headed wide with a glancing header from Brooking's cross.

This impressive opening was rewarded after 14 minutes when we took the lead. Brooking sent in a corner, Bryan Robson headed it back, Butcher headed it against the bar, and then Mariner dived bravely to head the rebound into the net. We thoroughly deserved this goal and were definitely in the driving seat.

They worked hard, though, and in one spell Shilts had to make three saves in one minute as first Alan Brazil had a shot at goal, and then Phil Thompson's back-header gave Shilts a fright, as did Graham Souness, when he hit a shot that Shilts did well to hold onto. Generally, though, the Scots were weak in a midfield battle in which Trevor Brooking was showing his terrific talents.

Phil Thompson and Terry Butcher stood like brick walls at the heart of England's defence. As far as Terry was concerned, he played one of the best matches he'd ever played for his country, and Bryan Robson played to his usual fantastic standard.

We had notched up yet another victory at Hampden – the oldest of our away venues, and we had won the Home Championship title once again.

The following year we travelled back to Hampden Park and this time we drew 1–1. It was the last ever Home Championship international – and what a battle it was! Bobby Robson switched to a 4-2-4 formation to give his forwards the much-needed support lacking in their recent games.

It looked as if we'd record a handsome victory, but as so often before in this fixture the Scots suddenly took the wind out of England's sails by scoring totally against the run of play. Gordon Strachan was as aggressive as ever in midfield and played a blinder. Spurs hard man Graham Roberts also played well, in one of just his six games for England.

All in all, of the 102 games where England faced Scotland in these championships, we won 40 and Scotland a close 39. Twenty-three ended up as draws. We scored 183 goals in total to their 166. Now that's what I call rivalry.

CHAPTER ELEVEN

MEXICAN HEARTBREAK

It was on 3 June 1986 when we stepped out into the Tecnológico Stadium for our World Cup match against Portugal in Monterrey. We were desperate to win, but fuck it – we lost.

It's a good job I had been well fed and watered in Canada because the weather in Mexico was steaming hot and I was about to lose some serious weight (don't say a word). I heard that Bobby Charlton had lost a stone when he was playing in Mexico City and I wasn't far behind with a 10-pound loss. This took me to 10 stone 12 pounds, which was a stone lighter than when I played with Arsenal. I have a feeling I was the correct weight for my height for the first time in years. In a decade, even. Scandalous!

Mexico was hot – bloody hot. You could have fried an egg on Ray Wilkins's head if he'd lost his hair that bit sooner.

I love the heat, but would prefer to swim and sunbathe rather than play in the World Cup finals. But, hey, life's not perfect. Joking apart – and sorry, Ray, I don't mean to offend – I'm just a lucky bastard who still has a good head of hair.

Anyway, moving swiftly on, the honour of standing in front of a world audience while the national anthem rings out loud into the air is a moment to be savoured. The pride you feel has no bounds.

Our confidence was sky high. We had been on a roll of late, winning the last eleven of our games. We should have beaten Portugal, who, at the time, were a very ordinary side. But we made hard work of what should have been a breeze.

Up until this day the weather had been perfect for us, but it was Sod's Law that it changed just before we kicked off, and the searing sun baked us.

The Portuguese played defensively and it became clear from the beginning they were going to rely on scoring on the break. Both Bryan Robson and Mark Hateley missed the target with shots in the first half.

Bryan, who was thankfully fit enough to play despite his ongoing problem with his shoulder, made some clever moves and gave the Portuguese a few headaches. We had seven shots on goal. Why, oh why, didn't we manage to convert at least one of them? I know we were the better team by far. But we were becoming more and more frustrated and playing their game rather than ours. All in all, we were stifled.

Gary Lineker almost scored early in the second half and just missed by a finger touch. A few minutes later, he was even closer to grabbing us a vital goal. He actually beat Benfica's goalie, Manuel Bento, before another defender hooked the ball off the line. It was painfully, agonising, close.

In the stifling heat of the second half, just as it was beginning to look as though it would end in a goalless draw, Carlos Manuel beat Shilton at close range.

I have to put my hand up and say I made a defensive error by allowing Diamantino to pass me – it was a rare error, but costly. He crossed low to the far post and Carlos Manuel was left totally unmarked and had the easiest of shots to beat Shilts.

We were so disappointed, as was the rest of the nation. It really was a terrible moment and I know all the pubs back home were filled with fans drowning their sorrows. I would have liked to drown a few of them myself.

We had to do better against Morocco. Well, we couldn't do much worse.

Three days later we played Morocco in the same stadium and again we walked out into a melting pot. The temperature was over the 100-degrees mark. Apparently, just before kick-off, our team doctor had poked his thermometer into the ground and it read 40 degrees Celsius. Shocked and worried, he didn't think it was right to tell us – he thought we'd be too alarmed. Damned *right* we would have! We were nervous enough as it was without the added anxiety of passing out with heat exhaustion, and Bobby Robson wholeheartedly agreed. On one occasion before, he'd been in the company of another doctor who had suffered a heart attack at high altitude. I for one am glad they decided to keep this little snippet of information to themselves until much later, when we were back in chilly Blighty.

The Moroccan side got off to a brilliant start, but, thankfully for us, they didn't take the chances that came their way. If they had, they would have thrashed us – but, as it was, the game ended in a draw.

The game was disastrous for us. Just before half time courageous Bryan 'Pop' Robson went in for a tackle and his shoulder popped out of its socket – again. Poor Bryan was in terrible agony. He was given attention behind the goal, but it was game over for him, and he knew it.

Then it got worse. Ray Wilkins got sent off. It was unbelievable. The normally level-headed Ray lost his temper after being penalised by the referee for a scandalous offside decision (honest) and threw the ball at him. It didn't warrant a red card – as it was a half-hearted gesture (honest again) – but off he went.

Ray has said since that this was the lowest point of his entire England career. I bet it was. It must have been very painful. As I said, good job he still had his hair or, to add insult to injury, he'd have got sunburnt as well.

You can imagine the dressing room at half time. Our spirits were low, but the most pressing problem was how hot we were. Bobby Robson said later that we looked as if we'd all just rolled off a barbecue. You can just imagine our relief when we saw there was a tin bath full of ice waiting for us, so we were given our half-time talk in that.

All in all, I think we did well to hold Morocco to a draw – being down to ten men in savage heat was one hell of an experience. The bottom line was that Bryan Robson was on the plane winging his way home, and Ray was suspended, but now we *had* to beat Poland. We played in the Universitario Stadium in Monterrey and beat them 3–0.

With Bryan and Ray out of the picture the boss decided to leave Mark Hateley and Chris Waddle on the bench and bring in Peter Beardsley for Mark.

By half time Gary Lineker had scored a hat-trick. His face was like a gleeful child's and this image was sent all around the world – it was very endearing. With the score ending up 3–0 to us, you could definitely say it was one of Gary's finest days. When the whistle blew for a desperately needed half time, we once again had to rely on ice and freezing-cold towels to draw the heat from our baked bodies.

Although Gary Lineker scored the goals in that important match, I have to say that much of the credit has to go to Glenn Hoddle. On the lead-up to one of the goals he made a brilliant pass to Peter Beardsley and set in motion a series of terrific passes that led to a cracker from Gary.

Glenn was very clever on the ball, and never more so than during that match. He was acutely aware that it was even more important than usual to keep possession in the intense heat. Brian Robson has said that, in his opinion, this was the moment Glenn showed the world his mastery in midfield. But for me it was the twosome of Gary and Peter Beardsley that was very special – awesome, even. They loved playing together, and it showed. Together they played as one.

Our next match – against Paraguay in the Azteca Stadium in Mexico City – also saw us win by three goals to nil. Gary Lineker continued where he had left off in our previous match – on a glorious streak of brilliance – and the effort would win him the tournament's Golden Boot for the leading scorer.

We were in the last eight now and next up was Argentina – and a match that would be the topic of conversation for ever and a day. I'll now describe it in detail – the truth, the whole truth, and nothing but the truth.

ENGLAND V ARGENTINA

There are two things a lot of people don't know about this game, which saw Maradona's infamous so-called 'Hand of God', and I am going to point the finger of blame at someone you may not have thought of – Steve Hodge.

The day before this crucial match, we practised a couple of tactical moves time and time again. It was well known that when their opposition were awarded free kicks the Argentinians ran out approximately 30 to 40 yards. We worked out a plan that would upset their tactics.

The plan was that I would run over the ball and heel it back to Glenn Hoddle, then, when the Argentinian defenders all ran out, our forward players would come with them and then Gary Lineker would spin back in, and Hoddle would chip me in, making it simple for me to square to Gary for a tap-in. It all went wrong in the match because Steve 'Forgetful' Hodge forgot to run out with the rest of the England players and was called offside. In training it had worked like a dream – but in the match it left us dreaming of what might have been.

Five of us stuck to this procedure when, a few moments before Maradona scored the illegal goal that sent us reeling out of the World Cup, he ran towards goal and one of us forgot to run, but instead just stood there: namely one Steve Hodge – Mr Forgetful. And that was what changed history. Steve Hodge ensured Maradona was onside and allowed the inexperienced referee to be manipulated into allowing the goal that put us out of the 1986 World Cup. The World Cup that, in my opinion, we could have easily gone on to win. That should have been our year – our glory.

It was white hot in the Azteca Stadium. The 115,000 crowd was noisy and everyone was anticipating something quite special of this World Cup quarterfinal clash between two old enemies.

Peter Reid had recovered from his ankle injury and Bryan Robson was also recalled. Terry Fenwick was back after his suspension and we were raring to go. Terry Butcher was on fire and got booked early on for a challenge on Maradona. The game was a tense affair at first, with few goal chances on either side. Peter Reid was probably the best player in the opening moments as he played with his usual impressive flair. The referee, who would later go on to devastate us with a mistake of monumental proportions, was already showing his weakness. The Argentinians were up to their usual antics of putting doubt into any official's mind, and this was a worry. To be honest, there was not a single shot worthy of a goal during the first half and at half time the scoreline was 0–0.

The second half was a different story, though – as anyone who knows anything about football will know.

It was 5 minutes into the second half when an explosive incident occurred that left us all reeling. Reports have said it was all down to one man – Maradona. But Steve Hodge had a bigger input into this goal than many people realise.

What actually happened was that Maradona picked up the ball, ran with incredible speed to just inside the England half and then ran at our defence looking to play a one-two. We had been practising the day before and told to race forward in a situation like this to push Maradona into the offside position. All of us except Steve Hodge did as we were instructed, but Hodge intercepted and flicked a looping back-pass to Peter Shilton. Peter rushed out to punch the ball clear, but Maradona leapt for the same ball and won it. Had Steve not flicked the ball back to Shilton but run in the other direction with the rest of us, Maradona would have been offside and a goal would not have been possible – hand or no hand. As history now tells us, Maradona beat Shilton to the ball and pushed it into the net.

Incredibly, the referee allowed the goal. It was a nightmare – a fucking nightmare. We all panicked and ran to the halfway line to plead our case. It was no use. Dismay turned into anger and then panic. Four minutes later, Maradona scored a brilliant goal – probably the best of the whole tournament. It was quite breathtaking.

He was so damn gifted and should never have had to resort to cheating.

Bobby Robson was astounded. He had been sitting on the touchline right opposite the incident and knew categorically that it had been an illegal goal. He threw on two subs and, with 9 minutes to go, Gary Lineker pulled a goal back for us. Then John Barnes crossed to him and he almost got his foot on the ball to equalise, but it didn't happen. We had played out of our skin and had nothing to be ashamed of, but we were out of the World Cup and the Argentinians were through to the semifinals. It was a tragedy.

I know it's true that we could hold our heads high. I know we had behaved impeccably both on and off the pitch. And it was true that after the disaster at the Heysel Stadium and all the negativity about our fans we were now building bridges – but it didn't stop the terrible hurt.

There was no way I wanted to swap shirts with any of the Argentinians. In fact, it all got a bit heated back in the changing rooms when some of our opposition were looking to exchange their kit for ours. Some of us would have liked a punch-up more than a jolly-up. Ironically, the only person eager to get his hands on Maradona's shirt was Mr Forgetful himself, Steve Hodge. He still has it and it's now worth a bloody fortune: it's estimated at a value of somewhere around £250,000. Deal or no deal. Oh, well, that's life. I wish I'd got it now, though.

Many years after this World Cup travesty, Maradona publicly admitted he'd cheated. He told about how he jumped and cheered and acted up to let the referee and other officials believe it had been a legal goal. He said he had to shout to some of his other team members to do the same. 'Come on – celebrate or they won't give it.' I know what I'd like to have given him. But the fact of the matter is: it was pure genius.

THE SUN SETS AND A NEW DAY BEGINS

I enjoyed Mexico more than Spain. I was a more mature player with higher fitness levels and was generally a more confident, all-round player. (And I'm not referring to the pies here.)

Spain had been especially disappointing as we'd not managed to score against either Spain or West Germany, yet had remained unbeaten. At least in Mexico we had demonstrated 100 per cent commitment.

There may have been better England managers than Bobby Robson but none have commanded the same respect or have deserved it as much as he did. Trust is a vital quality in a manager and we trusted him implicitly. My teammates were a fantastic bunch of players. We all got on so well, and I believe much of this camaraderie was down to his way of managing. In a nutshell, Bobby Robson is a really nice man. Like all England managers, he has his critics, and after this World Cup the knives were out for him. There was nothing new there – but, all in all, I think he did a good job.

Above: Malcolm 'Smoking' Allison. Another magical photo by Hy Money. What an icon Malcolm was! He was an original – though he reminded me in many ways of my dad.

Below: Me and Tony Healy doing keep-ups with our heads in training at Palace.

Above: This is me and my mum and Elaine when I won The Player of the Year 1979 award at Palace.

Below: A 'Glad All Over' day at Selhurst Park when the fans invaded the pitch after we beat Burnley 2-0 to win promotion to the First Division in 1979. One of the best ever nights for all at Palace.

Above: Celebrations in the dressing room at Selhurst Park after we'd won promotion. Jim Cannon is jubilant and passing round the champers. 'Not for me, Jim. Drinking's a mug's game.'

Below: The Crystal Palace team being treated to a lunch by Terry Venables in a little Italian restaurant in Croydon.

Above: This one is for you George Graham! It's me kicking a ball with my right foot in my England debut against Wales in May 1979, proving all my critics wrong when they said I had no right foot! George always teased I couldn't even stand on my right foot.

Below: This is me about to take a throw-in and telling my team-mates where to position themselves.

Above: A gentleman of football with his stars of the future. Legendary England manager Ron Greenwood is flanked by me and my good pal and team-mate at Crystal Palace, Billy Gilbert. I was in the senior team by now and Billy had been selected to play in the Under 21s.

Below: Me and Terry Venables doing a 'Laurel and Hardy' impression. We had some great fun together off-pitch, and fun in those days did not include alcohol.

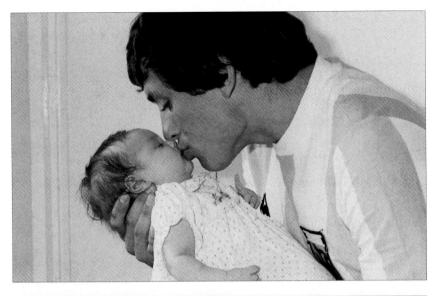

Above: 'Must be kissing an angel'. A proud dad with my first born child, Natalie. She was a dream baby and is now the mother of four beautiful children of her own.

Below: Terrific family shot of me with Elaine and our young family. Left to right: Elaine, Katie, me, Natalie and my only son, Harry.

MEXICAN HEARTBREAK

Glenn Hoddle and I made up nicknames for our squad members; some are obvious and others I will leave to your imagination. I've chosen to share these endearing 'aliases' to highlight the happy days we shared.

Bobby Robson – alias Rick: He had many nicknames but our favourite was Rick. He used to get in a muddle with our names and call me Kenny Statham. Once when we were at an airport he picked up a bag and went in search of Peter Reid, who wasn't even travelling with us on that trip.

Don Howe – alias Chuck: Don was as bald as our England team coach driver in Colorado, Chuck, and so he acquired the nickname.

Peter Shilton – alias Shilly: The newspapers had nicknamed him Shilly Shilly after he'd hit a dodgy tee shot in a high-profile golf match.

Viv Anderson – alias Busy: He never stopped bloody talking.

Gary Stevens and Trevor Steven – alias The Hustlers: They were never off the pool table.

Glenn and I – alias the Blues Brothers: Forever doing impersonations.

Mark Hateley – alias Psycho: No comment.

Bryan Robson – alias Pop: Because his shoulder kept popping out of its socket.

Chris Waddle – alias Barry Norman: He was a huge film buff.

Peter Beardsley – alias Ceefax: He knows everything that's on the television – including the time and channel.

Steve Hodge – alias Mr Forgetful: Even Bobby Robson was in on this one, because Hodgey was *so* forgetful. Bobby said, 'Put a tag on him at the airport in case we lose him.'

John Barnes – alias Digger: After Digger Barnes in *Dallas*.

Peter Reid – alias Freddie Star: He's a funny bastard.

Gary Lineker – alias Hero: No imagination needed there.

This had been a happy trip. We had all got on and there were no outside pressures to spoil our friendships. Bryan Robson's injury had been damn bad luck, while Ray Wilkins's sending off had been unfortunate. I had been privileged to spend time, both on and off the pitch, with some of the greatest legends of our time – lucky, lucky Sansom.

In Mexico we had been so near, yet so far. Although I hoped and prayed I'd still be the first choice for England at left-back in the next World Cup, there was no certainty of its happening. Four years is a long time, and injuries can end a career in a split second. Anything can happen to change your life, and I was smart enough to know all of this. I guess that's why Maradona's cheating hurt so bad.

Yet on the plane back we managed to get back into the spirit of things. We downed some champagne, played cards and generally fooled around. I told a few jokes, which fell on deaf ears, but my impersonations were getting better and better. I stood up at the front of the plane and in my best Columbo voice told Bobby Robson, 'My wife thinks you're terrific, Mr Robson.'

He laughed and then called me Dave before turning to Luther Blissett and calling across, 'What did you think of that Bluther?' I tell you: he may have been a great football manager but his memory was shit.

So, as the sun set on the 1986 World Cup and I lay in the Portuguese sunshine with Elaine and our children, my thoughts turned to my club – the mighty Arsenal. I was 27 years old. Soon I would be back at London Colney for pre-season training under new management. The 1986–7 season was going to be special – very special indeed.

CHAPTER TWELVE

ENTER GEORGE 'THE STROLLER' GRAHAM

RESPECT AND FEAR

As we stood in front of George Graham and listened to him telling us is no uncertain terms how things were to be under his management, we all wondered how long it would be before our new boss would win something big for Arsenal.

I was in Colorado with the England squad when I heard that Graham was the new manager. George had been a member of the Arsenal side who had done the Double in 1970–1, and Terry Fenwick couldn't wait to give me the lowdown on my soon-to-be boss.

'Bloody hell, Kenny! You're in for a rough ride, mate. He can be a right tough bloke – a proper disciplinarian.'

Not convinced, I said to Terry, 'Yes, but you've only ever played for him in a youth team. Everyone knows you have to be extra tough on kids.'

Terry just smiled and we moved on to more important things, like beating Portugal in our opening match of the World Cup. It would be some time yet before I had to stand in front of my new boss to find out the truth for myself.

I think many of the Arsenal fans have heard the 'don't call me

George, call me boss' story. But, for those of you who haven't, let me tell you. The message George Graham gave us was loud and clear: it was to be discipline, respect and repetitive defensive training all the way.

He had been at Crystal Palace and Queens Park Rangers, where he had been a youth team manager with his good friend, Terry Venables, before going on to manage Millwall.

We knew each other quite well, and, as we now lived just a stone's throw away from each other in New Barnet, we would occasionally have a glass of wine together. Strangely enough, we bumped into each other shortly before I'd flown off to the World Cup, but neither of us knew then that we'd be getting to know each other a whole lot better.

Now, as I sat thinking about my new boss, I recalled a conversation we'd had over a drink some months before, when we'd been chatting generally about our hopes for the future of the game. It gave me food for thought. I had accused him of being too negative and defensive and said I thought his teams should attack more.

His response had been loud and clear: 'I like my teams to have good shape.' Then he came back at me again: 'You seem to be frustrated, Kenny. All this talk of getting players forward tells me you're desperate to win things.'

'Of course I am,' I replied. 'I've never won anything in my life. I want to get my hands on a trophy. I want to take a cup-winner's medal home.'

I wasn't alone in my frustrations. George Graham wanted to be a winner every bit as much as I did, and we were about to enter a very exciting era.

We had the players – now all we had to do was go out and win.

THE NEW GAFFER

I have this vivid memory of George Graham that makes me laugh every time it pops into my head. It was in our Crystal

ENTER GEORGE 'THE STROLLER' GRAHAM

> Palace days and we were playing away at Sunderland's
> Roker Park. Dave Swindlehurst went in for a challenge and
> split his eye open. We all watched, alarmed at the amount of
> blood pouring down his face. George, with hand on hip,
> posing as usual, visibly shivered as he cried, "Oh! The blood!
> I can't stand it!"

The new gaffer arrived at Highbury wearing his pristine shirts and immaculate suits with his head held high and a spring in his step. George 'Stroller' Graham knew what he wanted and was determined to get it.

Many who had played in the Arsenal team with him in the early seventies were surprised by his appointment. Word was that he hadn't shown too many leadership skills as a player during his time at the club, and I can't say I spotted them at Crystal Palace, but when he arrived as manager it was clear something had happened in the intervening years to change him.

George had played with such ease that he had earned the nickname 'Stroller'. His playing style had matched his character – slick, graceful, but with an underlying sense of power. The fans had been delighted by the number of goals he scored. His shot could be savage at times, but on other occasions the same supporters would also turn on him and accuse him of being lazy – which was nuts, as George was anything but lazy. I think this criticism was more about his lack of pace.

I believed George Graham had got lucky when he was given the job of managing an Arsenal team full of talent. He was taking on a very experienced side and also had the added bonus of having enough funds to buy in new talent. There were also magical players such as young Tony Adams waiting in the wings at the youth academy.

His arrival to the first team was eagerly awaited, but the club was yet to find out just how much of an impact he'd have at Arsenal.

George took no time in making me his skipper, and he knew that by handing me that armband he would be getting 100 per cent of me. I had rarely played a poor game. My consistency was second to none. I was as proud as punch.

'Hello, George,' I grinned at the man whom I'd known for years.

'It's "gaffer" to you from now on,' he barked. He wasted no time in putting me right in my place. I was being given a wake-up call. We all were. George Graham was determined to make great things happen at Highbury. Alarm bells rang everywhere: on the training ground during the week and in the dressing room on match days.

The Gunners' campaign to win trophies had begun in earnest. The new gaffer was adamant we were going to win some silverware if it was the last thing we ever did. My God, we all got the message loud and clear.

He was right: we had been asleep. We'd taken our eye off the ball. Was George capable of pulling us out of the doldrums? Was he really a strong enough leader to get us where we belonged – back on top?

Well I tell you, something had happened to George Graham during his 3-year reign at Millwall. He had obviously finely tuned his managerial skills and was now about to set to work on us.

We were all desperate to win some trophies and no one more than yours truly. A domestic cup or League Championship medal had eluded me and that didn't feel right. I was winning England caps hand over fist, and rarely missed either an England or club game. I was consistent and remained injury-free. I never missed games because of being booked, and I had had one only sending-off in my entire career. In other words, I never compromised my place in the squad. What more could I do to win trophies? I could do the best I could with the efforts our new manager was bringing – that's what I could do.

I was still a young man, but also aware I was edging my way towards being a senior player. I held a great responsibility not only to deliver personally, but also to set a good example to the younger lads George was about to bring into the side – both from the Arsenal youth academy and from other clubs.

George was to make some inspired choices and set a precedent of good things to come. He was about to make some brilliant things happen, including signing some terrific players who would thrill us and ignite the waning passion of the Arsenal fans. And I was about to captain this new side. I took that armband with a pride no words could describe.

In the dressing room before our first match of the 1986–7 season – which happened to be against Manchester United – the gaffer gave us the talking-to of our lives. His message to us was that we were nobodies all the time we were failing to win big matches. If we wanted to be legends like Manchester United (who were doing really well), we had to wake up the Highbury giant who had been sleeping for far too many years. 'Go out and be the Arsenal,' he urged us with a passion in his voice that really made us sit up and listen. This guy demanded the best, so we had better get our act together and deliver.

So, when we ran out onto the pitch on the opening day of the 1986–7 season following a rousing team talk, where we had been told to emulate the Highbury legends of yesteryear, we went out there with all guns blazing. At last we had a game plan and that felt magic.

'Hustle them,' George had urged us, 'Squeeze them and don't let them play their game.' Midfielders were told to help out in defence and smother the opposition.

I can't say it was a great game for the spectators to watch, because it was very defensive. There were no goals until very late on in the game, but eventually Charlie Nicholas, who had the knack of saving his goals for big occasions, scored a cracker. The crowd went mad, we went mad – *everyone* went mad. You would have thought we'd just done the double. It was just fantastic. The air was filled with chanting and singing – Highbury, and especially the North Bank, had come alive. We'd beaten Manchester United.

I remember clearly the moment Paul Davis turned to me and said, 'We were in danger of going nowhere again this season, Kenny, but with this bolt of electricity the gaffer's sending through the place we could win the bloody lot.'

But for us to win 'the bloody lot' we needed to carry on as we had begun. George really had to get a grip with us and wipe out some of the complacent attitude left over from the Terry Neill days. But George was ahead of us in his thinking. He had a game plan and he was determined to follow it through.

His plan to push our opponents into the offside position worked a blinder. One hand went up, then another hand went up, and then the confused referee would blow his whistle. Fantastic – it worked really well. George wanted consistency. He wanted us to play the same way week in week out. Training focused on defence, and the back four were worked harder and harder with each passing day.

It's a bit weird really considering he'd played with such wild abandonment and amazing attacking flair. It was a contradiction in terms that his priority was now totally on defending – what was to be termed 'boring, boring' defensive play. But George was on a mission. He knew what he wanted and he went for it. He was taking no prisoners.

One day I sat outside his office for bloody ages waiting for an audience with him. I think he kept us all waiting in the corridor for ages for psychological reasons. He was well aware that whoever was sitting outside could clearly hear what he was yelling to the player inside. He'd rant and rave at the slightest of demands. The poor sod inside was getting a right dressing-down.

I knew there would be a similar showdown if I asked for better terms on my contract. It just wasn't happening. I knew Tony Woodcock had asked for a new contract – but that George had just totally blanked him. He didn't even speak to him as I recall – just gave a look that said it all. No way.

Charlie Nicholas was excited about this new inspiration sweeping through Highbury. This new Arsenal spirit was highly contagious. Charlie was also philosophical. With or without him, Arsenal was going straight back to the top, and there was a good chance it would be without him. Charlie was astute enough to know that he wasn't really George's favourite type of player.

Charlie was a showman who loved the big event. He had flair and individuality. George was after something more solid (he valued hardworking, solid players) and he also wanted youth. Charlie thought George was more delighted about our keeping a clean sheet than his scoring a goal against Manchester United, and I think there was an element of truth in this.

So where did I stand? I was certainly no longer a teenager. I was nudging thirty. I had been England's first-choice left-back for a decade and had earned more than enough caps, but how much longer would I be Arsenal's first choice?

There was a lull after this initial euphoria. Our match against Oxford was especially dire. Could our win against United have been a one-match wonder? Was it a case of beginner's luck? No, it wasn't. By late October we were off and running. Suddenly we were sitting on top of the League, and the Gooners were flocking back to the North Bank. It was rocking at Highbury all over again.

ARSENAL ARE BACK! ARSENAL ARE BACK! AND WE'RE GOING TO WIN THE CUP!

When I think about the prolific players I spent much of the eighties training and playing matches with, I feel very honoured: players such as central defender, Tommy Caton, who ended Arsenal's 2-year search for a replacement for Willie Young. George had to wait a whole year until he managed to clinch a deal all the fans had been praying for, but Manchester City had been reluctant to sell

Tommy. Arsenal badly needed someone to bring in alongside David O'Leary in defence, but until Tommy no one had come near to good old Willie's talents.

Paul Davis turned out to be a midfield master and a great asset to the side. Like me, he was a south London boy, although to be honest we didn't have an awful lot in common.

Then came the third round of the Littlewoods Cup. Manchester City travelled south and were greeted by a rousing Highbury crowd, who were desperate for their team to win this Cup tie. We wanted to be winners – all of us. It was tangible in the waves of chanting washing over the North Bank.

The referee tossed the coin and as usual I elected to have possession of the ball and start the action. The gaffer agreed – he liked us to have the psychological edge, and, my God, it worked on this occasion. We pulverised them in the first half.

As we kicked towards the North Bank, our favourite end of course, we honestly could have made it 6–0 during the first half – we were that inspired. City didn't know what had hit them. It's weird, but we always seemed to play better when we were running towards our fans at the North Bank. The crowds at Highbury were swelling again and attendance figures had crept up from 20,000 to 35,000. The whole place was rocking.

City had this really quick forward called David White. He got right behind me for a throw-in, which was bad news, as we had been working on stamping this out. I can remember the crowd chanting my name as I went to take that throw-in, and I was grinning from ear to ear at the change in our performance.

Yet, during the second half when we playing towards the Clock End, City managed to get back into the game, which infuriated George. He had a right go at us afterwards. 'You let them come back at you.'

He was right. We had been living dangerously and they could have easily scored, which would have rubbed out our clean sheet.

But they didn't score; and the end result was an impressive 3-0 victory for us.

The gaffer and I had a terrible row afterwards. It was the second time we had clashed since his arrival, and he told me I hadn't played well. He said it was a classic case of thinking we'd done enough and having taken our foot off the gas. Whatever, we were told we were *never* to make that mistake again. It was a bit of a bum end to what had been a triumphant Cup tie.

The next day we trained very hard. It felt like a punishment for our tame second-half performance the previous evening, but by the end of it we were well and truly hyped up for our next match against Charlton. It was a bit weird playing back at Selhurst Park, which Crystal Palace was sharing temporarily with Charlton. I remember peering out into the pouring rain and seeing so many of our supporters waiting for the game to begin and the feeling was terrific. At least half of the crowd were wearing the Arsenal shirts, so I'm mighty glad we whooped Charlton 2-0.

When newcomer Tony Adams scored a brilliant goal during the game there was a feeling pumping through my veins that told me we were up and running. Three more points. As the winning feeling began to spread through the club we just knew it would take a special performance from a good team to stop us in our tracks.

By November George had purchased some more young blood and, when we played Southampton in mid-November, some of them made it onto the scoresheet. Now we were top of the League and it felt fan-bloody-tastic. Viv Anderson found the back of the net, as did newcomer Perry Groves, and delighted both himself *and* the Gooners in the process.

Perry was about to become a cult hero with the fans. He was a fun-loving 'ginger' character who got nicknamed 'Tin-Tin'. The chorus of 'We all live in a Perry Groves World' was sung to the tune of the Beatles' lyric, 'We all live in a yellow submarine'.

And this was to become a Gooners anthem for many years –

even today, years after his retirement, they sometimes burst into song as they remember Grovesy.

At the beginning of the season it had been touch and go whether Tony Adams or Tommy Caton would get the nod to partner David O'Leary at the centre of defence, and Tony won. Although Tony wasn't as quick as Tommy, he still had great pace and was good in the air. He was fearless, determined and noisy, which is always a plus on the pitch. He used to shout instructions at the top of his voice and his confidence never wavered.

Tony was already skippering the England Under-21 side and I had this feeling he was en route to the captaincy at Arsenal – but not yet. *That* honour, at least for the time being, was in *my* safe hands.

As I said, the focus in training was on defending, but we didn't mind, as George's plan was working brilliantly and it was becoming the norm for Arsenal to keep a clean sheet. 'One-nil to the Arsenal' was another cheery chant to float through the air from the terraces. We'd defend, break away and score; and then batten down the hatches. It may not have been pretty, but it was effective and the fans knew that winning was the ultimate goal.

By March 1987 we were well and truly on the road to Wembley. Only our neighbourhood rivals, Tottenham Hotspur, stood in our way as we marched towards the first silverware the club had come within spitting distance of for years.

ARSENAL V SPURS: WEMBLEY, HERE WE COME!

We had lost the first leg of the Littlewoods Cup semifinal 1–0, so the pressure was right on us to win the second leg at White Hart Lane. The match was played on Sunday, 1 March, and was shown live on television. Glenn Hoddle would have to be shackled and Michael Thomas was given the job of marking him tight in midfield to prevent him from using those great long passes he was known for. At that time Hod was the best passer of the ball in

English football and we couldn't allow him the space and time to carve us open.

Despite the rain, the atmosphere was electric. I was so proud to lead the Arsenal boys out onto the pitch that day, and even prouder when all of us displayed great character and strength. Not even the critics in the Sunday newspapers, who said that we were going out of the Cup, could dampen our spirits – we were going all out to be winners. George Graham had been furious with the media comments – he didn't say so, he didn't have to, we knew his moods well by now.

His message to us in the dressing room was, 'You must be patient. We know we have to score, but, what ever you do, *don't panic* – especially if Spurs get a goal first.'

This was inspired advice, as Clive Allen scored, and, had we not been given this firm message, we might just have panicked. But we didn't – we followed orders and kept our heads. But those heads were a bit down at half time as we contemplated the 45 minutes ahead and wondered how we were going to pull this back. Then an extraordinary thing happened.

Spurs announced over their public-address system how their fans could apply for tickets for the final at Wembley. Then the buggers switched on their old FA Cup final song, 'Spurs Are on Their Way to Wembley', and the fans started to sing along. Well, that did it. Fuck this for a game of soldiers. We weren't going to take this kind of abuse. Our determination was now way over the top. With adrenalin rushing through our veins, we ran out onto the wet pitch for the second half knowing we were at war with the enemy.

It's very difficult to describe to you this rare feeling of 'playing out of your skin'. It happens rarely in a lifetime, and when it does you remember every moment of the experience as though it were in slow motion.

I got this goosepimply feeling, and I absolutely knew I would lead my team to victory. The young faces all around me mirrored my determination and we went for it – big style.

Strangely enough, we were more controlled in this all-important 45 minutes. In turn, we managed to pin them in their half and create more chances for ourselves. Viv Anderson scored, and then Quinny drove in the second. We were on level pegging in the Cup tie.

The replay was staged a few days later on the Wednesday. I stopped at the off-licence on the way to White Hart Lane and bought two magnums of the best bubbly they sold. There was this little voice in my head telling me, 'Kenny boy, you are going to Wembley to play in your first Cup final.' In my soul I was harbouring a powerful combination of hope and fate. This was the brain of 'Lucky Kenny Sansom' at work.

There had been silence, and question marks in the eyes of Spurs, at the end of Sunday's match. We wanted them to play their Wembley song again, and we wanted to beat them. We didn't want to have to come back from the dead for a third time. But Clive Allen made sure this was once again the scenario by pouncing on a low punch away from John Lukic and drilling in his third goal of this phenomenal semifinal Cup tie. 'Come on, John,' I thought to myself – this is not the match to have an off-night. I was about to hang my head and lose my faith for a moment, when Warrington referee Joe Worrell hissed, 'Come on, Ken, you can still do this.' I'm sure he wasn't biased in our favour, but that he, like the crowd, wanted an exciting match. I pushed my luck, however, and called over to the ref, 'If you're on our side, give us a penalty or at least a free kick in a dangerous spot.'

But in the end we didn't need any help to find our equaliser, as our sub, Ian Allison, worked himself into a shooting position. It nearly didn't happen, though; in fact it was all a bit messy. First he completely missed his shot, then he mishit it again, but to our joy the ball rolled over the line. There was nothing Ray Clemence could do about it.

The goal was in front of all our fans, so you can imagine the scene. As I gazed momentarily up to the terraces I saw an amazing sea of red and white as the Gooners jumped up and down in a mixture of relief and celebration. Then my eyes scanned across and fell on Chris Waddle, whose head was now on his chest. Tottenham seemed to be asking themselves, 'Surely not a third time?'

Then came one of the best moments in my career.

Rocky pounced on a pass from the left and, in injury time, he darted in and scored the winner. We were on our way to Wembley. It was pure exhilaration. Fan-dabby-dozy-tastic!

'How much longer?' I screamed at the ref. 'Three minutes,' came back the answer. *Three minutes.* The longest three minutes of my life. I could no longer hear the crowd. I was in a vacuum, and all I could think of was the final whistle and Wembley.

I had been suffering from a stomach problem, which turned out to be a hernia, but today I felt no pain – the adrenalin rush was counteracting any negatives and I felt as if I could jump as high as a house. Spurs hurled a free kick in my direction, but I headed it clear.

When the final whistle blew, the Arsenal players, fans and officials erupted as one, and I ran 50 yards to jump on Rocky's back. For once Viv Anderson couldn't get a word in edgeways – but I'm sure he didn't mind. Arsenal were on their way to Wembley, and I was on my first outing to Wembley in a Cup match. In the dressing room we downed a crate of champagne in minutes and couldn't stop ourselves from singing, 'Spurs are on their way to Wembley – *not.*' I have to admit we really gloated.

The players' room was like a morgue, but we soon changed that with all our boasting. However, if I'm honest, I must say did begin to feel a bit sorry for them – especially Clive Allen (who had by now transferred from Crystal Palace), who had scored three goals in a Cup semifinal but missed out on a trip to Wembley. But I couldn't let some other man's misery spoil my golden moment, so

I downed more champagne on the team coach and then carried on celebrating with the rest of the Gunners in a pub on the way home.

It was a very happy Kenny Sansom who slipped into bed that night. I lay there for ages going over and over the game in my head before falling asleep and dreaming of Wembley.

LITTLEWOODS CUP FINAL: SUNDAY, 5 APRIL 1987

It is the moment when the buzzer sounds in the dressing room telling you to line up outside the door in the tunnel that it hits you the most.

Recent form suggested Liverpool would win, but we wanted this so badly that we just had to keep believing we could pull this out of the bag.

What better way could we celebrate our centenary year?

I had played for my country at Wembley many times, but never for my club. Now my dream was coming true. As I drove down Wembley Way all I could see as far as the eye would take me was a sea of red and white. Red and white for Arsenal, and red and white for Liverpool.

Steve Williams was next to me making a video of the entire day, and I remember praying the camera didn't pick up the tension in my face. I knew it was there – I could feel every muscle, tight as a coiled spring.

The hubbub of anticipation inside the dressing room, and then as we waited to come out of the tunnel, was as exciting as I'd ever known. I gave myself a scolding: 'Come on, Kenny, you've been here so many times before with England. Surely you must be used to it by now.' Then I answered myself: 'But this is different, and I'm nervous beyond belief. My tummy's churning and I'm certain everyone can hear the rumbling.'

I remember wondering where Jan Molby and Steve McMahon were. I knew how much George rated them. And where was Rushy? I hadn't spotted him yet. 'Oh, stop it, Kenny, he'll show his face sooner or later,' I told myself.

There were so many thoughts flashing inside my head. It was like a running commentary that went like this...

There's a different plan of where we are to stand today because the guest of honour, Sir John Moores, is too ill to walk far, so we have to go to him before shaking hands; walking out into the spring sunshine is fantastic. This is kind of Boys' Own *stuff. I blink and drink in the crackling atmosphere, and I want this moment to go on for ever.*

We've been told the first 20 minutes are going to be vital. If we let Liverpool get a grip on us, we're in trouble – they'll never let go. And this happens. Things aren't going to plan and thank goodness for the 'Don't panic' message ringing in my ears. But then, horror upon horror, Rushy scores. Liverpool have yet to lose a match when Ian scores a goal and I know this fact is reverberating around our minds. What now?

I decide we must take the game to them and begin to push up in midfield. A couple of times I even end up on the halfway line in an effort to lift the tension from our play. The gaffer tells me off at half time, but I was going to stick by my gut instinct. I tell him I'll carry on the same way if necessary. Bold, daring or mad, I didn't care. I'm tapping into some part of me that I know I can trust.

We haven't being playing well in recent matches. We've been a bit tight. Something's got to happen to help us loosen up. Then it happens. Charlie scores and in a flash my nerves suddenly lift.

Liverpool are kicking off to restart the match after Charlie's goal and I tell myself that, if I don't enjoy the next few hours of my life, I'll never enjoy another thing in my life. Everything about me is in tune – I am charged up both physically and mentally.

Suddenly, Willow wants the ball again – Rocky is involved, as is Paul Davis, who's starting to spray passes around. It's clicking together just like it did in the early part of the season.

Is it my imagination or are we getting stronger? And do they really look jaded and strained with every passing minute? I'm shouting instructions – doing and saying everything in my power to spur us on to score a winner. I don't have a clue how long there is to go to the final whistle. Not a bloody clue. That happens sometimes when there's so much at stake.

Then, as if in a dream, Charlie scores again and the whole place goes wild. That ball seems to creep over the line, but over the line it goes.

As Charlie disappears under a human mountain I go berserk. I punch the air, dance around like a loony, and jump as high as the cloud I'm on. I do everything imaginable to release the euphoria.

Now I go back to the 'How long to go?' question. The referee, Lester Shapter, mouths over to me, 'Five.' Five minutes to go. No time. A lifetime. Still time enough for Rushy to score. Surely he won't rob us of our moment.

The lovely, wonderful, whistle blows. Liverpool droop and we jump. We've done it. We've won the Littlewoods Cup. Everyone is darting here there and everywhere and saying, 'You little beauty,' which was the gaffer's favourite saying.

The photograph of me leading the Arsenal up the Wembley steps to collect the trophy hit the headlines in all the newspapers nationwide. Lots of fans wanted to know why I was wearing a dodgy Arsenal cap, and I don't know why. Someone must have plonked it on my head and I had far too many wonderful thoughts racing through my mind to think about taking it off. All I wanted to do was get my hands on that beautiful Littlewoods Cup. Finally, I'd won some silverware.

Nowadays, that competition doesn't seem to be as important as it was back in the eighties, when it was a big deal. Today some of the top clubs, including Arsenal, tend to field a younger and more inexperienced side.

I can understand how this presents a chance for the kids to get a feel for an important match. But when I was a kid I'd watched great legends like Emlyn Hughes lift the Cup for Liverpool, and his face was always a picture of happiness. Now it was my turn.

I was told Elaine went hysterical when we won and was very noisy in celebrating our win on the coach. Good girl. She knew what this meant to me, and I, in turn, knew how much it meant to her. She'd been on a very long journey with me, so she deserved every mouthful of champagne she downed that lovely spring day when the Arsenal won the Cup.

This was to be my one and only Cup winners' medal – but a medal I will cherish for ever.

There was a fairytale end to this story.

Later that day, Viv Anderson, Tony Adams, David Rocastle and I took a taxi across town to attend the Professional Footballers' Association Dinner, where we were due to collect some prizes. It was another moment to be proud of – and I was proud. I had never missed being selected for the left-back prize in the PFA's divisional awards – two in the Third Division, two in the Second and six in the First.

Later, back at the party and drunk on happiness and champagne, we were astonished to see George Graham, who isn't a man to drop his guard too often, celebrating in style. He was so happy, and I will never forget the expression of jubilance written across his face. It lit up when Charlie's second goal flew into the net and the light never left his face all evening. I think his eyes were also alight with the prospect of more glory.

I just knew he would be collecting many more trophies at the Arsenal. But would I be there with him?

GET OFF MY BED, ROCKY – AND SHUT UP, VIV!

Whatever was wrong with my stomach wasn't going away. I felt weary and knew I wasn't in the best of health. My father had died from heart failure, and I was worried I had inherited a heart complaint. But my fears were laid to rest when Doctor Gilmore told me he was amazed at my high level of fitness. My heart was fine. Phew! Thank God for that. My dad may have given me some shiny shoes and a herringbone coat his friend Black Ray had 'acquired', but to have given me a dicky heart would have been taking the piss big style.

George was worried and called me into his office to tell me he was going to rest me for our next match against West Ham – as it happened, I was glad I wasn't involved in the 3–1 hiding the Hammers gave us.

It was a dark day indeed when the claret-and-blue whooped our arse. Our fans were devastated.

I guess we must have still been recovering from our Wembley win. (I'll never tire of saying 'our Wembley win'). Whatever the case, George was fuming and said the lads must never play like that again. He really tore into us.

Whereas the gaffer was not about to tolerate what he saw as a dip in attitude, I, on the other hand, found it difficult to see the lads being slagged off so soon after such a monumental Cup triumph. The whole season had been one long, hard, slog – especially for the younger players. I felt he needed to take everything into consideration before he started saying things he would regret.

The pain in my stomach was getting worse and worse. It was really affecting my play now – I'd even go as far as to say my performance was about 20 per cent below par. It was daft, ,really for me to have played all those matches and aggravate a serious injury. The result was that my pace was compromised, which in turn knocked my confidence. I had to rely heavily on my experience just to get through matches – which was ridiculous.

There were times, just before kick-off, when I'd have to gee myself up to blank out the pain. I don't think it would happen today. The boys of the twenty-first century are treated with kid gloves, and why not? But then again, when I really think about it, if a top-class player is fighting to keep his place in the side while bright young stars are snapping eagerly at his ankles, he too might try to deny even to himself that he could have an injury that will signify the end of his illustrious career.

My last match of the season was against Leicester in April, and we won 4–1. It was another great win, with Martin Hayes scoring two and Paul Davis and Charlie Nicholas the other two.

Gunner-to-be Alan Smith was still playing for Leicester in a bid to help in their relegation battle, but it didn't help on this occasion. I felt really sorry for the Leicester fans. They knew, relegation or no relegation, they were about to lose their best player. Alan Smith proved, in front of his new fans, that he was a class player. The Gooners were chanting his name and he gave a little acknowledgement wave back.

The match had been played in the morning, which meant getting home early to Elaine and the family. As I was tired, in pain, and worried about what was wrong with my stomach, I was glad to get indoors and put my feet up.

Eventually I made an appointment to see Dr Gilmore again. This time he diagnosed a hernia and said I needed an operation straightaway.

Although it was a relief to know what was wrong with me, it was also a right bloody nuisance. England were playing Turkey in Izmir the following week and I was eager to play, or not to be left out, or both.

Fortunately, Dr Gilmore gave me the nod to play for England, and I heaved a huge sigh of relief. There weren't many things that were much worse than *watching* England play from your armchair.

The gaffer was great when I told him I needed an operation, but that I wanted to play for England. He agreed straightaway. I should have seen his next move coming – but I didn't.

My terrific spell of glory had begun when I reported for World Cup duty in the summer of 1986, and it's incredible how much I had packed into this short space of time. It's no wonder that I suffered an injury. I had really worked my socks off. But what a roller-coaster ride!

World Cup hope had turned from despair into terrible disappointment, but back at Arsenal George had got results. He had bought discipline, organisation and huge determination to Highbury. We were no longer 'no-hopers': the Arsenal were back in the reckoning and this had much to do with his management skills. After a disappointing start to our season, we had moved on and had an incredible twenty-two-match unbeaten run. We'd won the Littlewoods Cup, I'd led the Arsenal up the Highbury steps and held the trophy aloft – just as I'd seen Emlyn Hughes do for Liverpool when I was a boy dreaming of playing top-flight football. This year had left my memory bank full of wonderful images that will remain until the day I die. I wanted to stay at Highbury for ever as well. I thought I'd be there till I could no longer kick a ball.

So just imagine my shock when I picked up the *Sun* the next morning and read a back-page story that told the nation Kenny Sansom was being sold – going to be cashed in for Arsenal to buy Nigel Winterburn from Wimbledon. I hadn't seen the paper till I walked into the dressing room and the lads started to ask me tricky questions such as, 'Where are you going?' Some were saying, 'You kept that quiet, Kenny.' I just stood there and fought my corner. This was all news to me.

Holding the newspaper in my hands, I went to see the gaffer. He shrugged his shoulders and denied any knowledge of anything. 'I know nothing. I have no intention of letting you go.' I know nothing, indeed! But in that moment I was heartened. There was no way I wanted to leave Highbury. I loved it there, and I wanted to sign a new contract.

I knew I hadn't been anywhere near the top of my form of late, but I was still in my twenties and once the hernia had been treated I knew I'd be back firing on all cylinders. Physiotherapist Gary

Lewin kept a close eye on me. I was to do nothing strenuous, just a little jogging and bicycle work – enough to retain a decent level of fitness. Gary is still the Arsenal and England physiotherapist at the time I write this, and probably the best in the world. It has been reported recently that his quick thinking and actions when he tended to Eduardo after the horrific injury he received when playing against Birmingham at St Andrews may well have saved the young lad's leg – and career.

I didn't have to travel up to Manchester for the game against City. The gaffer said it was fine to stay behind – and, being tired, I didn't mind at all.

I remember we had a barbecue, Elaine, the kids and I. Some friends came over and it was a smashing family afternoon. The only blot on the landscape was the news that was filtering through from Manchester via Teletext. I couldn't believe it. City just kept on scoring. There was no way this should be happening. City had been playing poorly and were in danger of relegation, so this was an embarrassment for us. As I sat there in the middle of a social scene with my guitar at the ready for a singsong, I could visualise George Graham's face. He would be bitterly disappointed. Between the commentary lines, I could hear this was a tired performance from the boys. Of course it was – they were whacked out. The end of the season couldn't come quickly enough. But first there was a job to do for my country.

The last time we'd played Turkey we had whooped them a staggering 8-0. We weren't expecting a replay of this magnitude, as we had been warned they were a much-improved side, but a 0-0 draw was, to say the least, a bit of a disappointment.

I don't think even Bobby Robson had expected them to be that good, but good they were and, to be honest, we were lucky to come away with a point. Of course, the media wrote their usual biased crap and insinuated that Turkey had played like turkeys and chose to ignore the fact that the Turks actually worked hard and produced.

The three-day turnaround trip to Turkey was intense, and it was good to be back on home turf. I had wanted to go. I was desperate to play. I was also bloody knackered. It didn't take too much energy for my next job, though.

Four of us – Viv Anderson, Tony Adams, Chris Woods and I – had been chosen to model the new England kit. This was a new one on me. I had never modelled before.

The only kit sponsorship I'd ever had was with Puma – I had worn their boots my entire career. This was the only money-spinner I had personally. The company paid me a certain amount every year and in turn they used my name to promote goods and when they opened new outlets. Hey, a guy has to have a few perks.

Now there was a small matter of an operation. By now I was in so much pain that coughing and laughing were excruciating. So it was a case of 'bring it on'.

The operation was performed at the Princess Grace Hospital in London, and was a success. The hernia, however, was a lot worse than had been expected. A stomach muscle had pulled away from the bone as a result of my having played too long with an injury. That said, I was assured I would be fit for the beginning of the next season. I'd be up and running – raring to report back to the Arsenal. Thank God.

I don't remember very much about being in that hospital bed. I was pretty much out of it. I remember Gary Lewin whispering, 'Goodnight' before drifting off, and I have vague memories of Elaine and her sister, Sheila, sitting by my bed as I dozed. I also thought I heard Elaine telling me that Manchester United wanted Viv Anderson, but I thought it must be a nightmare, as Arsenal surely wouldn't sell Viv.

'Hmm, some hope after the brilliant season he'd had,' I thought to myself. He'd made at least 10 points for us that season and was worth his weight in gold. How could he leave Arsenal for Man U when we all (including the fans) loved him so much. No, it was a silly rumour. I fell asleep again and this time dreamt of the Arsenal winning more major titles.

Then the boys came into visit me after caning QPR 4–0. They were in high spirits and chaos reigned for as long as the nurses would allow it! Viv never shut up. He pranced around in my dressing gown and ate all my fruit. Bastard. 'Get up, you lazy bugger,' he said, grinning. 'There's nothing wrong with you Sansom, you old fraud.' He was so funny.

Rocky tried to climb into my bed with me. He said he had a virus and needed a rest. Virus my arse! He was simply worn to a frazzle. The gaffer told the media he was suffering from an illness to protect him from the nosy newspapers. Whatever. I let him lie next to me for only a few minutes because he fidgeted too much.

When I think back to the antics and side-splitting laughter echoing out of my room and down the hospital corridor, I have to laugh all over again. It was good enough to be a comedy sketch. We may have been Arsenal heroes, but that day we were also a sorry sight. Gus had a broken nose, and Quinny had damaged ankle ligaments. We were the Arsenal Walking Wounded. How I didn't split my stitches open I'll never know – and it bloody hurt.

POOR OLD SPURS – AGAIN

Before the season came to an end there was a little matter of the FA Cup match at Wembley. Our arch-rivals Spurs were to take on Coventry.

It was a lovely sunny day and most of us got together – players, friends and family came over to our house for a jolly. In the morning we swam in our pool. Then we watched the build-up live on television as we tucked in to barbecued food and a few drinks.

Finally the big match got under way. Down went the sound on the TV and up went the radio. We preferred to tune into radio commentary, as it was more detailed and descriptive.

Quinny and I were bookmakers for the day, and I remember that the gaffer won some money for predicting Clive Allen would score first and put Spurs in the lead. It was a fantastic Cup final that ended in a 2–2 draw at full time. Coventry won in extra time and I honestly think they deserved to win. I'm not just saying that because I wanted Spurs to lose – I don't think so, anyway. Hmm, not sure.

Niall and I won £90, which came in handy for an equally smashing evening down the pub.

Poor old Spurs.

THE HEADLINES ARE BIG AND REFLECTING MY FRUSTRATION

Now, I know I can get the hump about speculation in the press, but the stories they were writing at that time were too big for me to ignore. There's no smoke without fire and all that.

The rumblings went on about Viv going to Manchester United and about Nigel Winterburn coming to Arsenal. I felt in the dark and my usually moderate temper was beginning to get the better of me. What the fuck was George keeping from me? I was his captain, for God's sake, and this, in my humble view, was disrespectful. I decided it was time I made my feelings known.

I picked up the phone on 21 May and asked, 'Why aren't you treating me like a captain? Why didn't you warn me you were buying a new left-back? If you'd told me I could have been prepared for the press on my doorstep and the constant ringing of the phone. I would've been able to hold my head up and say you were buying him to be a squad player.'

Although I was steaming inside I managed to speak assertively and put my point across without losing my rag.

There was silence on the other end of the line as George digested my words. Then he answered, 'Your position is not in question, Kenny. You'll be my first choice at the end of the season, and you'll still be my skipper. I'm buying Nigel Winterburn as a squad player and there's nothing else to it. Liverpool has a big squad, and *I* want a big squad.'

He also made it clear that what he did as a manager was none of my business. That's a fair comment – but I still maintain he should have forewarned me.

Even more annoying was that 6 weeks earlier any murmurs of Arsenal's signing Nigel had been scoffed at. Someone wasn't being straight.

You know, I never doubted my abilities on the pitch. Yes, I had been suffering from an injury, and, yes, I was tired. But I wasn't over the hill – far from it. I knew I had another 4 years in me, and I wanted, more than anything else, to stay at my beloved Highbury. Having faith in my own ability took away any pressure of really believing Nigel Winterburn was going to take my place in the side. But I couldn't deny the fact that for the first time in my career – at Crystal Palace, England, and Arsenal – I had someone challenging me for the left-back position.

While I understood that healthy competition is necessary to push a man to perform at his best, the threat was also an unfamiliar and deeply disturbing sensation. What I couldn't get my head around was why George wasn't focusing on looking out for a new right-back when his left-back was still the England first choice. It's at times like this that one is reminded of what a funny old game this can be.

A few days after my call to the gaffer we sat down and had a heart-to-heart. He told me he'd been cross with me for speaking to the *Sun* about my fears of inheriting a heart problem from my dad. Afterwards we joked that it was a case of 1–1 now between us personally and the air was cleared. We were back on the best of terms – or so I thought.

I had been hoping the tension was over, but it was not to be.

It looked likely that Viv *was* going to sign for Manchester United. I was gutted. We were all gutted. Why hadn't Arsenal offered him a contract earlier? But, in all fairness to Viv, to sign a 4-year contract with a big side at the age of 30 was a smart move.

I missed a couple of England matches at the back end of the season and noted how well Stuart Pearce seemed to have slotted into my place. Another left-back, Tony Dorigo of Aston Villa, was also playing really well and as he was about to sign for Chelsea – a club that would provide a big stage for him to perform upon; he too was one to be watched.

Elaine and I headed off with our children for a much-earned rest in our regular Hotel Montechoro in Portugal. I was so tired that I gave little thought to the youngsters climbing rapidly up the ranks and threatening my position. There were other considerations to be made to my family.

Poor Elaine had hardly had a moment to herself since our son Harry had been born, so she too was feeling jaded. I was planning on playing some tennis to build up my fitness levels as well as swimming and generally having fun with my little girls.

Lying in the sunshine, I reflected back on an action-packed year. I really hadn't expected George Graham to be such an inspiration. That man had surprised me by being a fantastic and inspiring manager. I was lucky. Arsenal was lucky. But my luck was about to run out – and fast.

CHAPTER THIRTEEN

THE END FOR ME AT ARSENAL AND ENGLAND

EURO 1988 – A DISASTER

The European Championships were a bloody nightmare. It was a case of national disaster and personal disaster. England were quite rightly criticised, and so was I. While 1987 had been a fabulous year, 1988 was an *annus horribilis* as our Queen would say.

I didn't have a particularly good tournament – full stop. The rest of the team weren't much better. The first of our three games was against the Republic of Ireland. Jack Charlton was managing the Irish side, and it was the first time they'd reached the finals – so they were on fire.

Our rhythm was thrown off course by nippy Irish players such as Liverpool's John Aldridge and Sheffield Wednesday's Tony Galvin. As for me – well, my game was just horrendous. It was actually the game that was to hail the demise of my career.

The Irish began by pumping long balls forward and it was from one of these long passes that they were to earn a goal – unfortunately, it was I who set it up.

The ball landed in a dangerous area, and, when Mark Wright and Gary Stevens both failed to get rid of the ball, I ran in and tried to rescue the situation. But I bloody miskicked it and it flew into the air. A sideways header by John Aldridge gave Liverpool's Ray Houghton a chance to loop the ball over Peter Shilton and into the net. They were over the moon, as all they needed to do now was show off the defensive solidarity that had seen them win their last eleven games – which is exactly what they did.

Although Glenn Hoddle skimmed the bar with a cracking shot and Gary Lineker played his heart out, we just couldn't score. I have to say that the Irish played a blinder, and thoroughly deserved the 1–0 win and, by the end of the match, the crowd at the Neckar Stadium in Stuttgart, West Germany, was alive with the green of the Emerald Isle.

But for us it was the most disastrous start to our challenge for the championship. We got a hell of a lot of stick from everyone, including the press. Oh, they had a field day.

My fitness and performance levels were dipping. I was in denial about my drinking and everyone was colluding with me. I could say I wish they hadn't. That I wish they could have been firmer with me and spelt it out loud and clear that I was destroying everything – but I wasn't hearing any words of advice anyway.

Although I didn't play well in this match it was nothing to do wish my spirits being low, as anyone can see on the Internet video channel YouTube, where I am larking about on the team coach doing my impressions and entertaining everyone. It's a shame my feet weren't as sharp as my jokes that day. On the pitch I was the joke.

In the next match we got whooped 3–1 by the Dutch. This was a great shame, especially for Peter Shilton, who was celebrating his hundredth cap, joining the ranks of Billy Wright, Bobby Charlton and Bobby Moore. Yes, the Dutch had a superb team, but I have to admit that we put in a dismal performance and got no luck whatsoever.

I remember clearly when Bryan Robson hit a clean ball over to Glenn Hoddle, who blasted the ball towards goal, only to hit the post, watch the ball dribble along the goal line and away to safety.

THE END FOR ME AT ARSENAL AND ENGLAND

The likes of Ruud Gullit, Marco van Basten, who scored a hat-trick, and other Dutch heroes were simply too much for us to compete with.

My last ever cap was won in June 1988 when we played against Russia in West Germany.

Now we had to face a humiliating match against the USSR. We were desperate to salvage some pride by getting a victory, but, no, it was yet another nightmare – we lost 3–1. Some journalists likened us defenders to 'horse carts'.

Tony Adams, by contrast, had a decent game and scored our only goal with a fabulous header. But, as Tony's England career kept on climbing, mine was most certainly falling apart. This was my eighty-sixth game representing my country – and my last.

It took only 3 minutes for them to take the lead and it was mainly due to a dreadful pass by Glenn Hoddle, which was snapped up by our opposition. The ball moved quickly on and Sergei Aleinikov put it in the back of the net. Our hearts sank.

They went on to create other chances and we had no answers. It looked as though we were on course for a real thrashing, but a surprise equaliser on the quarter-hour lifted our spirits and brought us back into the match. Glenn atoned for his earlier error by floating a free kick perfectly onto the head of Tony Adams, who headed home powerfully. Nine minutes later we almost took the lead after John 'Digger' Barnes left his marker beaten and fired a fine centre pass. Their goalie, Rinat Dasayev, was struggling as the cross came over and for a moment it looked like a dead cert, but Trevor Steven missed the chance to head one home. Oh, it was bleak.

To add insult to injury Alexei Mikhailichenko hit a beautiful diagonal cross out to Aleksandr Zavarov on the left, and when the cross came in Mikhailichenko followed up to score what was the nail in our coffin. The heart had gone from us and the Russians were on to a winner.

'They [the defenders] were plodding,' screamed the press. They were right. We'd lost our third match on the trot and our confidence was in the gutter – so was I.

I clearly remember drinking wine a few days into that tournament and Bryan Robson coming into the room and saying, 'OK, lads, that's enough. We have important games to play.' Honestly – I'm lost for words right now.

I wasn't the Kenny Sansom of old. I was a shadow of my former self and it was all down to the booze. I didn't know my England career was over. I didn't know anything much – except I needed a drink badly.

It had been a stressful time for Elaine and me. My poor wife had not only been bearing the brunt of my problems, but she'd hardly had a moment to herself since our son Harry had been born.

We decided to fly off to Portugal with our children. Elaine is a terrific tennis player, and I'm not bad, so we were looking forward to raising our fitness levels while having some fun and relaxation. Natalie and Katie were at the ages when they enjoyed holidays in the sunshine – swimming and dressing up. Natalie enjoyed getting messy on the beach, whereas Katie took after her mum and liked to dress up in pretty frocks.

As I lay in the sun I reflected back and even dared to look forward. What had begun as a fractious relationship with the new gaffer had turned a corner, and I was now of the opinion that he was a fantastic and inspiring manager. Arsenal had got lucky, and there was no doubt in my mind that the dark days at Highbury were coming to an end.

As for me, I was 29 years old, and my luck was running out. What was it that Terry Venables had said to me a decade before? 'The harder you work, the luckier you become, Kenny.' Were the gambling and drinking getting in the way of my hard work? I'd have to watch out.

THE END FOR ME AT ARSENAL AND ENGLAND

HIGHBURY – GAME OVER

> 'You never know how great it is playing for
> Arsenal until you leave.'
>
> DON HOWE

I lost my place in the Arsenal team. And then, to cap it all, Bobby Robson called to say, 'I can't pick you while you're not in the Arsenal team'.

It was such a miserable time. Elaine and I had to part exchange our beautiful house in Keston Park to keep our debtors from the door. So what did I do next? I had a drink. The roses were dying and we needed to plant some more seeds, but I'd forgotten how to live without the booze and there were no seeds to be sown.

Then my old friend Don Howe's words came to mind. 'You never know how great it is playing for the Arsenal until you leave.'

The 1986–7 season had been terrific. I'd finally won some domestic silverware and led my team up the famous steps of Wembley to hold the League Cup triumphantly high above my head. I'm glad I didn't have the foresight to see how rotten the following year would be. A year of injury and loss, and the beginning of a downward spiral that would continue until I finally reached crisis point.

I MESSED WITH GEORGE

You can't mess with George Graham and, in effect, that's exactly what I did.

Elaine, in desperation, went to see George in his office and begged him, 'We need help.' In tears, she implored him, 'You've dropped him, and this has made everything worse. He's still gambling heavily and now he's drinking far too much. Please, can't you do something?'

'I'm sorry, Elaine. Kenny has to help himself.'

'But others in the squad have done much worse, and they didn't get punished. They didn't get dropped.' She was in bits. 'I'm worried for his health. Can't Arsenal football club do *anything*?'

George said again, 'You have to help yourselves.'

Furious, and feeling badly let down by George and the club, I gave another interview to the *Sun*. The headline was a clear message to George: SIGN ME OR SELL ME.

The gaffer got the message loud and clear. 'I don't know you any more, Kenny. What's all this aggression about? You're behaving as if you're some big shot and it doesn't suit you.'

George was right. I was behaving like an idiot and the alcohol was making me aggressive and arrogant – two traits I deeply dislike in people. I thought I deserved better. I couldn't see I was being self-destructive. I was destroying my career. I was not being fair to Elaine. I thought back to all the times I'd been ridiculously selfish and for some reason the time I called her at three in the morning to collect me from Tramp because I couldn't get a cab flashed into my head. I closed my eyes and saw the vision of her sitting in the car outside with the children all bundled into the back. How dare I? Who the hell did I think I was? It was outrageous behaviour. But that's what happens with drink: your soul is dying, but no one would guess, as your behaviour is too unforgivable.

It was *I* who was my own worst enemy, not George and Arsenal. I didn't understood that till much later, of course. I'd taken the piss and now I was being punished. Rotting in the reserves, I would join a training session pissed – stinking rotten drunk. What a numpty! What a waste!

Elaine had asked for help for me, for *us*. Now it was my turn to storm into George's office. It was a real case of guns glazing. Had I been sober I would never have recognised myself.

I think, with hindsight, that I'd gone through so much – what with the injury, the operation and the anxiety that I was going to be replaced by Nigel Winterburn (it does nothing for your confidence when you sense you are just about to lose your job) –

and the fear of losing everything was too much. I'd lost control of myself, and that led to losing everything. Later, in rehab, I learned about the AA meaning of insanity. This was insane.

The tabloid headline had wound George up; perhaps that was what I wanted. I'm not sure. All I know is that I wasn't happy and something had to change. I had reacted to a situation that, in my opinion, would never have arisen had I been properly informed of George's reasoning. But that again was the arrogance of the booze and of always having to blame someone else.

But I do think that George had been keeping his cards close to his chest about Nigel Winterburn; and it wound me up, just as it would any player. But the gaffer was also letting me know that this was none of my bloody business.

The rumblings in the press kept on coming and before I knew it Nigel Winterburn was at Highbury and playing in the right-back position. How long would it be before I lost my position on the left wing? I'd held that position for nine long years. I was King Kenny of the Arsenal and I never ever dared look into the future and imagine I'd not be there. Daft as it sounds, I lived for the day, and until this period the day had always been bright and sunny as far as my football career was concerned. Now the dark clouds were gathering.

What made it all so difficult was that I had never doubted my abilities on the pitch. Yes, I'd been suffering from an injury, and, yes, I was tired. But I knew I had another 4 years in me, and I so badly wanted to spend those years at my beloved Highbury. The confusion was unbearable.

I was used to being 'first' – it was all I knew. No wonder I was in denial. No wonder I was falling into the bottle and pulling the cork in behind me.

TONY ADAMS IS SKIPPER

'OK, you've had your piece of flesh,' I cried. 'Now let me go.'

'No, Kenny, I'm not letting you go yet,' George replied. 'But I *am* going to take the captaincy from you. I don't know how you've got away with this bad behaviour for so long. I can only think it's because you're a nice guy.'

The meeting had been painful. When he asked me to return my armband I numbly did as I was told. All the fight had left me. The defender was defeated. Leaving his office with my spirits low, I saw Tony Adams waiting to see the gaffer. It was obvious he'd been summoned for a meeting to be handed the captaincy I'd just had taken from me. I wondered if Tony had heard the raised voices. Of course he had.

I smiled weakly at the youngster and he nodded in response. There was no gloating on his part. He knew my loss was his gain, but he wasn't the type to rub salt in the wounds.

Tony must have been so excited. He knew he was more than ready to take leadership of the Arsenal. People had been saying for some time that he was a natural-born leader, which he was – still is.

At the age of 28, I was the senior player and at 21 he was the rising star. There were a misinformed few who thought he was too young to captain a team as huge as Arsenal, but we all knew it was his destiny.

When he knew for sure that he was captain he walked straight up to me and asked me if I was OK with these latest developments. He was humble and modest, but also certain this was the right decision. There was no embarrassment on either part.

I told him, 'Tony, you deserve it. I'm fine.' (Much later, one of Tony's off-the-field mentors told me 'fine' meant fucked up, insecure, neurotic and emotional. Hmm, could be some truth there.)

Tony and I held each other in high regard. We had a lot in common, such as football, England, Arsenal – and a huge capacity for alcohol consumption. I wished Tony all the luck in the world, and that, as they say, was that.

I have come to realise that any team worth its salt looks harshly upon acts of disloyalty, and, although my speaking to the press had been a genuine act of grievance on my part, it was seen as quite something else by my club.

George Graham was now making it very clear that there was change afoot – and that change didn't involve me. He wanted a more vocal and aggressive skipper. A strong leader who would be the middle man to carry his demanding orders to the team. No one was to be in doubt of the new identity of the Arsenal. The late eighties and early nineties were going to be different and Tony Adams was the only contender for leadership. His innate character was perfect. He held the promise of something great, and it was obvious for all to see. How could I possibly have been anything but gracious, given all that positivity?

Tony is a true leader in every sense and I gather he always has been. Way back in his school days, when he'd been a gangly tousled-haired Essex boy, he was dishing out instructions to the other kids on the pitch. And, let's face it, it was only 'on the pitch' that mattered to him. He was football mad from the word go. His dad had been a decent player. If my memory serves me right he played briefly for West Ham. What I do know for sure is Tony's obsession with football began when he was a schoolboy not particularly enjoying the academic stuff (I don't think many footballers did in our day, and John Hollins knew that) – so he lined up his pencils, and they played against the rubbers.

Outside the classroom – in the playground or on the sports field – he chose two other handy players to play on his side and the three of them played against ten other boys. His tactical mind was in operation way back then as the biggest boy with a spring in his step went in goal, and on Tony's instructions the other one played in defence and he, as the third player, did the rest. Guess who always used to win. Yep, you've got it. Tony's three-man team. So, if anyone was going to take the armband from me, I'm honoured it was Tony Adams.

What next? I was approaching 30. The football pitch had been my second home since I was at primary school. Although my legs still had plenty of mileage in them I began to wonder (very secretly, not even daring to acknowledge it to myself) if my best days were coming to an end. But how could that possibly be? No, things would turn around. After all, I was lucky Kenny Sansom, wasn't I?

But, before I move on to football in the Northeast of England at Newcastle, I want to share with you the other side of my life, to tell you about my life off the pitch, tales of family, friends, teammates and the Kenny Sansom who managed to keep his personal life out of the press for the duration of his career. Here are my stories.

CHAPTER FOURTEEN

MY STORIES OFF THE PITCH

My thirtieth-birthday party was well orchestrated by Elaine and a stretch limo came to pick me up to take me to the Bibawood Club in Chislehurst. Six of us piled in to the motor, Elaine and I, my brother Peter and his wife Sue, and my sister Midge and her husband Paul. The champagne was flowing and everyone in high spirits. Our friends Pat and Ray, whom we had initially met in the Montechoro Hotel in Portugal, had come down from the Wirral, and our guest list was as long as it was varied.

The trouble was, the evening didn't go quite to plan. In fact it was almost a disaster.

Harry, who was not quite a year old, accompanied us to the hall and then the plan was for Elaine's niece Tracy (who often babysat) to take the children home at a reasonable time.

Elaine waved them all off at about nine o'clock and all seemed well. None of the children had coughs or colds so there was no reason to worry. But halfway down a dual carriageway Tracy looked into her rear-view mirror and to her horror saw that Harry was having a fit. It must have been very scary for her, as she had never seen a child fitting before.

She followed her instinct, which was to turn the car around, put her main beam on and drive the wrong way down the dual carriageway. Flashing all the way she drove as fast as it was safe to do until she arrived at Greenwich Hospital. From there Harry was rushed into a cubicle, where it was confirmed he was having a febrile convulsion. His eyes had rolled back and he was lifeless.

The first we knew about it was when Elaine received a frantic, late-night phone-call from Tracy, telling us to get to the hospital as quickly as possible. Well, you can imagine the panic. Although Tracy had tried not to worry us, she couldn't hide the terror in her voice.

When we arrived in casualty, Harry was lying lifeless on a cold, flat board. He looked dead. It was the most heart-stopping moment of our lives. Elaine was screaming, 'My baby, why isn't he moving? Why aren't you doing anything? Why are you putting those flannels on him? Stop it! Stop it!'

But, of course, they were doing everything in their power to bring him back to us, and the flannels were to help bring his temperature down, as that was what was causing the convulsion. Eventually he responded and came back to us. This was the best birthday present I ever had.

THE BLUE LIGHT OF THE LAW

Elaine and I had been out on a wild night in London and, just as we passed George Best's club, Blonde, an argument we were having spiralled out of control. This time I was so out of order that she screamed, 'Stop the car, I want to get out!'

I pulled over and before I knew it Elaine was off up the road in a terrible huff.

I don't know how much time passed, but I remember going to look for Elaine and not being able to find her. So I went back to the car and fell asleep. When I woke up I started to drive the car slowly to see if I could find her. The next thing I knew a policewoman was pulling me over.

Winding the window down, I smiled politely and prayed the cop was an Arsenal fan.

'Have you been drinking, sir?' Well, she would say that, wouldn't she?

It's amazing how quickly you can sober up enough to find an excuse.

'Yes I have, officer, but I haven't driven the car. My wife was the driver and I just moved over to the driver's seat because I *was* going to drive, but then remembered I'd had a drink – at the Arsenal football dinner.' (Well, it was worth the shot.)

Then, like a vision of loveliness, Elaine came into view. 'Here she comes now. Come on, Elaine, come and get back in the driver's seat,' I called out, hoping she'd cotton on as I sneakily slid over to the passenger side.

Elaine, sharp as ever, did exactly what I'd asked. Which was very fortunate, as a big police van came round the corner, I suspect to carry me off for the night.

The policewoman shook her head and said to Elaine, 'Your husband's a very lucky man.' You can say that again.

Drinking and driving is an absolute no-no and anyone who does it is a fool. I have been that fool. So I guess I *do* have another regret – besides our not winning the World Cup in 1982.

I have been guilty of drinking and driving and any youngster reading this please heed my warning, because there is a moral in the story I am about to tell you.

On one particular night, Elaine and I had just enjoyed a wicked evening out and, although we were only 20 minutes from home and could have easily called a cab, I chose, in the wisdom of a drunk, to drive home. I can't remember a bloody thing about the incident, so I am going to hand over to Elaine to tell the story...

Kenny had drunk a lot – a hell of a lot. He was at that annoying stage of drunkenness when he believed he knew everything and everyone else had it wrong. That's why taking even one drink is dangerous because, if you are like Kenny, once you start there is no stopping.

With him dressed in his white evening jacket and me in my posh frock, we climbed into our Mercedes and headed down the steep hill away from the venue we'd been attending. It was dark, so we couldn't see the magnificent view of the River Thames on our left, but what I did see was a copper waving to us, and I was certain, by the expression on his face, that he wasn't after Kenny Sansom's autograph.

'Ken, didn't you see that copper?' I asked as we turned the bend.

'What copper? I didn't see any copper.'

'You should have let me drive, like I suggested. I haven't had anywhere near as much booze as you.'

We started rowing, which was nothing unusual in drink. We liked a good clearing of the air, and I think secretly we enjoyed letting off the steam that usually led to making up and our being all lovey-dovey again.

But this time I was really, really angry. Probably, because I was terrified of his getting nicked or killing us on the deadly hairpin bend he'd just swerved round.

'Stop the car! I'm getting out,' I screamed. But, before I could run away, I saw a sight for sore eyes standing in front of us. It was another copper and he was standing in the middle of the road; his arms forming the shape of a crucifix. The other copper must have radioed ahead to let them know an absconder was on the loose and heading towards – of all places – the police station.

I wound the passenger window down. 'Yes, officer?'

The young man (they seem to get younger and younger) looked straight through me and his eyes settled on Kenny. A look of surprise made him appear quite comical. 'You're Kenny Sansom, aren't you?' It wasn't a question – he knew it was Kenny Sansom all right.

Kenny managed a nod, and when he finally found his voice, he added, 'We've just been attending a football function. It was a charity do.'

The young copper shook his head sadly. 'Hey, listen, I'd let you off with a warning, but it's my colleague's shout. He's the one that told me you were heading my way.' He looked up at the blue light shining over the police station as if to say, 'You daft bugger, why did you come this way?'

Then a senior officer strolled out of the station and joined us. I expected him to say, 'Evenin' all' like Dixon of Dock Green. And do you know what? He did. But he added a bit more.

He said, 'Good evening. I'd like you to blow into this bag, sir.'

You can imagine. I thought my heart was going to beat straight through my chest which, by the way, was barely concealed in my low-cut Versace number.

After Kenny had blown as softly as he could manage into the breathalyser machine – as if a pathetic effort would register less alcohol – we were invited into the station. I guess it would have been presumptuous to expect a cuppa – but that's exactly what we got. It was tea all round.

According to the police Kenny's alcohol level measured exactly on the thin line between pass and fail.

It couldn't have been possible. No way. He had drunk for England as usual. We were clued up enough to realise it was Kenny's fame that was saving our bacon. It shouldn't have been that way, but, as you know, fame buys you perks.

The police were most accommodating. They allowed me to park up our car and then the original officer – the one I'd ignored earlier – piped up and said, 'I'm going your way. I'll give you a lift home if you like.'

I had had a lucky escape. But had I? In the long run, would it have been more beneficial to my wellbeing to have been arrested and locked up? I would perhaps have learned a valuable lesson. My name would have been in the papers and I would have had been forced to experience some deeply embarrassing headlines in the tabloids, as Tony Adams did some years later.

Tony's was a very different story, but that's for him to tell – which he has, in his autobiography, *Addicted*. In his book he tells his story with great honesty. If there was ever a warts-and-all story to be told and closely listened to, it belongs to Tony.

Tony is, without any shadow of a doubt, a man who has more guts than any other I know. Integrity should be his middle name.

On the pitch he was motivator who reigned supreme in defence for an incredible 669 matches. Any youngster wishing to learn the art of football as a defender could do a lot worse than study Tony Adams's game.

When we look at the young guns of today, especially boys like Theo Walcott, we need to remember that Tony's debut for the Arsenal also came at the tender age of 17 – just weeks after his birthday. 'Who *is* he?' asked Charlie George. 'This guy is in a different class.'

While Tony was orchestrating and organising defensive matters beautifully on the pitch, he was slowly and insidiously drowning in his personal life. As far as his game was concerned, his dedication to Arsenal never floundered and in return Arsenal stood firmly by his side when he was in trouble. Which is just as well, because when he smashed up his car, got breathalysed, convicted of drink-driving and then sent to jail, he needed all the support available.

I have heard some people say, 'I've had two lives – the "before" and the "after". Prince Harry, at the memorial of his mother, Princess Diana, spoke poignantly about how he and William looked at their lives and saw themselves in two very separate lives: the life *with* their mother and their life *without* her.

I witnessed the before and after of Tony Adams, and my admiration for him has no bounds. There is no question that being incarcerated in one of Her Majesty's prisons gave him the opportunity to wake up and smell the coffee. This was his lowest moment, but it opened doors for him to exist in a world devoid of alcohol and allowed him to begin his journey down the road to wellbeing.

This was a long time ago now – way back in the mid-nineties and around the time I was risking everything by drinking too much and gambling away our material wealth. I was in that comfortable but dangerous place called 'denial'. *I* wasn't an alcoholic. *I* was in control. *I* was simply one of the lads having fun. How I conducted myself was 'normal'. We were *all* downing champagne and having a flutter on the horses – weren't we?

Had I been charged and arrested when I was clearly over the limit and, consequently, made to confront my addictions, how different would my life have been?

It's a question to ponder rather than answer. There *are* no clear and concrete answers where addictions are concerned.

A FUNERAL

My dad died of heart disease. Well, actually, that's not quite true. He went into hospital with an inherited heart problem but died as a result of the tuberculosis he contracted on the ward. I'm sure there are plenty of people reading this who have lost a relative to some bug or other they picked up in hospital.

I cried when he died. After all, he *was* my dad. Blood is thicker than water and all that. I also went to his funeral, but Elaine refused to accompany me. She was firm in her choice. 'I didn't like him when he was alive. He was very rude to me. I'm not going to be a hypocrite.'

And he *was* rude to Elaine, and not just behind her back but to her face.

During the spell when I was in touch with him he used to refer to her as 'that little Irish tart'. I don't know where he got the Irish idea from, as she has no Irish in her at all. All I can think of is she has beautiful sparkly blue eyes, rather like the Irish.

If he came to visit us he would try to entice me to go out with him. In front of her he'd say, 'Come on, son, let's go and find some *real* women.' Can you imagine that? How dare he be so rotten? So you can see why my wife wouldn't go along to see him laid to rest. I love that woman's principles.

Of course, everyone was pissed at the funeral, and the characters present looked very dubious – just like my dad.

After my dad's funeral I took my sister Maureen to Tramp nightclub, where we drank ourselves silly and then I drove us home in my Mercedes 280SE. I'd just had a CD system fitted and we turned the music up as loud as it would go and then parked bang in the middle of Westminster Bridge. With the windows wide open and Elvis blaring from the car, we heard Big Ben strike three in the morning. We sang our hearts out in a morose drunken singsong that must have lasted a good half an hour.

Can you see that happening today? I don't think so. What were we thinking? It just goes to show how different life is in London two decades on – we'd have been locked up and the key would have been thrown away.

SHOWBIZ SHENANIGANS

Not only have I been privileged enough to spend most of my life in the company of some of the world's greatest football legends, but Elaine and I have also had some terrific times with some of the most talented people in the world of showbiz.

Some meetings with the rich and famous, such as Frank Bruno, Michael Caine, the pop band Oasis and many, many more, have been fleeting. Other stars have become firm friends. One of our favourites is the hugely talented British actor Karl Howman. Karl is probably best known for his character Jacko in the television sitcom *Brush Strokes*, although he has a string of acting roles to his credit, and today concentrates more on directing. Karl is a trustee at Charlton FC, and, like me, he does a lot of charity work.

Golf days and after-dinner speeches are probably my favourite functions, and it seemed it was the same for him. It turned out we both lived in Keston Park, so, when we met at the opening of the David Lloyd centre in Foots Cray, it was no wonder we clicked.

Karl was also into football in a big way – so this love of footie was what really got us talking. The fact that we are two family men with several children added to the things we had in common.

The comedians Hale and Pace were also at the opening, as was the tennis player turned GMTV presenter, Andrew Castle. Frank Bruno was among the guests and his raucous laughter could be heard above everything else.

I played in one of the tennis matches and was partnered by old-timer and one-time Wimbledon player Buster Mottram. He turned to me in his posh voice and asked, 'Left-hand or right, Kenny?' I told him I would prefer to play on the right, so that was that sorted out. We played against Andrew Castle and his partner, and my claim to fame was passing him down the line and winning the point. He's never forgotten and never forgiven me – especially as, whenever I am a guest on GMTV, I manage to slip it into the conversation.

After this Karl invited us to a barbecue over at his house. Since my daughter Natalie's boyfriend, Mark, was a fan of Karl's, they were asked if they wanted to come along as well. They jumped at the chance, of course.

The sun shone on the day and the guests sparkled. Ray 'The Daddy' Winstone and his wife (another Elaine), who are firm friends with Karl and his wife Clare, were also there. The gangster the late Tony Lambrianou was also a guest and he and I had a long chat about the East End. He knew my uncles Terry and Fred, and said he liked them both very much. I wasn't sure whether this was good or not. Whatever the case, all I know is that we had a terrific time and they were all lovely people. It was heartening to know you were with very successful people who had reached the top of their professions, but that they were still down-to-earth, normal, decent people. Brilliant.

HONG KONG PHOOEY

In 1983 Arsenal flew out to Hong Kong to play a friendly match. It was clear right from the moment they welcomed us that it was a big deal for them to be entertaining us. They were so friendly and such wonderful hosts that when, at the end of the trip, they invited us to appear on television we agreed. It would have been rude not to.

We arrived at the studios, where we were going to go out live to the Chinese nation – and let me tell you (you probably know anyway) it's one hell of a big nation. I was interviewed, as were Terry Neill, Pat Jennings and my good mate Graham Rix.

The producer turned to us and slowly and clearly spelt out how they were going to set up the interview so as to make everything easy for the Chinese population to understand us. He said to us, 'I'm going to tell you your individual questions in English before we go on air, but when we go live the interviewer will say it in Cantonese. Is that OK? Do you understand?'

We must have all looked a bit vacant because he went on to give us an example.

'Mr Neill, what is it like to bring an English team to Hong Kong?'

Although we all nodded we were really none the wiser. It was in danger of being a muddle from the kick-off. So Terry Neill was asked his question in Cantonese and replied in English. I was impressed. The system seemed to work well.

Graham Rix, who had a slight injury problem, was asked in Cantonese, 'Are you going to be fit for the match, Mr Rix?'

'I'm hoping so,' smiled Rixy. 'I'm very keen to play.'

Above left: Kenny the Pearly King, with equally pearly white teeth. They're all my own – and I've still got them all!

Above right: 'Handsome Sansom' on a modelling assignment. The upside is I looked very smart – the downside was that I'd never ski-ed in my life, except across the pitch at Selhurst Park one snowy winter, for fun.

Below left: Me doing a 'Harry Worth' (the lovely old comedian) whilst on a modelling assignment.

Below right: Me and my Puma! Good job he was a Palace fan or I would have been the one stuffed! I wore Puma boots for my entire career.

Above left: A Classic photograph of Terry Neill, Arsenal legend and manager in my early days at the north London establishment. I'd love to know what he was thinking when this photo was taken.

Above right: The Highbury Days and the George Graham era. Here is the Gaffer looking very laid back. I think he'd downed a few glasses of Chablis but as you can see he still looks dapper – even if he was a little blurry eyed. The vodka is on the shelves – this really was the drinking era at Arsenal.

Below: 'I see no ships.' George Graham took us on a pre-season trip to Scotland. Left to right: John Lukic, Alan Smith and me.

Above: Me looking pleased with myself just after I'd finished playing a match for England.

Below: Diego Maradona (on my left) was just 19 here when he took Wembley by storm in 1980. I was 22 and like everyone else was staggered at his skills and exceptional pace. During this game he had a terrific run past six players. Unfortunately I gave a controversial penalty away. I was amazed – I was certain my tackle had not only been fair, but also pure class.

Above left: An early shot of me under the England colours.

Above right: Me and my old England pal, Glen Hoddle. He was my room-mate for quite some time as we both had long and successful careers playing for our country.

Below: Mum was chuffed to be snuggled in Kevin Keegan's arms as he is her number 2 hero.

Above: In action for England, this time against Wales in 1980.

Below: Lining up in Mexico with the rest of the England lads against Argentina in the heat of the 1986 World Cup quarter-final.

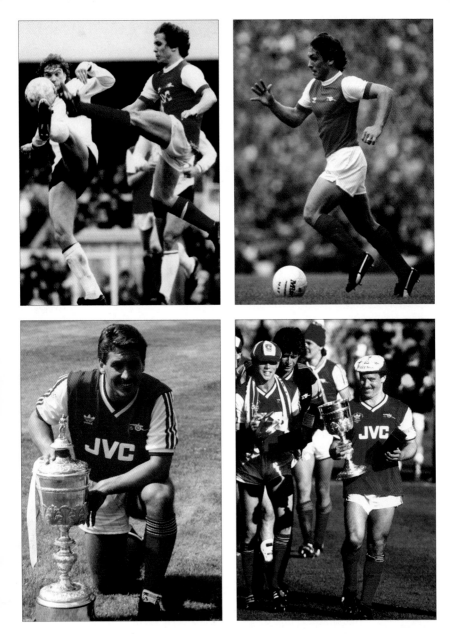

Above: In action for the Arsenal, top left challenging Hoddle for the ball in the North London derby.

Below: Me and the lads celebrating winning the League Cup final against Liverpool in 1987.

Me in my prime for England.

Above: Up against my old nemesis Diego Maradona in a seniors' game a few years ago.

Below: Still pointing the way for my team-mates as an Arsenal veteran!

'Mr Pat Jennings, there's been a lot of talk about your big hands. Can we see them?'

The goalkeeping legend replied, 'Yes, I've got big hands.'

Well, I tell you. I don't know how I kept a straight face. I was so busy trying not to laugh that I totally forgot what my question was and what I was supposed to answer.

The next thing I hear is my name followed by all this Chinese chatter.

'Kenny Sansom, I hear you played in the 1982 World Cup. How was it playing for your country? Was it exciting? Were you proud?'

The unfamiliar words seemed to go on for ever. I didn't have a bloody clue what he was on about. I leaned forward in my chair, as if *that* would help.

'Pardon, sorry, what was that?'

Everyone looked at everyone else in disbelief. We were live on air and we'd all frozen, which in hindsight was better than laughing – which we were all dying to do. In fact I could sense Pat Jennings's shoulders going up and down in silent laughter. Then Terry started to laugh out loud. It was a *One Flew over the Cuckoo Nest* moment with everyone sitting in a circle not quite knowing what to do next.

The Chinese presenter, live on air, groaned as someone (and I don't know who) hissed much too loudly, 'You've fucked it all up, Kenny.'

Moving swiftly on to Plan B the interviewer repeated the question in English: 'So, what's it like to play for your country?'

So, yes, you could say I well and truly fucked that one up.

SELLING SEX IN INDONESIA

Indonesia was an experience and a half. I had never seen anything like it in my life before.

Being brought up in south London in the sixties and nurtured by all around me through the seventies and eighties, I had been protected from the monstrosities occurring around the globe. I read the news and listened to bulletins on the television, but focused mostly on sport or comedy programmes.

All of a sudden, we're strolling down an Indonesian street and some young kid comes up to me and points to a young girl who couldn't have been more than 8 years old. 'My sister,' he grins.

I was about to ask for a pen so I could give him my autograph, when he went on, 'You want wanky, wanky? I sell her. She very good.' Aghast, I simply shook my head.

I had to get out of there. It was horrible – disgusting. But this scrawny little kid just kept on asking the same question over and over. He was so desperate for money that he was selling his little sister for sex. I wanted to be sick.

I thought back to the girls I was at school with, and then to my own two little girls before gazing back down into the big brown eyes staring up at me and smiling. I shuddered and hurried on. It was a terrible feeling to witness something like this at first hand. I would have had to experience it to believe it. There was absolutely nothing I could do. Men apparently paid for sex like this all the time.

Yet, as someone pointed out to me, 'Kenny, it's horrific, but this is life here. If a little body is all a family has to sell to keep them alive, they'll sell.' My God had I ever been protected from the real world!

When I had been the same age as the two kids I'd just met, I'd been enjoying caravan holidays on the coasts of southern England. These had been the days of penny slot machines, candyfloss, toffee apples, smutty postcards, and one-armed bandits – when days were sunnier and went on for ever. We filled hour upon hour with football, swimming and riding bikes. It was a lifetime away from the world of these unlucky little children.

This encounter with poverty made me think back to my Faversham, Canvey Island and Margate adventures. The two

Elaines were always around somewhere and all the boys wanted to be with them. As I said earlier, they were terrific dancers. I, on the other hand, kept my skilful feet very still, saving them for the football pitches.

My Elaine was petite and smiley with the palest blue sparkly eyes. She was irresistible and we fell in love to songs such as 'A Certain Smile' by Johnny Mathis.

MEMORIES IN MUSIC

Songs are important when you're young and in love, and it's funny when you look back and find a lot of your memories revolve around them. They say you remember only the very good or very bad things that happen to you and I think that's true. I can recall special moments or really horrible ones, like the police collaring me and David for breaking into the chandelier factory, but the in-between stuff is just a blur – or a blank space.

But when I hear a song that reminds me of being young it takes me right back there. I'm sure at least some of you out there understand where I'm going here, and can relate to what I'm on about – I certainly hope so.

When a record you recognise comes on the car radio and you are not ready for the memory, it can throw you. Suddenly you are back in the moment. All through my teenage years in the seventies the music was brilliant, and Elaine and I loved our music.

'Lean on Me' by Bill Withers has stood the test of time, as has Barry White with soulful melodies such as 'Can't Get Enough of Your Love, Babe'. I loved the music of great legends such as Nat King Cole, and Frank Sinatra doing it *his* way is one of the best tunes ever.

Elvis – the King – is everyone's favourite, and when he crooned I just melted. The voice of Johnnie Mathis is another that can bring me to tears.

KENNY SANSOM

HOLIDAYS

Holidays are another thing that trigger memories. I was 11 years old the first time I ever went on a plane. Mum took me and my brothers and sisters away to Majorca. It was one great round of swimming and football. (What else?)

There were Irishmen, Scotsmen and Welshmen – men from all over the country – talking with all sorts of strange accents. I was a cockney lad and couldn't understand a bloody word.

My brother David and I went in for all the competitions going. Guess who won the Tarzan competition. Yep, you've got it: I did. And they didn't even get to see me eat a pork chop. I thought I had a wonderful singing voice – but I didn't win that contest. I liked being up there and showing off – and at least my mum thought I was fabulous.

I did win a prize for something. I won a pretty crazy game where you had to walk along a greased pole without falling off. Well, I could do that one standing on my head. I think I won a bottle of Pomagne, but I gave it to my mum and my sister Margaret, who were both very happy indeed to knock it back.

It was like having a bottle of Moet for them – but there were no champagne flutes, only plastic cups. They weren't complaining: they lapped it up.

Swimming in the pool in the sunshine was a real treat – the sea in Majorca was much warmer than the sea at Margate. It gave a whole new meaning to taking a dip.

We children were allowed to go into the bar in the evening with our families. This was so much better than standing outside a pub with a packet of crisps and a bottle of Coke down by the Elephant and Castle.

Later on, of course, I travelled the world several times over exploring Europe as well as places like Mexico (why did I have to mention Mexico again so soon?), Canada and China.

Elaine and I had a very special holiday in Ibiza once. We stayed up in a mountain log cabin that had a sunken bath and a shag-pile carpet. It belonged to an eccentric man called Mr Pike and I remember how he loved a drop of Chivas Regal whisky and a bottle of Dom Perignon.

He was very generous and shared it all around. He shared lots of things around, actually. He insisted one day that we take his yacht out to sea. Well, that was an offer we couldn't refuse. It was a fabulous eight-seater – really luxurious. All was going well until I looked around and there were tits and bums everywhere. Elaine's face was a picture – actually, so was mine. Then some bright spark suggested we all strip off and swim back to shore. Off came everyone's kit. We had no choice. It was a case of grin, strip and jump.

Elaine and I discovered our love for American holidays. Once we were there on 4 July, Independence Day, and that was very special. We loved Florida – Clearwater and St Petersburg in particular.

My mum loved going to the States – and Florida was a favourite of hers, too. The only trouble was she used to tend to like wandering off on her own, which was a bit of a nightmare, as this was a whole lot different from her familiar walks in south London. A number of times we'd have to send a search party off looking for her and by the time we'd find her we would be in a terrible state and about to call out the police. She, on the other hand, would return full of stories about what she'd seen or what she'd done. She was bloody fearless – hang on, she still *is* bloody fearless.

We were in Mexico. Yes, she was there for the World Cup. We couldn't have kept her away if we'd tried: she would simply have got there under her own steam. She'd have tapped someone on the shoulder and said, 'Excuse me, but my son Kenny Sansom's playing football for England in the World Cup – could I have a lift please? Anyway, she met a Chinese man who she said fell in love with her. She said he asked her to marry him. I'm not sure whether this was a tall story. But she maintains to this day that he used to write to her with undying love. Good old Louise.

KENNY SANSOM

WHITE CHRISTMAS

Christmas as a child was magical. And, until I grew up and heard other people talk about their horrible childhood Christmas holidays, I thought everyone had a beautiful time. Chestnuts roasting on an open fire, stockings (or socks) hanging on the mantelpiece waiting for Santa to fill them with nuts, tangerines and selection boxes, and *A Wonderful Life* showing for the millionth time on Christmas Eve – these were what I knew.

How great James Stewart was in that ultimate classic of the good guy's hardship, the greed of the bad guy and a guardian angel who saves you! Then Clarence the angel gets rewarded for all his efforts, and we know this because a bell tinkles on the Christmas tree every time an angel wins his wings.

Even today that message of good conquering bad makes me emotional. When I watch people getting applauded for something they've done well – for achieving their goal against all the odds – I cry. If they fail in their endeavours I am almost as inconsolable as they are. Watching their disappointment hits a real nerve inside me. Seeing the winner being showered with confetti as they realise their dreams is also a tear jerker, but at least they have made it and not fallen at the last hurdle

Christmas 1986 – a child is born
Christmas Eve
Christmas Eve at Arsenal was a special time for the Junior Gunners who have been lucky enough to be invited to Highbury to meet their heroes. The lucky little Gooners would come to Highbury to watch us train and afterwards get to ask all the players all sorts of questions. We sign footballs, give them presents and do everything in our power to make their day as enjoyable as possible.

During my time at Arsenal, Charlie Nicholas was the kids' out-and-out favourite. He responded to them superbly. His natural qualities simply shone through. At question time he was quizzed the most. We were all asked different things and the stock question is always to name your best game or worst defeat.

I answered that my most enjoyable games would have to be during the World Cup, while my worst defeat was our 6–1 thrashing at Everton the season before. It had been dire.

The kids watched us train and Charlie was, as usual, up to his daft tricks. Theo Foley, assistant manager, took us for a warm-up around the Highbury pitch, and Charlie, acting the goat as usual, decided to cut across the grass and win the race. But he'd failed to notice the pitch had been watered. Halfway across he slipped. His rubber-soled shoes were totally inappropriate for the terrible conditions and, to the delight of the boys, he fell flat on his face. He didn't get up, but instead just lay there in the middle of Highbury for ages.

It's no exaggeration to say that the kids laughed until they cried. It was great to watch the special relationship they had with Charlie.

I'm certain the management at Arsenal never really got to grips with just how much Charlie, with his bubbly character, meant to the loyal fans. They simply adored him.

After a long pleasurable day at work I went home to my family, where my heavily pregnant wife, Elaine, was having those Braxton Hicks contractions, heralding the early stages of labour and the birth of our third child.

Christmas Day

Like all parents of young children, our kids Natalie (now 8) and Katie (5) woke us up at some unearthly hour on Christmas morning by excitedly opening their presents from Santa.

Christmas wouldn't have been Christmas without the extended family all around us, and Elaine's family were especially great that year. They were going nowhere – determined to be around in case the new baby arrived.

Elaine was so tired. The build-up to the festive season had been hectic, so she was grateful for the extra hands.

Our Christmas Day was the same as it is in most households: opening presents, clearing away rubbish, a turkey and stuffing lunch with Christmas pudding, and mince pies to follow.

But come six o'clock I had to leave to report to the boss for a night with the team at the Noke Hotel – our usual place to stay the night before a game. We were playing Leicester the next day, and it had already been decided between the lads and the boss that we'd avoid the temptation of excesses on Christmas Day by spending the night together. Not ideal but not exactly a chore.

Boxing Day, and a new arrival

It was a morning kick-off and what a rotten match it turned out to be! We drew 1–1 with Leicester, with Martin Hayes the scorer of our only goal.

It wasn't a good game. We should have had a convincing win, especially as their defender Russell Osman limped off leaving them a man down. I prayed we wouldn't look back at the end of the season and wish we had won that Boxing Day match. Especially as I came within a hair's breadth of scoring as I thumped a shot on goal, but straight at their keeper.

Oh, boy, did I ever get stick from the lads for *that*! But that was nothing unusual.

When I'd left our home on Christmas afternoon Elaine had been in some discomfort, and it was obvious baby Sansom No. 3 was on the way. It's funny how you get a bit blasé about things like childbirth after you've already seen a couple being born. I'd been full of anxiety when Natalie was born, a little worried when Katie arrived, and, by the third time, was taking it all in my stride.

There had been no hiccups when the girls came along, so I didn't anticipate any this time. I also knew Elaine was in good hands. As I left on Christmas Day I got the look that said, 'Off you go, I'll be OK. Look at all the support I've got. It's not as if Leicester were at the other end of the world.'

By the time the coach got back to London Colney, Elaine was in hospital and our child not far off being born. Graham Rix gave me a lift to the hospital, and I remember it was just after three in the afternoon when I ran through the hospital doors.

Three hours later, at 6.10 p.m. on Boxing Day, our son Harry William entered the world. Our one and only little boy had joined our family. I think the hospital staff were surprised how much Elaine and I cried.

On the way back home I stopped off at the off-licence and bought several bottles of champagne to wet the baby's head. All the family were around to share in the celebrations, and although I knew we had to play against Southampton the following day I also knew I'd get by on a natural high. I had a son – I only had a bloody son.

The next day we played Southampton at home. As it was our centenary match, there was a celebratory atmosphere all round. All the famous faces from the past were there, so it was vital we win. And, to our huge collective relief, good old Quinny got the one and only goal of the match late in the game.

Southampton played really well, with Mark Wright playing as a spare man covering all dangers and winning a lot of Niall's knockdowns.

I went home on cloud nine and called in at a couple of pubs along the way to tell my drinking buddies about our new arrival.

Then when I got home Elaine's family, who had been holding the fort, joined me in well and truly soaking the baby's head. Then later we held Harry's christening in our sunny south-facing garden, where a hundred people got burnt down one side – very painful and deeply unattractive.

FOOTBALLERS BEHAVING BADLY

The eighties were full of bad behaviour all in the name of 'bonding'. There were countless incidents of not only boozing and gambling, but also a few close calls where some of us could easily have found ourselves behind bars abroad – and some did.

I am choosing to share two examples of Arsenal legends and cult heroes out on the town, and a couple more of the shenanigans on foreign shores when travelling with the England squad. Let's go with the Gunners first, shall we?

As I've said before, and many of you know anyway, lots of the Highbury players, especially in the seventies and eighties, indulged heavily in drinking binges – and no binges were heavier than the ones that took place before Cup ties in 1987 and 1988.

In 1987, before we won the Littlewoods Cup, beating Spurs (funny how I can't stop saying that), we all jetted off to Portugal. The following year it was Puerto Banús on the Spanish Costa del Sol. We returned from that particular shenanigan to be beaten by Luton Town in the League Cup. That's how bloody hard we partied.

First of all, let's go to the resort of Montechoro in Portugal.

Montechoro madness: 1987, with Arsenal

George Graham decided us take us away for a few days for a 'team-bonding' holiday before we played Liverpool in the Littlewoods Cup final; I think George was looking to top up his tan and get a little golf practice in.

I was to room with Ian Allison and the whole of the team had been booked into the Montechoro Hotel, where Elaine and I, along with our girls, had holidayed for the previous 3 years. Obviously, I knew the hotel and surrounding area really well, as we used to go for long walks. It will come as no surprise to you that I also knew where all the best bars were located.

I knew the manager of the hotel really well, so I used my influence to get Ali and me some good accommodation, a suite of luxury rooms, which made the other lads jealous.

We split into three or four groups and then each went its separate way in search of entertainment. Ali and I found ourselves in a German bar I knew very well called the 19th Hole, and during the course of the evening we met a lot of people – as you do when you are in holiday resorts. Three of them, however, were special characters. Ali and I nicknamed them 'Jacket', 'Bond' and 'Miss Moneypenny': Jacket because the man was wearing a jacket with more colours on than the rainbow; and Bond and Miss Moneypenny because they used to meet up once a year for a naughty but nice romantic time.

It was a brilliant night but, unbeknown to us, elsewhere it was not going so well. I didn't realise there was trouble in the camp until the following morning.

I was summoned to the reception area to take a call. Apparently the caller asked for me because I was the Arsenal captain at the time. It was someone from an English newspaper and he said, 'Kenny, we hear there's been some trouble in Portugal concerning your players.'

I replied, 'I'm sorry, I can't help you. I've heard nothing.' This was the truth. I was in the dark on this one.

Later that morning as George Graham was playing a quiet game of golf, a buggy came flying across the green and informed him that four of his players had been thrown in prison. I wasn't there, but I could just imagine the expression of anger written across George's face. But also, knowing him as I did, I knew he'd take it all in his stride.

The four players in question were Charlie Nicholas, Graham Rix, Rhys Wilmott and Viv Anderson. Allegedly, they had got into a fight in a nightclub with some marines (the lads don't go halfway, do they?) and they all got kicked out.

'Phew! That was a close shave,' gasped Charlie – but it did not end there.

The marines got into their car and went looking for the lads and when they found them they drove the car straight at them. Again, as the story goes, they were trying to protect themselves and so they started to throw bricks, stones and anything else handy at the car. The police arrived on the scene and promptly banged our boys in a cell. Ouch!

When the worst of it was over and the lads had been released, George called us all together for a meeting and said that, if we each paid for the damage for the marines' car, the incident would be forgotten. The repairs came to £900, which with eighteen of us on the trip came to £50 each. George's logic was that we were in a team and therefore all had some responsibility. If I remember rightly, only one of us did not want to put his hand in his pocket, and that was Paul Davis – tight git! Just joking, Paul.

Anyway, back in London on the day of the Cup final against Liverpool, Ali and I walked into the dressing room to find among the pile of good-luck telegrams one especially for us. It went like this: 'To Kenny and Ian. Good luck for today. I hope you beat Liverpool, love from Jacket, Bond and Miss Moneypenny.'

That was a lovely thing to do. It really touched us – thanks very much.

Puerto Banús: Spring 1988

Team-bonding holidays were by now part and parcel of most football clubs' preparations before a big match, and all squad members were expected to participate. We were due to play Luton the following week in the League Cup final. No football matches are easy. Nothing is a dead certainty. But we were certainly glad to be playing Luton instead of Manchester United or Liverpool.

My drinking was getting out of hand, but I didn't know it. Everyone close to me – especially Elaine – was alarmed to witness the change it had on my attitude. I thought I was the centre of the universe. I felt I was above the law. Alcohol was giving me a distorted view of the world and my place in it. I was getting above myself and I guess I was getting on some people's nerves. I was getting on George Graham's nerves – that's for sure. And I was about to push my luck too far.

The night before we were due to fly off for a 'bonding holiday' in trendy Marbella, I got well and truly slaughtered. I must have arrived home at about three in the morning and, much to Elaine's distress, I announced I wasn't going to Spain with the others.

An hour later, David O'Leary rang our doorbell, only to be told by my wife that I wasn't going to Spain.

A sober David O'Leary knew this would mean trouble, so he tried for ages to persuade me to get dressed, have a coffee, and then go with him to the airport. But I was having none of it – I knew best.

I was growing tired of these 'away jolly-ups'. My idea of fun was now much more about being out on the town in London with Elaine and friends, or just a few of my chosen teammates. Likewise, my days abroad in the sunshine were usually family affairs.

I was coming to the end of playing for England. I had done a hell of a lot of partying, and even more travelling. It had been fantastic and thrilling. It had also been lonely with lots of spare time on my hands.

Ten years of hotel rooms had given me plenty of time to bond with my teammates as we played cards, drank champagne and generally misbehaved. Practical jokes and wind-ups had kept us all laughing, but I think the laughter had been thinly disguising the sense that something was missing – that it all wasn't quite real.

As far as I was concerned the last thing I needed right now was a 'fun-in-the-sun' crack in Marbella's infamous Puerto Banús – where the rich and famous join other hellraisers for drinking, drugs and wild, wild women.

Most of the lads were up for it, though, and I understood why. From what I've seen of the leather-skinned males in Marbella, and what I've heard about the goings-on, what man in his right mind wouldn't jump at the chance of an all-expenses-paid party in Europe's most famous playground? Me!

When I didn't show up at the airport there were many who weren't surprised – but George Graham apparently kept looking over his shoulder expectantly. 'Where's Kenny, Gary?' he asked our physio, Gary Lewin.

Poor Gary just shrugged. He didn't have a clue.

'Get him on the phone. Tell him if he doesn't show he won't play in the final,' barked George. 'And I bloody well mean it.'

Gary phoned our house and a flustered Elaine answered. 'He doesn't feel too good, Gary,' she said.

'I suggest he gets his bag packed and catches the next plane down to Malaga. The gaffer says if he doesn't come he won't be playing in the final.'

Elaine slammed the receiver down and gave me the bad news. I knew it wasn't a threat. If George had said I wouldn't play – skipper or no skipper – I'd be dropped.

So I panicked but, after sitting with my head in my hands for a few moments, I came to my senses.

Well, as much as I could with a few litres of wine flowing through my veins. 'Pack me a bag, Elaine. Find out what time the next plane leaves for Malaga. Drive me to the airport, Elaine.' My orders were endless. Poor Elaine was, as usual, on the receiving end of my demands. She deserved better. But she knew I loved her. She knew she was my girl and that this was my way when I was in drink.

I didn't want to go and leave her behind. My dependency on her was increasing alongside my escalating alcohol consumption, and she was astute enough to know this. She loved me unconditionally and at times I abused that love. But in those times I couldn't think beyond the next drink.

I don't remember the flight over to Spain, but I know I was drunk when I landed. I was dressed in my Arsenal blazer – not conspicuous then. What an insult to the club! I didn't have a clue where the team was staying, only that it would be close to Banús, probably somewhere in the Port itself.

So I braved the bustling crowds and pushed my way over to a

Spanish woman behind a desk who, it turned out, didn't speak very much English. As I spoke no Spanish besides *hola* and *cerveza*, to say we communicated in Spanglish would be a gross lie. It wasn't that good. We didn't communicate, full stop.

I asked her, 'Excuse me, can you tell me where the Arsenal football team are staying?'

Her response was a squint, a shrug of her shoulders, followed by a shake of the head, and a curious *'Señor?'*

Can you imagine that happening today? The whole of the Spanish mainland would know where the Arsenal football club were staying and the press would be camped outside waiting to catch the boys getting up to mischief.

So I looked around for, well, I don't know what. Inspiration, maybe?

I think a few people tried to help the poor Spanish girl. They wouldn't want to help me – *I* was a disgrace. I think there were a few instances of *'donde?'* (where?) and *'de nada'* flying around, but the wheres and whys were getting ridiculous. If we had been speaking in pidgin French it would have been a scene straight out of an episode of *Only Fools and Horses*. Perhaps I should have asked for a bottle of Châteauneuf-du-Pape – at least I could have sunk back into oblivion.

I know I took a cab next. I think the debacle in the arrivals lounge had sobered me up a little.

'Puerto Banús, *por favor, señor,*' I said to the swarthy little man, but had to repeat the request in a raised voice to be heard over the Gypsy Kings. He nodded and we were off up the road that's been dubbed 'the graveyard of Europe'. There's a new toll road there nowadays, but when the only road available had been the N340 the death toll had been frighteningly high – especially in holiday time. We were now in April and it was hot. Dehydrated, I knew I needed a thirst-quenching beer.

I shut my eyes and before I knew it the taxi was pulling into

Puerto Banús. It was early evening and the sun was going down behind the mountain. I knew there wasn't a hope in hell of finding my teammates' hotel, but I took a calculated guess that sooner or later they'd turn up at the Sinatra bar on the first line of the port – directly in front of the million-dollar boats and yachts clinking in the harbour.

I shook off my Arsenal jacket, took a seat looking out to sea and ordered a much-needed *cerveza*, and drank in the crazy atmosphere of Banús.

I haven't a clue how long I sat there in the fading daylight. Watching the world go by in a haze, my eyes kept darting to the corner of the Salduba bar, praying the boys would come into view.

I wasn't looking forward to my bollocking from the gaffer, but I was keen to establish I'd still got my place in the final. The thought of their winning and my not being their skipper was too painful to contemplate. If anything was going to sober me up, that would be it.

Then they appeared. George was strolling just ahead of the others, and when he saw me jump up to greet him he gave me a stony stare and pointed over his shoulder. He dismissed me by saying, 'See Gary Lewin.'

He couldn't be bothered to talk to me, and I can't say I blame him.

That few days were oh so crazy – just as I knew they would be. If I was in the mood to drink, I was in the best possible company.

We stayed in the Andalucia Plaza, which was just across the main road, and close to the casino (very handy).

My memory of the whole mad episode is hazy and much of what we got up to has been fitted together like a jigsaw puzzle by each of us. Paul Merson remembers bits and Perry Groves can seriously remember when Mers threw him in the sea in the port – in among the fishes and multimillion-pound boats.

Why did Mers throw Grovesy in the sea? Because he could. Well, actually, it all began as we sat, very drunk, in the Salduba bar on the corner of the front line of the port, and Grovesy asked Mers if he could have his money back that he'd been looking after because Grovesy had no pockets in his shorts.

Mers stared at him as if he'd got two heads. 'What?'

'I want my money,' repeated Perry.

'*Your* money? What do you think you've been spending these past few days, thin air? All our money's gone on booze and food and clubbing... and... ' Then, in one quick move, Mers grabbed the tomato-sauce bottle (in the shape of a tomato) and began to squirt him with it. Perry squirted him back and then we all joined in for a free-for-all. Then Mers picked Grovesy up and in front of a busy front line he threw him into the sea. How Grovesy managed to clamber out, and how it didn't end up in the *Sun*, I'll never know. But it didn't end there.

We decided it would be a laugh to take a boat out to sea – perhaps do a little fishing like the scene in *One Flew Over the Cuckoo's Nest*. So up the gangplank marched Mers, Grovesy, Tony Adams and I and, um, can't remember who else. On board we rummaged around looking for keys to start the boat and then we all decided to have a little siesta. We all fell asleep and thank goodness we didn't manage to find the keys and set sail in what could have been the property of some dangerous drug baron. I kid you not.

As things turned out, what with Luton beating us, I wish I'd stayed on the bloody boat and sailed off into the sunset.

Colorado

The England squad enjoyed our card school and wherever we went we knew the procedure on arrival. Check in, drop our bags in our rooms, and meet in the lobby 15 minutes later to begin a marathon card game. These card schools were very big among all football teams in my day. Sometimes we were away for 3 weeks at a time and every spare moment would be taken up playing cards.

On long trips we'd play seven-card brag, where you'd have to win two three-card brags. No money was ever handed over till the end of the trip (a point system kept the score), so quite a big win (or a big loss) could accrue. The winner of each individual game would win £5 from each of the other players. The art of the game was to end up with one man on zero and one man at the top of the points table.

Back in 1980 on a trip to Europe prior to the European Championships we'd been in Italy for a 3-week period and I'd had a heart-stopping moment when I could have lost a serious amount of money on a single night when we were playing what was turning into a dangerous game of three-card brag. It got to the point when I was losing by £650 and starting to panic. The money was piling up in the middle of the table until it reached £2,200. Suddenly I got lucky with a pair of twos (in three-card brag it's very strong indeed). Two of the other players had good hands as well – one with a high pair and another with a run. You can imagine the smile on my face when I turned my cards over and I'd won the lot. Obviously, I had to pay out some losses, but I still came away a very happy man. Anyone who is not involved in gambling may not know that any gambler will tell his stories of winning – but rarely about his losses, which are many.

Before the 1986 World Cup in Mexico we flew to Colorado, and what a terrific time we had, all great mates together and no friction between us whatsoever; it was brilliant. Of course we were training and socialising and enjoying the whole experience, but the thought of the next game of seven-card brag was never far away.

The week before we went off to Monterrey to play in the World Cup the wives came out for a holiday. It began with a hitch, though, when Michelle Lineker and Elaine were detained at the airport because they both had problems with their passports. Michelle had got the wrong visa and Elaine's was due to run out.

The other wives arrived minus the two so-called offenders, telling us they'd been sent home. Sent home! It sent me and Gary into a spin, I can tell you. We panicked and tried in vain to make phone calls, calling taxis and running around like headless chickens.

Then, after a great deal of side-splitting laughter on the girls' part, they confessed that Michelle and Elaine had talked their way out of trouble and out they jumped. Nice one, Elaine.

We travelled around more during the week the girls were with us and ate in some great restaurants and hotels. Elaine and I remember clearly a story the owner of one hotel told us about why his hotel, called the CaRLTON, was spelled with a small *a* in it.

'I used to be very poor. You could say I was a down-and-out and at my very lowest moment I had no option but to beg for food. I walked into this hotel, and the name of it began with an *a*. They shooed me away as if I was a piece of dirt on their shoe.

'After that incident I slowly regained some control of my life until I eventually became a wealthy man, owning a chain of hotels. But I couldn't bring myself to put a capital *A* in the name – so they all became little *a*'s. Now I am in a position to give something back I ensure a chunk of the profit I make from my hotels goes into my charity that builds homes and hospitals – anything to help those in unfortunate positions such as I once found myself in.'

One of the great things about travelling the world is that you meet so many interesting people and that gentleman certainly stays alive in my mind.

I spent a lot of lovely time with Elaine on this holiday. She was 3 months pregnant with Harry at the time, and all was well in our world. As the romantic song goes, it was 'Love, love, love' all the way. We didn't want it to end, and the other players felt the same about their wives. When the time came for us to kiss goodbye and wave them off to the airport there were lots of tears all round. Honest – there were tears running down most couple's faces. It was like a scene out of a movie. As their coach drew away we were standing there peering up through the windows waving and mouthing, 'I love you.'

As soon as the coach turned the corner I shouted, 'Come on, lads – whose deal is it?' It wasn't that we didn't genuinely feel sad about the departure of the girls – but, hey, we loved our card school, too. Whoever said footballers were fickle?

A MEMORABLE TREAT

We went on another trip to Vancouver and were staying in a beautiful hotel and being really spoilt by the Canadians. The Expo Show was on and there was a brilliant atmosphere, with beer tents and stalls and more beer tents. When we'd seen enough, Glenn Hoddle and I decided to slip off and have a Chinese meal. Some bloke who was probably in his fifties had been chatting to us and seemed impressed that we played football for England. Overhearing our plans, he chipped in with, 'What're you up to for dinner, then?' He was a solicitor or lawyer, something of that ilk. 'I'll treat you to dinner in the revolving restaurant at the top of Vancouver Hotel if you like.'

It was off the cuff, spontaneous, great.

You should have seen the place – it was a million dollars. When the lift stopped at the top of the building he went over to *maître d'* and asked for a window seat for his special guests and got one. You should have seen the view. It was absolutely magnificent.

This guy had been to every World Cup since 1958 and now he was in Vancouver to watch the Canadian match before going on to the World Cup finals in Mexico. I can't for the life of me remember his name, but I remember him. And if by any chance you're reading this, thanks for a lovely evening.

CLOSER TO HOME

Being afforded the luxury of worldwide travel was great, but there's no place like home. Throwing parties and having barbecues on sunny days were what we loved best. But going out on the town and treating family and friends to swish restaurants, where they might never otherwise have been.

Elaine's parents rarely ate out (not many families did back then – it wasn't something their generation did), although they had the odd takeaway and ate at a Berni Inn on birthdays – so we loved to take them out for dinner. They were salt-of-the-earth people and Elaine, being the blue-eyed baby of the family, was cherished dearly and I guess they spoilt her a bit – so now it was our turn to spoil them.

The first time we took them for a Chinese meal was funny. The scene could have come straight out of a comedy script. Again, it wasn't planned, but just kind of happened.

Elaine and I went to this Chinese restaurant regularly and knew the boss, Danny, really well. So, when he came over and saw Elaine's dad Bill was struggling with his chopsticks, he said, 'Are you all right there, sir? Can I help you?'

Instead of offering a knife and fork he asked him, 'Are you left-handed or right-handed?'

'Right-handed,' says Bill.

'Oh that's why. My mistake: I gave you left-handed chopsticks.'

Alice smiled at Bill. 'No wonder you can't use those ones, Bill,' she said.

Family!

Another story will probably resonate with many of you, as boys in drink tend to collude with each other and behave worse than they would alone.

Bill and Alice had come over to us for the weekend at our home in north London for Sunday lunch. When meal time arrived there was no sign of me as I'd met up with my dad in the Orange Tree (a great pub that the Gooners will know well) and, well, I was running late.

The women were getting twitchy, so Bill said, 'Don't worry, I'll go and get him.'

'He'll probably be in the Orange Tree,' said Elaine knowingly.

When he walked into the pub, Bill was greeted warmly by all, and I said, 'Come on, Bill. Have a drink and then we'll get back.'

Bill agreed. I'm certain he wanted a drink, but if he hadn't I don't think he'd have had much of a choice. Well, you guessed it: six or seven drinks later Elaine appeared in the doorway with a face like thunder and some harsh words. We went home with our tails between our legs to a well-done dinner – but at least it hadn't been given to the dog.

It wasn't only Elaine's parents we treated: her sister Sheila and her husband Gordon also enjoyed many a night on the town. One of the highlights was going to see Shirley Bassey at her Talk of the Town show. What a performer! What an entertainer! Gordon and Sheila absolutely adored her – and quite rightly. No wonder she was made a dame. We had front-row seats and it was almost as if we had our own audience with her.

Suddenly it seemed as if she was being bothered by something and soon after she announced, 'I'm having trouble with my eyelashes – does anyone want them?'

A young man about four rows back came flying down the gangway, determined to be the proud owner of Shirley Bassey's false eyelashes. But Gordon was a man possessed. He jumped up and cried, 'Hey, hold on, you're not having both of them. Don't be greedy. I want one.' And get one he did. He was over the moon – you'd have thought he'd won the lottery – and to this day Shirley Bassey's eyelash is nestled in his wallet. God knows how many times he's brought it out to show.

Afterwards we went to Langhans – one of our regular London haunts. Once we were inside, the waiter smiled at me and called me by my nickname, 'Hello, Mr Chablis, what can we get you?' (Besides a crate of Chablis, that was.)

I turned to Sheila. 'We've got to have the bangers and mash. It's delicious, and at ten pounds a head it's a bargain.'

So there we were tucking into our sausages when I noticed Cliff Richard arrive and sit two tables away from us. I nudged Sheila. 'Hey, Sheila, Cliff Richard's just arrived.'

She stopped eating and peered across the room, 'He looks just like him, Kenny?'

'It *is* him, Sheila.'

'No, it can't be. But I tell you, he's his double.'

Today we have lots of tribute artists who earn fortunes imitating famous people, but it didn't happen so much – if at all – back then in the eighties. And to this day Sheila cannot be certain whether she saw the real Cliff. I'm certain, though. It was Peter Pan himself. I don't think he had the sausages, though, the fool – he didn't know what he was missing.

CAB DRIVERS AND ME AND BOBBY MOORE

Although I've told you about the times I stupidly drank and drove, more often than not I'd end up in a London black cab – so I've travelled in more than enough in my time.

Cabbies are usually chatty guys with a lot to say, especially if they recognise me.

Once I got into a taxi in Billericay in Essex with my friend Tony Hoskins, who was a West Ham fan (I never was too fussy who I mixed with!), and the driver instantly recognised me.

'Hello, Mr Sansom, it's a pleasure for me to have you in my cab – I'm a West ham fan.'

Here we go. Now I've got two of the buggers in my company – and at very close proximity. Was I about to suffocate? So the cabbie went on. 'Sir Bobby Moore was my hero. I worshipped the ground he walked on. He was fantastic.'

I started to say something about Bobby Moore, but he quickly interrupted me, '*Sir* Bobby Moore, you mean.'

On and on he went. I think we went through the whole of the West End with him going on about our 1966 World Cup hero. 'He often used a pub I used to go to all the time, you know. When I first bumped into him he was standing by the bar. I'd already had a few beers in another boozer, so I had some Dutch courage. I walked straight up to him and said, "Hello, Mr Moore. I'm a great West Ham and England fan, and you're my hero." He said to me, "Thank you very much," and I wanted to say more – to keep on talking to him, so I asked him if I could tell him something else and he was very kind and nodded, so I went on to say, "If I caught you in bed with my wife I'd tuck you in and make you a cup of tea, Mr Moore – you were *that* good."'

What a character! What a pleasure to meet that particular cabbie!

Let's stay with Bobby Moore for a moment, because there was a funny coincidence a couple of months later when I was playing golf at the Royal St George's in Sandwich, Kent, and was telling my mate Michael Oates about the Bobby Moore story. All of a sudden this bloke appears next to me and all very excited he says, 'Hello, you're Kenny Sansom, aren't you?' It wasn't really a question. He knew it was me all right. Then he added, 'Kenny, you don't know what you've done, do you?'

I shook my head, 'Sorry?'

'What you did in your football career – it was fantastic.'

He kept on repeating himself as if he couldn't quite believe he was standing on a golf course next to me. Suddenly he cried, 'I'm going to telephone my wife. She'll never believe this. And I'll tell you what: I'm going to let you take her out for dinner.'

I was unusually struck dumb for a moment, not quite knowing how to respond.

Then he looked glum and said, 'No, on the other hand, if you saw my wife you wouldn't want to take her for dinner.'

I still think it's bizarre that these two stories of famous footballers and fans' wives should occur in such a short space of time. Very strange indeed.

CHAPTER FIFTEEN

SAMANTHA FOX OR FATIMA WHITBREAD – YOU CHOOSE

O nce I was invited to take part in the BBC's *A Question of Sport*. In those days it was hosted by David Coleman. It was being filmed in Manchester and, since I was already up there because we'd been playing up North, Elaine flew up from Heathrow and met me in the hotel.

When she arrived I was already having a briefing from David Coleman and a drink to wash the information down. We were joined by the Welsh marathon runner Steve Jones (another contestant) and his wife, and we all socialised till the early hours and a good time was had by all. We weren't too concerned about a hangover as the show wasn't being recorded until 3.30 on the Sunday afternoon, which gave me ample time to recover.

Elaine and I just about made it down for breakfast at 9.30 and as we sipped our black coffee we were amazed to see Steve Jones and his wife jog in through the doors. 'We've just been for a three-mile run,' grinned Steve, not at all out of breath. We nearly fainted just at the thought of it. How fit is that!

Two shows were filmed that afternoon and one of the athletes in the second show was Fatima Whitbread, who was there with her stepmum. She seemed very nice, but we did no more than exchange a few pleasantries. We all sat in on the briefing, where we were told to wait a few moments before answering our questions on air. It was all about keeping the suspense levels high. If you knew the answer it wasn't good to jump straight in and make it look too easy.

We were given a glass of wine before the show. They said it was to calm our nerves, but I didn't have any. I have always loved TV and radio work and the adrenalin associated with the work more than topped up my diminishing alcohol levels from the night before. I did all right, though, and thoroughly enjoyed the whole experience.

When the time came to fly home, Elaine and I and Fatima and her stepmum all checked in at Manchester airport, flew back to Heathrow and then said, 'Goodbye, it was nice meeting you.'

Two weeks later there was a knock on my door. I opened it and came face to face with a *News of the World* reporter, who looked me right in the eye and said, 'We've received a story saying you're having an affair with Fatima Whitbread. Can you confirm whether it's true or false?'

I stared back at him and scratched my head thoughtfully before calling Elaine. 'Elaine, can you come here a minute? This man wants to ask you something.'

Elaine arrived by my side and I asked the man to repeat what he had just asked me. Well, tears were running down her face as she screamed, 'That's the funniest thing I ever heard. Where did you get that idea?' She wasn't crying: she was laughing her head off.

'You were seen with her at Manchester airport and then later at Heathrow,' said the man, looking very sheepish. 'I think I must have got it wrong.'

'What do you think?' was my final question before we shut the door on the red-faced reporter, who was no doubt thinking of killing whoever had given him the tip-off.

SAMANTHA FOX LOVES ARSENAL

It's not often you get offered to spend the night with a Page 3 icon such as London's Samantha Fox – but that's exactly what happened to me when I was the Arsenal captain.

By now you know what a social animal I used to be. I had as much energy off the pitch as I had on it, and when you are out and about at golf dos and, charity days and special dinners, you meet all sorts of interesting people – and some more interesting than others.

Elaine and I were at a charity fancy-dress competition in the mid-eighties and one of the judges was the Page 3 glamour model Samantha Fox.

I was dressed as – wait for it – Andy Pandy, and Elaine had gone as a clown. She wasn't a regular clown, but had had her face painted professionally as the white-faced porcelain sad clown who had tears running down her face. She really looked fantastic, but unfortunately she didn't feel the same way – especially when she saw Samantha Fox with her breasts popping out of her barely there blouse and wearing a skirt that wasn't much bigger than a belt.

I kept telling Elaine not to be daft and that she was my girl and I thought she looked great, but she couldn't hear me. I don't think she was alone in feeling intimidated by a sexy young thing baring all. Lots of wives and girlfriends, especially when they are in celebrity circles, feel uncomfortable at some time or another. Covered from head to toe in a clown's attire, she could have kicked herself for not wearing something more alluring.

It didn't help when Samantha came over and told me what a huge Arsenal fan she was and asked for my autograph. Then she stayed talking to us for quite some time and asked if I could get her some Arsenal tickets.

So there I stood dressed as Andy Pandy, with Elaine as the White-Faced Clown next to me with genuine tears threatening to spoil the painted-on fakes, while Sam thrust her ample breasts (nothing fake about *them*) at us. She was one sexy lady, that's for sure.

I said I'd try my best to get hold of some tickets for the next home match at Highbury and she gave me her phone number. I know. A few days later I called to say I'd got the tickets and we arranged to meet in a pub in north London.

I got there first and was drinking with a couple of pals of mine when she walked in – looking every inch a Page 3 girl. My mates were impressed and my ego was flying through the roof. I challenge any man to say they'd feel differently.

We all had a few more drinks – no change there, then. I handed over the tickets and she asked how she could repay me. At least I think that's what she said. It was a long time ago when I was in my prime – when I was King Kenny of the Arsenal and thought I was invincible. So I let her take me home to her house for coffee. Well, she'd said she wanted to show me something and that it was all very delicate. She was looking a bit down, so I was a gentleman and went back to hers. I knew it was all very innocent, because she told me her mum would be there.

Back at the Fox household we had some more drinks and chatted a lot. She showed me her photo album and pictures of her taken long before she was famous. There were some really cute ones of her as a baby and others of her as a toddler. Some that were taken when she was still quite young showed her in callipers. She explained she had suffered with a problem – I think it was with her hips – and had to wear these awful walking aids for some time to correct the problem. It was all quite sobering, actually. Really it was.

All the time this was going on her mum was upstairs and there really was an air of innocence to all of this – until she asked me if I wanted to stay the night.

Elaine never believed that nothing happened, but I can assure you, as I've assured her for years, nothing did. Strange as it might seem, she didn't fancy me 'in that way'. In fact I've always been a bit paranoid that it might have been me who sent her running into the arms of another woman.

I know of other players who have got into hot water with their wives for something they have supposedly done – it can be really tricky being a professional footballer at times. It can also be a bit of a burden being Handsome Sansom. I wasn't surprised when I heard Samantha preferred women to men. I just hope it wasn't me who turned her off blokes.

CHAPTER SIXTEEN

GOING NORTH OF WATFORD

Before I knew it, Nigel Winterburn was playing in the left-back position that had been mine for most of the eighties. And what happens when you dropped from your club side? Yep: England moves on, too – in my case with Stuart Pearce.

With the attitude 'what doesn't kill you makes you stronger', I packed my bags and waved goodbye to my beloved Highbury.

It was very different from leaving Crystal Palace. When I left Selhurst Park I was a young and eager lad who was still incredibly immature. I went with the flow and rode the wave unquestioningly. I was moving to north London to play for a giant club – how could that possibly be difficult? It just all seemed par for the course.

Leaving the Arsenal was different. I had been there eight long memorable years, and you could say that both Elaine and I had grown up there. Two more children, Katie and Harry, had joined our first child, Natalie (but you've already read about my lovely kids), making our family complete – well, until later, when the grandchildren came along to liven us up all over again.

We had moved house so many times I'm surprised we could

remember all the addresses. We'd gone from south London to Epsom Downs, where Natalie was born. From there we'd gone to Barnet, where we purchased a medium-sized home and then a bigger, more luxurious house. Our next move was to Keston and to a haven we loved the most. Instead of selling up, we decided to rent the Keston house out and the plan was to rent in Newcastle until we were certain we would stay. The only time I'd ever travelled north of Watford was to play an away match, so it was a bit daunting.

We had to consider moving the children out of school and that wasn't easy, especially for Natalie, who was older and had made friends she wouldn't want to leave behind. As far as I was concerned the children wanted for nothing, both materially and emotionally. I was the daddy – the breadwinner. Elaine was the mummy who was never far from their sides, catering to all their needs.

For all these reasons it was a terrible wrench leaving our sanctuary. The Sansoms were relocating to Newcastle. How about that? I never thought I'd see the day we moved out of London or the suburbs. Way back, when I'd been a young teenager and Liverpool had been interested in signing me, it was the London boy in my heart that hurriedly signed for the Arsenal.

I moved to the Northeast before Elaine, who had to sort out the move and all it entailed. This wasn't an ideal situation, but it was my work and there was no alternative.

The Newcastle United manager, Jim Smith – a great guy – met me in the lobby of a local hotel at around 5.30, and asked me what I'd like to drink. Now that's what I call a welcome.

'Gin and tonic, please,' I replied.

'Make that two,' he told the barman, and we took our seats for a long evening. Well, it was a long night, actually, as we didn't stop drinking and talking, probably about rubbish once the clock had struck the witching hour. The showbiz agent Eric Hall had been with us at the beginning of our session, but, not being a drinker, he made a hasty exit and left us before it got too messy.

It was a fascinating evening that saw Jim and me telling each other some secrets that are never to be told. The tales were for our ears only. But one thing he told me that I'll share is that when he'd been a player he made it a firm rule never to have sex after a Wednesday because it weakened his legs for the Saturday match. Hmm.

Most footballers have their own personal restrictions about when you can or can't have sex, or a drink, or both. Some are stricter than others when adhering to their self-imposed rules.

Jim liked a swig of brandy 15 minutes before a match. He said it was for 'Dutch courage'. Jim was old-school, as were so many whose paths I crossed, and, pretty much without exception, they all liked a nip of brandy from the communal flask. I have many fond memories of Jim – he had such a way with words. One in particular stands out. 'That fucking Dunwoody let me down again.' Yes, we were similar in many ways.

For those of you unfamiliar with gambling or horse racing, Richard Dunwoody was the jockey of the time, and Jim's going on about his latest bet was his idea of a team talk.

I remember once that we were playing away at Southampton, and, as Jim and I walked past a group of Saints fans, one of them shouted across, 'Oi, Sansom! Who won the three fifteen?'

I scratched my head in wonderment as I called back, 'It's only two o'clock, you idiot!' I tell you, if the Geordie fans are the most loyal and passionate and adore anyone who wears a black and white shirt, the Southampton boys are the dumbest. All fans have a certain personality of their own. The Scousers are funny bastards with a terrific sense of humour. Manchester United have the reputation of being quiet, whereas the Portsmouth fans never stop cheering. The Gooners are of course the absolute best, whereas Spurs? Well, what can I say, boys?

Seriously, it saddens me how much the gulf between the fans and the players has widened in recent years, but that's the way it is, I'm afraid. It costs a small fortune now for the young fans to go to matches and watch their heroes play either home or away. The money now generated has made footballers superstars. Which is a great shame for the young fans desperate to get close enough to get their programmes signed. Autographs still mean a hell of a lot to young and old alike.

Elaine was down. I could hear it in her voice when we spoke on the phone. She was trying to be bright, but you don't know someone all your life and not pick up unspoken words – especially if the tone of their voice is listless. It wasn't like Elaine to get stuck in the doldrums – she was always the backbone of our family and I didn't want her cracking up.

One afternoon after training I downed a few drinks and then jumped into my sponsored Ford Sierra to begin the 5-hour drive down to London to see my family. I knew they needed some support and I too was missing them.

Elaine takes over the story...

I was down in the dumps. It was a hell of a wrench upping sticks and moving into the unknown – especially with three young children to take into consideration. I'd go anywhere with Kenny – there is no question about it. We had rarely been apart, so I missed him terribly. One evening there was a knock at the door. It was late, so I wondered who the hell it could be. I wasn't expecting anyone.

As I walked up the hallway, I could see the outline of a man behind our frosted-glass front door. Well, as I got closer, the outline of Kenny was unmistakable.

'Kenny! What the bloody hell are you doing here?'

'You sounded down,' he sniffed. He was in tears.

'Have you been drinking?'

'Yes.'

'Daft bugger.'

'I took it easy. I drove all the way in the slow lane.'

It was madness. It was pure insanity. My drinking was beginning to affect me, but I was yet to hit rock bottom.

I can't tell you how gutted I was at leaving the Arsenal. I was devastated. I loved the club, my fellow players and the loyal fans, who lit up the Highbury ground for home games and travelled miles to support us in away fixtures. Those fans who chanted 'King Kenny' would change their tune, of that I was certain. I had traded in the red and white Arsenal kit for black and white stripes, and in that sense I had gone full circle – for those had been our Brandon colours back in the sixties when the playing fields had been home to us bright young things.

Sound old, don't I? In actuality, I was not quite 30 when I joined the Geordie boys of the Northeast. Yet the fact that I had been engrossed in football since I was 8 years old – and my competitive play had spanned 3 decades, one of which had been representing my country – made me feel a bit ancient.

That said, after recovering 100 per cent from my hernia operation, I was fit and raring to go again – which is pretty bloody amazing given the abuse I gave my body. Thank God for the good genes.

Elaine and I were so surprised when we arrived in Newcastle. We absolutely loved it. As two born-and-bred cockney Londoners in the heart of Tyneside, we had assumed we'd be outsiders. But we had seriously undermined both the place and the people.

Elaine would come back from the local shops or the park with the children and look at me with an air of astonishment. 'Kenny, these people can't be for real. They're too nice. I keep being asked, "How are ya, pet?" and "Away... are ya havin' a grand day, lass?" These people don't talk: they sing.'

She thought at first they might be taking the rise out of her, or finding her cockney accent quirky and simply wanting to listen to her voice. But as time went on and she met more and more people it finally dawned on her that these were genuinely wonderful people.

We felt so relaxed among the Geordies that we decided not to bother renting, but to buy a home and settle down 'oop' there.

Mind you, the night life could be a bit hair-raising. Stringfellow's or Tramp it wasn't. The disco scene in Newcastle in the nineties was something else. A club called Don Dino's comes to mind. You didn't need a membership to get in: you needed a scar. When Elaine went to the loo she was the only girl without one.

In Newcastle it's the birds who chat up the blokes. It was a case of women's liberation out of control.

Elaine's no wimp, but she didn't exactly take a shine to the 'geezer birds' – probably because she didn't want to get scarred. She came back from the loo that night with a pale face – the blood having drained from her. 'I think we should get out of here' was all she said.

The house we purchased was really special, and I was happy to go to the training ground every morning in the knowledge all was well on the home front.

When I joined Newcastle in 1989 the Magpies were in the old Division One, but relegation was just around the corner, shattering everyone involved with this passionate club. But, whatever division the boys were in, the fans rallied round, adoring and worshipping the players just the same.

The Brazilian player Mirandinha was at the club during the 6 months I was there. He was a great attacker of the ball but could be a bit of a liability at the back. Before one game, Jim Smith urged me, 'If you get a throw-in, Kenny, for God's sake, whatever you do, don't give it to Dinha.'

Well I did get a throw-in and, as I looked around, I could see Dinha standing in the correct position begging for the ball – so I threw it at him thinking, 'Surely he can't be *that* bad?'

Dinha picked up the ball and skilfully dribbled away, straight into a striker on the opposing side, whereupon they scored a fabulous goal. I was screaming inside, 'Mirandinha, you bastard!'

But I was also mad at myself for not following Jim's clear instructions. We both needed a stiff brandy after that bloody game.

Another piece of off-pitch advice Jim gave me was never to mix whisky with red wine. He was forever repeating this little gem. Then he'd turn to me and ask, 'What you drinking, Kenny?'

'Gin and tonic please, Jim.'

I liked Jim – I liked him a lot. He was a funny bastard and there was never a dull moment when he was around.

I didn't care much for the training ground, though. Fuck me, it was windy! It didn't matter what the weather was like, as soon as you ran out onto the pitch the wind whipped up a gale. I became convinced there was someone standing in the shadows pumping a wind machine in our direction.

MY BEST EVER MATCH AT HIGHBURY

The sun rose and the day dawned bright and sunny. It was a perfect spring day – but it wasn't. It was a day I had been dreading ever since I packed my kit and walked away from my beloved Highbury. I was going back to play *against* the Arsenal. How could I do this?

My loyalties felt torn and divided. I was no longer a Gunner, I was a Magpie. But I knew that as soon as I stepped out on the Highbury turf I would feel a terrible wrench.

My mum was in bits and, for the first time in my entire career, she purposely stayed away from north London. 'If you think I'm coming to Highbury to hear those lovely fans boo you, Kenny, you're very mistaken. Not a chance.'

I tried to persuade her, but, typically of Mum, she was having none of it. She didn't watch it on the television, and didn't even listen to the radio. She was that afraid of the booing she felt certain was to come my way.

Wild horses, on the other hand, couldn't keep Elaine away. If ever she heard someone slagging me off in the crowd, she'd turn on them: 'I suppose you think you can do better do you – muppet.' Her fiery side knows no bounds. And this day was to be no different.

I can't tell you how fast and hard my heart was beating in the tunnel as I waited to emerge into the sunshine for my day of reckoning. With every step, I could feel my legs turning to jelly. My new teammates picked up on my apprehension and were brilliant. My ex-teammates took the piss. Bastards!

When I ran out onto the pitch my whole being was on fire. Every emotion possible was running through my veins – but fear was the uppermost. Within seconds these fears dissolved into thin air as I heard the Gooners chanting, 'King Kenny, King Kenny!' and clapping. I can't tell you the relief. And ask anyone who knows me and they'll tell you, 'This was Kenny Sansom's finest moment at Highbury.' The fact the fans still loved me meant the world to my family and me. Elaine was jumping for joy and my mum kicked herself for not having come to the match.

As for me, I played out of my skin in my old arena. You should have heard the gasp from both crowds of supporters when I shocked them all by blasting a shot against the post. I only bloody scored! But it was disallowed. 'Offside,' ruled the referee. 'Offside my backside!' I yelled back. But the referee wasn't listening. Do you realise that, had my goal stood, Arsenal wouldn't have won the League that season. So I guess it was a blessing in disguise.

The Gunners had not been playing at their best of late, and today they were really struggling against our defence (of course they were!). But, to be honest, we too were underachieving and battling against relegation. The pitch was in an awful state – the 'mudflats', as Perry Groves now referred to the Highbury ground, made the going hard. Today the ground is lush, but 25 years ago it was a mess with sand bumped all over the place.

Their young team looked exhausted and their play wasn't flowing as it might have done under better conditions. In the end,

Brian Marwood scored for Arsenal. It was a late winner. It was also scored while a weird kind of atmosphere was engulfing the ground. A whisper that a drama of catastrophic proportions was unfolding somewhere else started to circle the stands. For this day – *this day* when I feared I would be booed – a devastating incident, not so far away, was claiming the lives of many young football fans, and changing the lives of hundreds more.

For today was 15 April 1989 – the day of the Hillsborough tragedy. The day we all became aware that something fundamental would have to change in our national sport. It was also the day we all hurried home to hug our own children and pray for those who had lost their lives in a human crush.

All-seater stadiums were now a must. Like all the other football grounds from one end of the land to the other, Highbury had to alter the layout of their terraces. The structure of the North Bank was to change, and the Clock End, too, was to alter – but there would never be any changes to the spirit of Highbury.

(Until, of course, when the lovely place came down in 2005. But I guess the spirit remains in the new apartments that have been built on the site.)

After Hillsborough, the heart of football remained in tact right across the board. The losses were grieved. They are still being grieved – events like that never truly go away. Hillsborough touched everyone, but most of all the good people of Liverpool, where no one walks alone. I don't suppose there's a kid alive who didn't get an extra-special hug on the night of 15 April 1989. I know mine got very close moments with Daddy.

EVERTONIAN HUMOUR

> 'Get out the fucking way, Sansom. Go on, move your fat
> arse – I can't see the fucking pitch.'
>
> EVERTON FAN

Ah, don't you just love the people of Liverpool? Whether you're part of the Red Army or come from the other side of Goodison Park and wear blue, the gutter humour is loud and clear. When they have something to say, they just let you have it.

Newcastle were playing away at Everton and, as I stood on the line about to take a throw-in, I heard the great Liverpool accent loud and clear, as did everyone else: 'Get out the fucking way, Sansom. Go on, move your fat arse – I can't see the fucking pitch.'

Can you imagine? But my sense of humour was greater than my vanity and I howled with laughter. Mind you, had I not joined in I would have looked a proper idiot as half the bloody stadium heard the shout.

Leaving Newcastle was a difficult decision. They are a fantastic club. My old England teammate Kevin Keegan has recently returned to the fold. With other legends such as Dennis Wise and Alan Shearer by his side, let's hope it happens for them. What I do know for certain is this: that all those Geordie fans want is to watch their team play some magical football and, when Saturday comes, to enjoy an afternoon watching their heroes.

It's going to be a tough call to get Newcastle up to where they belong, in top-flight football. One thing is for sure: it won't be for the want of trying.

Newcastle were relegated, which was a blow, but I would definitely have stayed on had there not been a cocktail of reasons for going back to London – one being a great offer to go to Queens Park Rangers and be coached and managed by my old friend Don Howe and his No. 2, Bobby Gould, which was far too palatable to turn down. I was going back to my roots; I was going home.

It was just as well I didn't know where else I was going.

Downhill.

CHAPTER SEVENTEEN

ALL OVER
THE PLACE

'He's here, he's there, he's every-bloody-where...
Kenny Sansom!'

We were on the move again. Some of the high-profile wives of footballers today have a lot to say about moving here, there and everywhere, and about how cracks can appear in relationships because of the constant changes – but Elaine just got on with it. *I* was her husband, *this* was my job, and *we* were a family. End of story. That's not to say she wouldn't have liked to stay longer up in Newcastle, because she would have. She really loved everything about it there. But there were no moans or groans. The Sansoms were simply packing up and moving on again.

We firmly believed that the children were fine with this, as they didn't protest. They just went along with the changes as if it was normal to keep on changing schools. It wasn't until very much later that they voiced their opinions, and, when they did, it hurt. Had they tried to tell us and we didn't hear? Were we naïve in thinking all we needed to do as parents was to keep us all together? Did Elaine and I miss the obvious – that they needed to make firm and lasting friendships with their schoolmates? The answer is a very loud yes – but we were blinkered and missed the writing on the wall. Had we realised the fallout would impact on their ability to make firm friendships in their adulthood we would most definitely have thought twice about our multiple moves. But our priority was to keep a roof – any roof – over our heads.

I have learned so much recently – and I'll tell you about that later – but back then, in 1990, when Natalie, Katie, and Harry were of school age, we were still young and we did what we thought was best for us and our family. But, as I said, more about that later.

WEST LONDON

We had lived in south London, north London, and now were moving into west London. The only part of London we'd steered clear of was the East End – probably because my dad and his cronies were there.

This time we made our nest in Isleworth, which was near to Sky TV and a stone's throw from Loftus Road, Queens Park Rangers' ground, the home of my next club.

Trevor Francis, who was managing QPR, was really keen to sign me up. But there was the small issue of a medical first. The timing couldn't have been worse as I'd just returned from a three-week holiday in Cyprus, where I had discovered a beer called Keo Ken, which was of course, to me, delicious. Although I was tanned and fit on the outside, my insides must have been a right old mess.

After examining me, the medical officer shook his head and told me my blood pressure was way too high and he would have to report this to Trevor.

So there we were, three of us sitting in the Royal Lancaster Hotel with the very diplomatic Trevor opening up a bottle of red wine and smelling the cork to test the quality while listening to the medical reports. 'Don't worry about his blood pressure. Is he otherwise fit?'

'As a fiddle,' said the MO.

'Then I'm signing him.' Trevor offered me the money, I signed, and we drank the wine. High blood pressure or not, I was still a great asset to have at left-back.'

Like Crystal Palace, QPR were a great family club. I had a terrific time there and, to top it all, we had a blinding team. I'm going to stick my neck out and say that any of today's teams would have found us hard to beat. If we had been in the Premiership we would have held our own.

Don Howe (who, remember, followed me everywhere) was managing the side, with Bobby Gould, the old Coventry player who had a brief stint at Arsenal in the late sixties, as his number two.

Don and Bobby knew each other well, as Bobby had played under Don at West Bromwich Albion. They had both recently arrived at the club after managing the Wimbledon side that had shocked everyone (including themselves) by beating Liverpool in the 1988 FA Cup final at Wembley. Nobody had seen it coming. Liverpool, who had just won the League, had also won the FA Cup three times, and were therefore odds-on favourites. Laurie Sanchez got the crucial goal just before half time. After receiving a free kick from Dennis Wise he headed the ball into the net. Their goalie, Dave Beasant, was a hero for deflecting all the Red Army's shots on target and, to top it all, he saved a penalty. It had been Bobby's finest moment.

In goal at QPR we had the main man himself, David Seaman. Soon he would be off to join my old team at Highbury, but for now he was our man. Before any attacker made it through to the goalie, they had to face David Bardsley, Paul Parker and Alan McDonald. In midfield we had the brilliant Ray Wilkins, terrific Simon Parker, the former Liverpool man Nigel Spackman and the great character who is Peter Reid. Our attackers were phenomenal. There were also young stars such as Les Ferdinand and Andy Sinton.

These were crazy days off-pitch. Peter Reid was such a funny bloke and a great mate. We had lots in common and when we were drunk we convinced ourselves we were hilarious. Mobile phones were just becoming available and all those early purchasers thought they were right flash bastards. We'd look around in pubs and take the piss. One day, when we were in the London Apprentice in Isleworth, we noticed a group of yuppies with their mobiles the size of bricks. Steaming drunk, Peter, Nigel Spackman and I picked up a banana each from the bowl of fruit on the bar and started chatting into the bananas. Pathetic, I know, but, fuck me, we laughed till we cried.

Of course it was only a matter of a few months before we too had our mobile bricks attached to our ears. The days of not being tracked down by frustrated bosses or furious wives were now to become a thing of the past. Oh, well, all good things must come to an end, I suppose.

I was with Queens Park Rangers for a very happy 18 months, and even managed to score in the 1990 FA Cup run. So, all in all, it was a smashing era. But by the time I left I was looking down the tunnel towards the end of my career as a player – but there was still life in the old boy. I still loved playing too much to stop, even if I *was* carrying too much weight.

COVENTRY

Coventry was another family-oriented club, and the fact that my old friend Terry Butcher was managing them and Mick Mills, my old England teammate, was also in the team along with Cyrille Regis made the prospect of my becoming a Coventry player highly attractive.

I wasn't happy, though. I was feeling empty and any away matches or trips abroad without Elaine and the children were becoming even more difficult than usual.

If I hadn't wanted to go to Marbella with George Graham and the Arsenal boys, who were people I knew really well, I certainly didn't want to go to abroad with Coventry. But George had taught me a lesson and, if I was required to go, then that was what I'd do. So I went. I arrived home late at night in a vest and shorts.

The day had begun in bright sunshine with me happy to be where I was, but, as the day wore on and I pumped more and more booze down me, I became morose and homesick. I had a thousand pounds cash in my pocket, so I jumped in a cab and made off to the airport. There I asked for a ticket for the next plane to London, only to be told that the quickest way was via Switzerland. Still in my shorts and the vest, which had the word 'Daddy' across it, I boarded the plane and drank my way back to London, where I asked a cabbie to take me to Stratford. 'East London? he asked. 'No, Stratford-upon-Avon,' I slurred. 'That'll cost you, mate.' He turned round, saw who I was and just drove. By the time I reached home the grand had all but gone.

Once again I gave Elaine a fright by turning up late at night and off my face. She wasn't expecting anyone, and our security in that house was tight, so for someone to get as far as the front door was virtually impossible. That said, she welcomed me with open arms – but we both knew this was bizarre behaviour. Was I crumbling? Of course I wasn't. I was King Kenny of the Arsenal. Actually, no, I wasn't. Who was I?

In fact it wasn't long before I was back in London – playing for Brentford. It seemed I could never be away from my roots for too long.

I had to face the fact that I had become an ex-player. Now I had to keep telling myself, 'It's very important to keep smiling, Kenny.'

I had played my last game as a pro – I was now in free fall. I have no idea how I would have coped with this stark realisation without the cushion of the haze of alcohol. Never before had the numbing effect been so needed. I was a drunk and I was still gambling. Yet the enormity of my situation was still lost to me. My best friend was still a man called Denial, and I stupidly thought he'd never let me down.

Some days I drank whisky. This was a terrible thing to do, as Chivas Regal in particular made me behave like an absolute arse. Accusations such as 'You're just like your dad' were thrown at me and I can't tell you how upset I became. The last person I wanted to be likened to was my dad. As far as I was concerned he was a villain and I was a hardworking footballer who just so happened to like a drink – along with most around me. But I guess I now know that I was also plain stupid.

So, against my better judgement, I decided to go and play for Chertsey Town – an amateur club in the heart of Surrey. They were a nice bunch of lads who welcomed me with open arms. But I was in a bad place. My flash cars were gone, and we were hanging onto our fabulous family home by the skin of our teeth.

I was so broke that I didn't even own a car, so a mate gave me – yes, *gave* me – a discarded car of his own so I could drive up the A3 to Chertsey. I was grateful and embarrassed, but not necessarily in that order. I was beginning to know what it felt like to be a has-been, but it was too harsh a notion to acknowledge fully – so I had another drink.

CHERTSEY TOWN AND DOWNGRADING

I was driving a Proton – a Proton, for fuck's sake! I was a drunk who couldn't leave the gambling alone and I was fucked. Now, I rarely say 'fuck it' and I don't believe in swearing for the sake of it, but, fuck me, I had plenty to swear about during the nineties.

Do you know what? I was playing for Chertsey Town – an amateur side – supposedly for fun. It was fun most of the time but I was miserable inside. One of the players even had the cheek to point out to me that my boots were dirty. The fucking cheek of it!

So, as sharp as the sharpest tool in the box, I quipped, 'Yeah, it takes a lot of cleaning to get the Wembley turf off your boots, mate.'

This wasn't like me at all. Was I changing and becoming a nasty bastard who swore all the time? My mum would go mad if she heard me being so rude. But fuck it! I was fucked.

It wasn't the greatest experience, driving a Proton with alloy wheels and electric windows that didn't work. It was a bit like Don Howe's great truth about not realising what you've lost till it's ripped from you. Fuck, I missed my Mercedes. I'm not a snob – not in any way, shape or form. I am still as down to earth as I was when I got caught nicking marbles from a chandelier factory with my kid brother. But anyone out there who has gone from Buckingham Palace to Coronation Street overnight will understand the sheer misery of downgrading *everything*.

The luxury house was gone, and that had broken our hearts. The smart cars were gone. Elaine's designer clothes had to be worn more than once – very embarrassing if you're sitting at the top table at the Ritz, but not such a big deal if you're off to the bingo trying to win the mortgage money.

If this book has suddenly turned into a black comedy, that's because our life was now something we had to laugh about to stop ourselves from going mad. Something else stopped me from going mad – the booze. Or was it the booze that was responsible for my misery? Certainly not: the booze was my mate. Wasn't it?

All I know is that, when I think back to those dark days, I can honestly say I don't know if I could have survived this time sober. I looked to the drink to help me escape to a comfortably numb place.

You will read later in this book that the time eventually arrived when I had to address my alcoholism, but during the nineties, as I went through my late thirties and early forties, I hung onto my crutches for grim death.

I enjoyed the feeling of being drunk. I wallowed in my misery while wearing a painted smile all the time I was in public. In private I allowed my mask to fall away, which made life hard for Elaine. She worried about me, the kids, the money – everything.

Holding our world together must have been really tough on her and sometimes I have to wonder how she managed to stay the course. But the truth is – she loved me. She wasn't in love with the public face of Kenny Sansom. Instead, she was still in love with the young boy she'd met way back when we were kids in school. She'd always made allowances for me. Right at the start she had intuitively understood my fear. Remember, I was too scared to walk her down a dark alleyway. Now I was in a different dark place and I was still scared. I had no direction and was still desperately in need of someone to show me the way.

Things had always been easy when I was younger. People gravitated towards me, as did opportunities. I was born with a gift and had always been looked after. First my mum, then Elaine, then Malcolm Allison, then Terry Venables... The list goes on and on. Hotel rooms were booked for me, as were my flights – both domestic and worldwide. I had food put in front of me when I was a kid, and was allowed to eat with my fingers. As an adult I had received similar indulgence. I thought I was lucky. I thought I had it all. The downside was that I had become a pampered child who didn't have a clue how to take care of himself. I was what is now commonly known as a 'dependant'. Shame I was unaware of this little gem for so bloody long.

CHAPTER EIGHTEEN

GLENN ROEDER – A STRANGE DEFEATIST ATTITUDE

'No one is perfect – not even Thierry Henry. Some
say you can't teach a genius like him anything. But that's
nuts. I don't believe anybody is beyond learning something
new. I think there's room for improvement and Thierry
could score more with his head.'

I truly believe the above statement. There is always room for improvement. It's all about attitude. Lose the negativity and look at the positive. But, as I moved away from being a player and into coaching, it struck me there were too many people involved in football with negative attitudes.

When I watched Terry Venables sitting alongside Steve McClaren on the bench during the second half of our match against Croatia, I winced. It was agonising to watch England crash out of the Euro 2008 Championships; it was also excruciatingly painful to see what I perceived to be anger and frustration on my old boss's face and I wondered what was going on in his head. I'd had a similar experience of being number two to a man who nearly drove me insane with a dodgy attitude.

I had been privileged to be managed by the best in the business, and I'd learned by example. Now, as second in charge to Glenn Roeder, I was about to experience something different. I was to be less than impressed.

There are very few people I take a dislike to. I usually find something good in them to focus on, and have the philosophy of trusting someone till they ruin that trust. Usually, it works for me. Sometimes it doesn't.

I read an article recently where the journalist stated the obvious: 'Glenn Roeder's managerial career has been fraught with difficulties.' You can say that again, matey. The piece was written after he had been appointed manager of Delia Smith's Norwich City. The Canaries groaned – apparently none too pleased with his arrival. I don't blame them.

Glenn moved to Watford when he was in the twilight of his career as a player-manager and, having cut down on my drinking and focused on my fitness once again, I was asked if I would like to be second in charge – as a player-coach.

We *could* have had a lot of success together, and at first it looked as if we might be getting somewhere. The fans at Vicarage Road were welcoming and I think they were full of high hopes for their club, but it wasn't long before it all went pear-shaped.

I was determined I was going to be a bloody good coach – perhaps even manage a side in the future. Not a premiership side. Not straightaway anyway. But I knew I had coaching skills because I had all the qualities necessary to teach young kids the game.

I communicated well, especially with the youngsters, and even if I say so myself, I've got the patience of a saint.

I had been a skipper for England and Arsenal for more years than I could remember, so I was well equipped to lead and manage quality players. I had also marked the likes of Maradona in the World Cup, so I was not about to be intimidated by a single, solitary person.

GLENN ROEDER – A STRANGE DEFEATIST ATTITUDE

I'd played for England and I'd played for Chertsey Town. I communicated from grass roots to the heavenly hand of God. This was my chance to change my lifestyle and get stuck into passing on all the skills I'd been taught by the masters of the game.

I can't say I ever really warmed to Glenn, which was strange, because anyone who knows me will tell you I am dead easy to get along with.

I often wondered whether this was something personal between us or whether he was generally guarded with everyone. In my opinion he wasn't a great team player. Others making suggestions or choices seemed to tip him off balance. I had one hell of a lot to offer, but my suggestions were falling on deaf ears.

Before Glenn was handed the job at Watford he'd been player/manager at Gillingham. After one season with him in charge they were second from bottom of the League and only narrowly missed relegation by beating Halifax Town.

They were sitting on the bottom in the last match but one of the only season with him in charge, and no one was smiling.

He'd been a good player – but not outstanding. There was a certain class about his style of play. He had his own particular way of stepping over the ball and escaping from tricky situations, which became known as 'the Roeder Shuffle'. He captained Queens Park Rangers to the 1982 FA Cup final, but must have been gutted when he missed the replay due to suspension. But his disappointments didn't begin or end here.

As a Woodford (Essex) boy, he had tried but failed to earn an Arsenal scholarship. This must have been a crushing disappointment. But he didn't give up and went on to play professional football for Leyton Orient. After his stint at Queens Park Rangers he transferred to Newcastle where he stayed for 5 years, playing almost 200 matches for them.

During our first season at Watford we finished seventh in the League, which wasn't too sad, as when we joined it had looked as if relegation was on the cards. But the second season was a disaster.

Take for example his decision to buy Craig Ramage (otherwise known as the 'Showboater'), for what I personally believe was a ridiculous sum of money. That money should and could have been spent far more wisely. I might just as well have not opened my mouth because my comments, advice and suggestions fell on deaf ears.

The fans either loved or hated Ramage – there was no in-between. It was a case of all or nothing.

There was no doubting his flair; there was a certain amount of wizardry to his play, and on a good day his skills were reminiscent of Gazza. But, like Gazza, he could also have some godawful days.

I recommended time and time again we should sell Ramage, but it appeared that Glenn was reluctant, fearing that he'd get stick if Ramage went on to do well at another club. We never sold Ramage while I was there – neither did we buy anyone else who was useful. I had no say in it.

He could and should have used my knowledge. I know in my heart of hearts we would not have been relegated had he been generous enough to share the load around and enable us to work as a team.

On one occasion we went to Bramall Lane for an away game against Sheffield United. It was the first match of the new season.

We travelled up the on the team coach on the Friday and later had a few drinks in the bar with the boys. The chat was pleasant and the atmosphere generally relaxed. I was the first-team coach – that was what I had been employed to do. At the pre-match meal I felt a part of the team and everything was hunky-dory.

I knew we had the players to hurt the Sheffield United boys individually, but at half time we were 2–0 down and it was clear all was not well within the team.

During the first half Craig Ramage had given the ball away on several occasions. I suggested that during the second half Welsh footballer Lee Nolan, who was playing on the left wing, should be shifted to right wing to get us back in the game.

I was angry. If I'd had my way I'd have ripped the lazy bugger apart during the half-time break. But the minute I opened my mouth Glenn Roeder stepped in and interrupted me. 'I'm the manager, Ken. I'll have the first say.'

What was the purpose of my employment?

I learned to keep my mouth shut and subsequently lost enthusiasm. For the first time in my career I treated my job as something to get done – no more, no less. It was a tragedy for me and a tragedy for Watford – because they went down during our second season.

I'm certain had we worked together as a team we would have finished higher in the league table. No question about it. But instead I had no choice but to stand by and watch the poor players become demoralised and depressed. As for the fans – they were heartbroken. Where's Elton John when you need him? Singing, I suppose. Perhaps I should take up singing. I do a great Elvis impersonation.

SUPER KEV

One of the finest characters I met during my disastrous period at Watford was the talented Kevin Philips, who has rightly earned the nickname, 'Super Kev'.

Kevin began his career as a young right-back at Southampton and his abilities as a striker were quickly noted by Watford, who purchased him for a mere £10,000 from a semi-professional team called Baldock Town.

I got to know Kevin when we travelled back from a team trip to Portugal. We sat next to each other and it was a very sad time for him, because his dad had died while we were out there. He struck me as a sensitive young man, and I'm glad he went on to have a great career at Sunderland, where he became a hero when he scored thirty goals in the 1999–2000 season, earning him the European Golden Boot – the only Englishman ever to win the honour. Although he was small in stature, he had two great feet and was good in the air. He made 209 league appearances and scored 115 goals for Sunderland. He was forever getting hat-tricks and his goal average was more than one goal in every two matches. It was a shame he managed to earn only eight caps for England, but at least they were for the full team. Not bad.

When Roeder was sacked, so was I. I left Watford scratching my head in confusion, and moved swiftly on. I walked into a bar. Ouch! It hurt. It was an iron bar.

Life was certainly hurting for us Sansoms. My friends Booze and Denial weren't being so friendly. They were letting me down. Now I was really beginning to feel alone. I was scared that everyone was going to leave me. I kept on drinking until one day I drowned in the stuff. Now I needed some true friends, for those I'd thought were on my side were not: they were in fact the enemy.

ARSENAL FOOTBALL VILLAGE IN SPAIN

I was still very much involved with the Arsenal. I loved working at Highbury doing the Legends Tours of the stadium (now the Emirates Stadium in Asburton Grove, London) and I became part of the team interested in building the Arsenal Village down in Casares, about a half-hour drive south of Puerto Banús. On one of our trips out to Spain I met someone who would impact on my life.

There was a whole crowd of us and after a long day down at the Village we decided to go and have an equally long night in Banús. We visited Sinatra's Bar for a drink or ten, ate some great food in one of the many restaurants and then headed off for a popular nightclub called Marvellous.

Most of the others had gone ahead of me. I was doing my usual 'having a bit of alone time', strolling past the boats and among the hundreds of other people milling around, simply watching the world go by.

Eventually, I arrived at Marvellous and instead of joining the rest of my crowd, who were down at the far end of the bar, I ordered a drink and stood alone. It was then that I noticed a crowd of lads intimidating a group of young girls. They were getting more and more rowdy and I could see that the mother of the girls was looking more and more uneasy.

I walked over and told the lads to clear off, which to my amazement they did. I didn't know I could be so hard.

The mother thanked me and we chatted for a while before I went off in search of Elaine and everyone else who was having a great time dancing. It wasn't my scene – I'm more of a John Revolting that John Travolta. My feet were made to kick, not dance.

Before I left (which was not long afterwards), I sent a bottle of wine over to the mother and her daughters and left.

I thought no more of the incident until a few weeks later when I went into LBC Radio to do my Saturday-afternoon show and there was an email for me. It was from the woman whose daughters I'd saved (sort of) from the yobs and she was thanking me for my 'heroism', and for the wine. Did I want to meet up so she could buy me a drink?

Why the hell not? It was all innocent. I didn't chase other women and had never felt the inclination to cheat on Elaine and have an affair.

The woman's name was Denise; she was a couple of years older than I, and she was very attractive. We talked, had a drink, talked some more, had some food, and kept on talking. We got along like a house on fire – but it was no more than a friendship on my part.

The friendship grew and I realised how much I liked being with her. It was all very easy, but I never thought it would grow into something more. I was wrong. We got closer and closer and by the time my drinking hit crisis point I was wondering whether I would be happier with this genuinely calm and caring woman. Life at home with Elaine was full of friction and recriminations. The gulf between us was growing wider.

I knew my job at LBC was coming to an end. Richard Parks had bought the station and was making major changes to the structure. Shows and jobs were being axed and I too was in for the chop. It felt as if my life was coming to an end. Depressed, confused and crying all the time, I drank more and more. I also turned to Denise more and more.

On the Saturday when I was scheduled to record my very last show I knew I was too sick to do the job. I called Elaine and told her how I was feeling. She was furious and told me we needed the money and I *must* do it. She had a point – but I was broken. I called Denise and she rushed to London, where she mopped me up and gave me the confidence to go and do the show.

Things were changing. I was changing. But I was going nowhere. I was a married man and it never entered my head I would ever leave my family. So we soldiered on. I had very little contact with Denise over the following months. Yet to say she wasn't on my mind would be a lie. We had forged a strong bond.

I had to sort my life out, though – and if I didn't sort my health out I would be a goner and no good to anyone at all.

CHAPTER NINETEEN

TONY ADAMS – A SPORTING CHANCE

A few years ago I played golf in Tony Adams's charity golf day for the Sporting Chance Clinic. On charity days you often end up playing with people you've never met before and on this particular day when I turned up I was introduced to three guys and one of them was called Kevin Carlier. I thought he was a stranger, but he said to me, 'I know you, I come from Orpington. I've actually been to your house before.'

'Really – are you sure?' I studied his face, but didn't recognise him at all. We had a chat and laugh. I probably did a few impressions to impress him as we strolled around the greens and by the time we reached the nineteenth hole we were getting on like a house on fire. We ended up coming third and winning Hugo Boss jumpers.

I recall that I sank three pints of John Smith's as we mused over life in general. Kevin could sense I had a problem (he wouldn't need to be a rocket scientist) and invited me to go for lunch with him a few weeks later. I noticed he was dropping subtle hints about my excessive drinking but he never judged or criticised. He never actually said, 'You should stop this drinking, Kenny.' Instead, from time to time, he'd ask Elaine, 'How are you? How's Kenny doing?'

They would put their heads together and two and two would make five. It was an impossible situation. The saying 'You can lead a horse to water but you can't make it drink' had never felt truer as far as they were concerned.

All Kevin could say to Elaine was, 'When he reaches crisis point, which he will – that's if he doesn't keel over first – call me and I'll get in touch with Sporting Chance.'

My old mate Georgie Best, whom I used to love chatting to in Tramp, had passed away at the age of 60. George and I would be pissed as parrots, but we still managed to have long conversations that seemed to make sense – I think. At this point in my life I was hurtling towards the same tragic premature death as Bestie. A terrifying thought, as I was still in my forties.

One morning, not long after I'd made friends with Kevin Carlier at Tony's golf day, I was at my tennis club when my friend Andrea, who was a qualified GP, came over to me wearing a solemn expression. I knew she and Elaine had been conspiring to get me into treatment and I had actually given in to pressure and had some blood tests done to see how my organs were shaping up. She had bad news that meant I wouldn't be playing tennis that day – but that was the least of my worries. My tests were back and physically my insides were beginning to resemble poor old George Best's – a lot.

'What do you want to do with the rest of your life, Kenny?' asked Andrea, and just as I opened my mouth to answer she added, 'Don't bother answering, because you won't be alive to do anything if you don't give up the drink now.'

I wasn't far off dying. I now recognised the pain in my side for what it was: my liver groaning, my body giving up the ghost.

Suddenly, I knew this was it. My shocking moment of reckoning had arrived. 'I can't do this any more,' I sobbed to Elaine as I sank my head into my hands in despair. Then I took a closer look at my hands. They were mottled because of my poor circulation.

Elaine reached for the phone and called my sister Maureen. Then she phoned Kevin. The moment had arrived. 'It's time,' I conceded.

Kevin Carlier called Peter Kay, the director of Sporting Chance. When Kevin called Elaine back he said, 'Promise me you'll call Peter Kay at Sporting Chance in the morning. I've left a message on his answering machine saying you would be calling.' The message said, 'I'm calling on behalf of Kenny Sansom. I think he's ready.'

TONY ADAMS – LOST BOY TO WISE MAN

'If it wasn't for Tony Adams my brother would
have died a premature death.'

MAUREEN SANSOM

Tony Adams is a sporting legend and a hero who has been honoured by the Queen with an MBE. Any fan of Arsenal and England doesn't need reminding of his terrific footballing ability and brilliant leadership skills.

Tony finally retired from playing football in 2002, while still flying high. Not for him the trawling of the echelons of the lower leagues. His testimonial against Celtic at Highbury was truly a celebration of a terrific career that saw him play more than six hundred games for his club – the only club he'd ever played for. Tony Adams was quite simply born to be a Gunner.

But for those of you who are not diehard Arsenal fans and are not aware of his struggles with alcohol, I am going to tell you about Tony Adams the friend. Today, Tony is a wise man. But before this wisdom grew he was a lost boy.

Just like me and many other famous sporting people, Tony began his career before he had lived through those tricky teenage years where you learn to grow into a man. Teens are years of opportunity – when you can make lots of mistakes and (hopefully) learn form them. Professional footballers are pampered, taken care of by managers, trainers and other sporting bodies such as the FA (sometimes) and PFA (always).

We are told what to do, where to go and when. Officials hand us plane tickets, take care of our passports (they are shown collectively at the airport), and in many instances (especially today) they tell us what and what not to eat.

If we are playing well any indiscretions of behaviour are overlooked, which means we don't learn from early lessons. I am not telling you anything that hasn't already been well documented by Tony. Yes, the press pounced on his drink-driving conviction, and, yes, there was the usual tut-tutting. But the honesty and humility he showed matched his warlord attitude on the pitch. He put his hands up and asked quietly for help. Not for him were the huge tabloid stories of rehab. Instead, he just slipped away and grew up.

Having seen what therapy had done for him, and not being totally in agreement with some of the larger rehabilitation centres, he decided to set up his own charity and to keep it small and personal. He knew whom he wanted in his team but it took some time to find the right premises at the right price.

Unbeknown to me, Tony had been harbouring the wish for me to go into treatment, and when I finally decided it was time he welcomed me with open arms. Once upon a time I had handed him the precious Arsenal captaincy; now he was handing me back something even more precious – a chance to get my life back.

Elaine used to go on and on about my getting help. I used to think she was nagging. I had become one big problem, which was causing everyone who loved me untold misery.

A conversation that had erupted into shouting the week before replayed in my brain. I had been sitting at the dining room table when the bickering had turned into nastiness.

'It's all about you, Kenny – as usual.' Elaine was really going for it.

Shocked, I turned to my daughters, desperately seeking some approval.

It wasn't forthcoming. The normally calm Natalie was angry too. 'You just left Mummy not knowing where you were. You just disappeared and we were scared. So after four days we came searching for you – me and Katie. You don't remember, do you, Dad?'

I thought I detected a grain of her normal empathic nature, but couldn't be sure. What I was certain about, though, was her evident disappointment in her daddy. No longer hiding her anger behind her love for me, she was threatening to explode.

'We searched all the local hotels until we found you. The lady on the reception gave us the key to your room, and when we turned the lock we were so scared about what we'd find. When we saw you fast asleep, naked on the bed, with empty bottles strewn around the floor, we were actually relieved. *We were relieved, Dad.*'

Katie wasn't so kind. I could almost smell her disgust. I had hurt her mum; I had hurt her, too.

'The woman on the reception gave us the key to your room. When me and Natalie opened the door and saw the window wide open, we thought you'd jumped.'

Unable to recall the episode they were talking about, I had to take their word for it. I had been a naked rambling drunk who had apparently thought it was funny.

But now I was quite rightly being slapped in the face with hard facts. I was a disgrace. Big Shot Kenny Sansom, who still got asked for autographs, who was still perceived to be an Arsenal legend and a stalwart for our national football team, now stood emotionally naked in front of his family trying to absorb the enormity of what was being said.

I cried. I cried hard. But my family were used to this morose side of my character and were unmoved. Funny Kenny, the joker, the impersonator, was no longer a laugh.

My attentions had then turned to my son Harry, and all I could see was misery. He had nothing to say that wasn't being said in his sad eyes. I had let him down. I had let them all down – but most of all I'd let *me* down, and if I didn't sort myself out how could I even attempt to heal the terrible rift?

It was time to claw back some pride. It was time to listen – to stop joking around and be serious. But how could I do that? I was approaching my fifties and a grandfather of five little ones, but I was a boy at heart. 'Normal' to me was being looked after. It was all I knew.

But I wasn't an alcoholic – of that I was certain. Alcoholics were ill. I wasn't ill. Those who had dared to challenge my denial had hit a brick wall time and time again. But now I could physically feel the bricks crumbling.

PETER KAY

Peter Kay had agreed to meet me to discuss 'where we go from here'. Peter is Tony Adams's right-hand man and chief executive of Sporting Chance. He's not the funny Peter Kay who sings 'Show me the way to Amarillo', but the serious guy who, a long time ago, almost died from alcohol and drug abuse. So he wasn't about to dance down the road with me for a drink in his club in *Phoenix Nights*, with sweet Marie waiting for us.

Oh, no, there were no sha-la-las the morning we met – tentatively on my part, determinedly on his part – to talk about my getting some treatment for my little problem, or, as Peter preferred to put it, to 'talk about your crisis point'. This head-to-head was going to be as serious as it gets.

As he sat opposite me in the café in the Carlton Hotel in London I noticed he was looking fresh-faced and concerned. His blond hair flopped over one eye and, as he brushed it back haphazardly, he asked, 'So, Kenny, how can I help you?'

I was thrown. I didn't really think he *could* help me. Although I had picked up the phone intending to call Tony Adams myself, I had put it down again and it had been Kevin who had taken action and called this meeting.

Now, as I sat uncomfortably shifting in my seat, I felt as if there was some kind of conspiracy going on. In that moment I decided Maureen and Elaine had ganged up on me and set the whole thing up. I wanted a glass of wine to blur the edges.

The whole scenario was surreal. The atmosphere in this high-class establishment was suddenly suffocating me. The piano player tinkling away in the corner was in a world of his own – oblivious of the seriousness of this setup. What a wonderful world he must live in, I presumed silently. Presumptions and assumptions, I was later to learn, were stupid notions. I ordered a coffee – I'd have the wine later when Peter had gone back to the clinic.

'How would you feel about coming back to the clinic with me right now and checking in for some treatment?' Peter wasn't at all authoritative, neither was he condescending – quite the opposite. He was gently asking the impossible, though. I was going nowhere but to the nearest pub once we said goodbye.

Elaine and Maureen, who had been drinking cappuccino across the other side of the room and also listening to the tinkling of the piano player, rejoined us, and Elaine's inquisitive gaze darted back and forth between Peter and me. How could I refuse to give this thing called rehab a shot?

I left agreeing to check in to Sporting Chance (which is set in the lush grounds of Champneys health clinic) the following Monday morning. I felt as though I had 4 days of freedom left. What I didn't realise was that, in reality, I had 4 days left in hell.

Peter went and reported back to Tony. 'Kenny's coming in next week.' They were both hopeful. They were both sceptical. They both knew the game well.

THE FINAL COUNTDOWN

On the way back home from the Carlton, after Elaine and I had said goodbye to Maureen, I went off to the betting shop while Elaine shopped in Tesco. I'd asked her to buy some wine for later, and knew she would because she always did as I asked. She figured if she didn't buy it now she'd only have to go back out later when I was desperate.

I went to the bookie's and put on a bet. I was back in my comfort zone – the familiar sounds and smells washing away my earlier fear of the unknown. All thoughts of incarceration in a sterile ward had been banished to the recesses of my unconsciousness, where they belonged. That was where I liked them, tucked away where they couldn't get to me, leaving me safe with my delusions.

That night I had a drink, but not much more than a glass or two of wine. Elaine was holding the pills Andrea had prescribed to help me come off the alcohol safely. Apparently, if I took them, I wouldn't get withdrawal symptoms. 'You won't shake and sweat and vomit so much,' the doctor told me. *Oh, that's all right, then.*

I took the pills, and I drank the wine.

The next day, I took the pills, drank lots of water, and just a little wine.

By the Monday morning my system was alcohol-free. Which is just as well as they wouldn't have admitted me had there been any trace of drink inside me.

I was diving head first into the unknown. The worst of it was, I *still* didn't believe I was an alcoholic.

CHAPTER TWENTY

REHAB, AND 'WHO THE HELL IS KENNY SANSOM?'

Elaine and I stopped in a small enclave on the edge of the golf course on the borders of Hampshire and Sussex where the grounds of Champneys health clinic begin. I'd asked Elaine to pull over for a moment so I could gather my thoughts.

Across the grass, about 300 yards away, stood the big imposing mansion that I assumed must have been the home of the lord of the manor many years before. It was a beautiful building and I suppose anyone driving down this lane for a weekend break to get pampered would be filled with excitement – but not me.

To keep my fear under control and my anxiety in check I had a good talk to myself with my old internal friend, the one who always colluded with the part of me who wanted the easy way out.

I don't have to stay here the full 28 days. I could just give it a go and if it gets too much I can call Elaine and she'll come and get me. I'm not an alcoholic. I just like a drink. There's nothing wrong with downing a drop of wine every day. I'll give my liver and kidneys and rest and then go home.

'Have you got my mobile, Elaine?'

Elaine was horrified. 'You're not allowed mobile phones, Kenny. It's part of the treatment.'

'Come on, Elaine. I've got to say goodnight and good morning to you. The rest of the time I'll keep it hidden. It'll be all right.'

Elaine gave me the phone and as I pocketed the forbidden item my eyes were drawn to ghostly figures dressed in white robes. They seemed to be gliding around the grounds like troubled spirits searching for heaven. It was really spooky.

Was *I* searching for heaven? I didn't know. I didn't know anything. But I thought I knew everything, and that was the trouble.

CHECKING IN

'Hello, Kenny, I'm James.' The man, who must have been somewhere in his fifties, held out his hand and warmly welcomed me to what was to be 'home' for a short time – just a couple of days or so until everyone realised there was nothing wrong with me.

I slipped my hand into his firm grip and was shaken by the confidence of my new therapist.

'I'll be meeting up with you for one-to-one sessions,' he told me.

I envisaged that he and I would be shut away in a room talking about 'my problem' for days on end and groaned at the prospect. But, much as I didn't want to admit it, I did find him easy company. This man, I told myself, will be sharp enough to realise I'm not an alcoholic.

'This is Chris,' he said, introducing me to a smart young man. 'He'll show you to your room.' There was another man called Julian, who also was part of the team.

Elaine opened her mouth to ask if my request for a single private room had been successful. We had been told I might have to share, as it was on a first-come-first-served basis, but I was in luck: there was a single room free.

'We have a single room available,' smiled Chris. 'Come on – let me show you around.'

I guessed Chris to be in his twenties. He was a trendy young thing and didn't look as if he'd had a problem in his life. It was weird being shown around by a twenty-something who appeared to be full of confidence. He was also a picture of fitness and health – how could I have possibly guessed that he, like everyone on the team at Sporting Chance, had a history of chaos and mess? That everyone here spoke my language and I had nothing to fear?

We left the small cottage where James and Chris shared an office and trudged across a cobblestone area towards a slightly bigger house. Chris, still leading the way, held the door open and I entered a kitchen/diner area. 'This is where you can make yourself a cup of tea or coffee, or just chill out.'

Next, I followed him into a cosy front room with sofas and a television. Through the windows I could see for miles and miles. The sky was dark, but the fields lush and fresh. These were views of England at its best.

'Over here in this space is where we have group therapy,' said Chris. 'There are only four of you here at any one time – five at a push. It was Tony Adams's wish to keep the clinic small and intimate, making it a unique treatment centre. In many ways our priorities are quite different from other rehab centres. But you'll find this out for yourself as time goes on – when you've settled in.'

'I might only be staying a few days' was my response. I hoped I sounded more confident than I felt.

'OK,' said the wise young man.

Up the stairs we went and when he opened the door to a small, neat and spotlessly clean single room I was pleasantly surprised. It was nothing like a hospital here. There wasn't enough room to swing a cat, mind you, but, then again, I didn't anticipate swinging a cat anyway. I love cats.

The view from my bedroom window was even more stunning

than it had been at ground level, but the storm clouds were gathering and I shuddered at the thought that this might be an omen. I didn't have to stay long, though, I reminded myself. Just long enough for them to realise I wasn't an alcoholic.

On the way back to reception, Elaine and I passed two of my fellow sportsmen who were allegedly struggling with their own addictions. I instantly felt I would get along with them. It might sound weird, but it didn't take long for us to bond (that's what you do in rehab) and become supportive of each other. I don't intend to talk about my new friends. Confidentiality is of the utmost importance in therapy, and trust, I came to learn, is a must.

Elaine and I said our goodbyes, and, I'm telling you, that was tough. She knew she had to leave me there, but inside she was screaming to stay with me.

Nothing could have persuaded her to take me back home with her, though. I knew she wanted to stay there with me just as much as I wanted her to stay. I wanted to be spoon-fed through the journey into the unknown and out the other side.

I knew she would be crying as she drove away. But I also knew she would be full of relief and praying this would be the start of our new life – in sobriety.

FIRST NIGHT, AND A NEW DAY

I slept fitfully that night. It was most peculiar going to bed sober and alone. Being drunk in my woman's arms had always felt right. I knew I'd been having horrendous nightmares, but couldn't remember any of the content – just the panicky feeling of a man about to bunge-jump.

I went down to breakfast and there I met a man who introduced himself to me (we'll call him 'Dave', though it's not his real name). Dave handed me this big thick book called *Alcoholics Anonymous*. It is known in the world of alcoholism as 'The Big Book'.

'The stories in this book will help you to see you're not alone.

They've been written by recovering alcoholics and point out the devastation of alcoholism. It's like... you must take one day at a time and the longer you stay off the drink the more likely it is that you'll achieve sobriety.'

I thought about doing a Norman Wisdom impersonation to lighten the subject, but he was on such a mission he probably wouldn't have even noticed. Perhaps I should sing a little Elvis – something like 'Heartbreak Hotel'.

'And don't go in a pub. Just walk on by, like Dionne Warwick, and don't look back. It would be like going into a barber's shop not needing a haircut. The longer you're in the barber's the more likely you are to have a haircut.'

I thanked Dave for his advice and told him I thought he'd just made a great analogy. No longer hungry, I decided to take myself off for a walk.

'We'll be meeting for a reading from *The Promise* at eight o'clock. It's a daily meditation book,' said James as I disappeared through the door. 'We do this every morning,' he called after me.

I wasn't exactly thrilled about the prospects of my first day in the rehab clinic. I was resistant and reluctant. But I *was* open to giving it a go.

If therapy had worked for so many other people, including the great bunch of professionals I was now among, I at least owed it to those who loved me to get well.

Elaine's words were reverberating around my head as I took my seat in the 8 a.m. meeting. I was going to take this very seriously and go home a changed person. I looked out of the window again and it was still stormy. Then as I was gazing at the sky I heard a man's voice saying the following words: 'It's only when there is nothing but praise that life loses its charm. And I begin to wonder, what should I do about it?'

The group members had my full attention now. The 'promise' of the day had jolted in my brain. Someone was saying, 'You see, balance in all things offers the greatest satisfaction. Most people don't realise the full value of variety in our lives. We need to experience the struggle of uncertainty. We must get something out of the pain.'

This was a revelation. I hadn't thought about life this deeply before. Then someone else read another pearl of wisdom: 'Today will be a mixture of joy, boredom, perhaps both pain and sorrow – each element will give me reason for growth.'

'We're all in the same boat,' said the therapist. 'There's no one to judge or criticise in this room. Kenny, how are you feeling?'

I nodded. 'Fine,' I said.

'Do you know what "fine" stands for?'

I shrugged and he went on. 'It stands for Fucked up, Insecure, Neurotic and Emotional.'

So, next time someone asks how you are feeling, you need to think about it for a moment before telling them honestly how you feel. 'Fine' is superficial, whereas 'actually I feel like shite' or, alternatively, 'full of energy' will help you connect with the person asking.

I didn't tell any jokes in that meeting, and neither did I cry. Afterwards, I took myself off to the gym and enjoyed a light workout, and then it was time for my one-to-one minus my football boots. This was going to be a whole lot harder than my physical one-to-ones with Terry Venables at the Crystal Palace training ground.

'I was wondering,' said James during our very first one-to-one (therapists wonder a lot), 'how you were feeling about being here.'

I looked across from my armchair to his and started talking about the wonderful food Champneys served up. 'I love the food here. The fish is out of this world. I never realised I liked salmon so much. And my bed – it's so comfortable. I like the lads as well – nice bunch.'

Then I started to go on about the professional footballer who was staying in the next room to me – the guy I'd noticed in group therapy who had been very upfront about his... gulp... alcoholism.

James let me carp on for a while before he leaned forward and quietly said, 'But I was wondering how *you* were feeling, Kenny.'

I was taken aback. Hmm. How was I *feeling*? He'd got me there. So I tried again. 'Well, I'm feeling good. I haven't got a hangover and those pills Andrea gave me have really helped with my withdrawal symptoms. A few weeks ago I had sharp pains in my side and I felt really sick – you know, nauseous. But now I'm fine— Oops, I mean, good, that is, er, healthier.'

I looked out of the window of the small counselling room we were in, and I wondered. How do I feel? As the low summer clouds rolled by I thought about those lonely afternoons in the pub playing the fruit machine with one hand and nursing a pint glass of wine in the other and I felt a deep sense of sadness. The stillness in the room disturbed me – it was claustrophobic and troubling. I wanted to fill the gaping hole with chatter – with jokes and impersonations – but James had sussed me.

Still, what mattered most was that I wasn't an alcoholic.

'It's good I haven't had a drink for a while.' I was groping in the dark now. 'I'm sure that once I've given my liver a chance to regenerate I'll be right as ninepence. I'll be able to drink in moderation, just on special occasions, or if me and Elaine are out for dinner.'

James wasn't impressed, and it showed. 'Kenny, do you think it's the first glass of wine that is the problem, or, say, the seventh?'

'It's obvious,' I laughed. 'It's the seventh.'

'Wrong.'

This was daft – everyone knew that the more you drank the worst it was. Wasn't that why I was here – because I drank too much? Because they *thought* I was a bloody alcoholic? I was feeling a bit irritated now, but I didn't want it to show, so I smiled.

'Let me explain something.' James sat back comfortably as if he was going to tell me a story – like in the kids' TV programme *Jackanory*. But James had something to say.

'When you take your first drink you are surrendering your power to alcoholism.' The statement annoyed me. Grrr! I'm not an *alcoholic*.

'It is in this moment that you lose control – when your willpower is compromised and the demon voice inside tells you it's OK to have another and another. Your enemy is not the seventh drink: it's the *first*. Because *that first drink* is the little bugger that steals your power.'

Now it was my turn to sit back in my chair. Again we fell into silence, only this time I used the quiet moment really to think about what James had just said.

If the wine stole my power, then I was a slave to the drink. I wasn't in charge. I was out of control. My life, therefore, wasn't my own. Was that why I felt as if I was in hell so much of the time?

It was just as if a light had pinged on in my brain. I was on my way.

INSANITY

Being in male company was what I knew and suddenly it was as if I was away with the lads awaiting a game against West Germany. The other 'inmates' (as we referred to ourselves) and I got on well together. I especially liked chatting to the other professional footballer. As you can imagine – we had loads to talk about. It was also good to be able to talk to people who had problems similar to mine. Of course, we were all different, but we also had lots in common – like drinking. I felt as if we should be playing cards, but I guessed that would be considered another addiction – which, of course, it is.

In group therapy we had to sit in a room together and share thoughts and feelings. At the beginning of each group session we had to say our names and how we felt that day. All this 'how you feel' talk was beginning to register. The more sober I became the more I was *able* to 'feel'.

Has anyone out there seen that movie *28 Days* with Sandra

Bullock? Well, let me tell you, suddenly I was a character in that movie. It scared me, but I also felt strangely relieved. Sandra Bullock was the joker who was the life and soul of the party until she got a life. I was astounded as I watched the movie and observed her interaction with the horse. It reminded me so much of my very first moment of loving Elaine – of her horse refusing to budge and of my being able to help her with that small problem.

Now, almost 35 years on, our problems had grown – could this mountain be climbed? Only I could know the answer to that. The good old Kenny Sansom who loved Del Boy and Rodney, and enjoyed nothing more than to stand at the front of the plane entertaining the troops as we flew home from playing against the rest of the world, was now sitting firmly on his arse in trouble.

'It must be time for a joke,' I said, trying to break through the stifling silence. 'What was the one Terry Venables liked the most? I'll tell you that one.' I couldn't remember. So in my best Del Boy voice I uttered the most ridiculous words – 'Bonnet de douche, Rodney. Bonnet de douche – and a bottle of Châteauneuf-du-Pape.' In real life this means, 'Shower hat, shower hat – and a bottle of the best red wine!'

Everyone looked at me as if I'd just grown two heads. Then this other bloke floored me by announcing, 'I'm Steve [another made-up name] and I'm an alcoholic.'

Shit! I was in the room full of real-life alcoholics.

If I had ever attended an AA meeting I'd have known that this was the bog-standard opening to an evening of sharing life experiences – but, having given this foundation a wide berth, I was in the dark.

Then this other guy added, 'And I'm an alcoholic.'

Whoa! What was going on here?

Everyone was looking at me again. You would have thought I'd have felt awkward, but I didn't. I announced once again that I was called Kenny. No one appeared to mind that I wasn't an alcoholic.

It would be fair to say that for the first time in my life my jokes weren't well received. Perhaps *I* was the joke. I would have to think long and hard about that crazy notion. I liked being the life and soul of the party – but then so had Sandra Bullock in *28 Days*, and she soon learned that being the life and soul of the party came at a high price and she didn't need to be so funny once she'd got herself a 'real' life.

Was I about to turn a corner?

HI, I'M KENNY, AND I'M AN ALCOHOLIC

The 28 days at Champneys went surprisingly quickly. There were as many white robes gliding around the gleaming corridors of the health centre as there had been in the grounds the day I arrived.

Using the gym in the health centre and eating the delicious healthy food was making me feel good. I had even used a knife and fork and not even thought about using my fingers. Mum would have been very proud. My mum had always been proud. The thought brought a lump to my throat. Was I *moving on*, as they say in the therapy world? *Was I on a journey... growing... healing?*

Now *there was* a trail of thoughts to make me choke on my mineral water – which, by the way, was beginning to taste good. I was also having fun.

We all jumped onto Lilos in the pool and kicked the ball around the field. It was like being back with my Brandon team on a Sunday afternoon. All that was missing were the back-and-white-striped shirts and a slice of orange. It was as if time had melted away, and I was thoroughly enjoying the company as well as the *feeling*.

There was one time when we were all sitting around the pool reading our copies of 'The Big Book', when I thought back to the discussion we'd had earlier in group therapy on the subject of insanity. I think I had been there about 10 days when James asked us what we thought about the concept of 'being insane'.

We had been studying Step 2 of the AA twelve-step programme.

James wanted to know what we thought the definition of insanity was, and to give an example.

I said, 'It's someone who wears a white jacket and has lost the plot.'

The therapist looked at me thoughtfully. 'So you don't consider drinking seven bottles of wine a day an insane thing to do?'

I reluctantly conceded he had a point there, and it was a bit of an uncomfortable moment. It had become more and more uncomfortable as the session progressed and James read out parts of the Step 2 information. It was all about a power greater than us being able to restore us to sanity. It was about having knowledge of a problem, not necessarily resolving it; that there has to be some action – some willingness – on your part to *be* different as well as to *think* differently. We had to admit we were powerless over our addictions and this in turn made us feel wretched (hell came to mind) and helpless. I *was* helpless, and I *couldn't* help myself. To conquer Step 2 I needed to be open-minded to a solution that had never occurred to me before. The bottom line was that I needed to admit I was powerless to my addictions. I suppose this all linked with my gut feeling that Drink and Denial were not my friends, but instead enemies that were forces working against me.

Now, as I sat in the sunshine by the pool, I began to think about 'being insane' again. Was I insane? My gaze settled on the beautiful women sunbathing and reading their 'Big Book', while sipping water instead of wine. It just didn't seem right. I'd never experienced anything like this before. To my right were my three newfound friends and they too were engrossed in their educational reading. I couldn't concentrate on the words in front of me, which wasn't surprising, as I don't think I'd ever read a book from cover to cover before. There had never been the time. There had never been the inclination.

The silence was strange. The whole scenario seemed abnormal to me. Was it because it was all so different that I was feeling uncomfortable? Was part of being insane about being different? I had to say something.

'I'll tell you what's insane, shall I? I think I've sussed it.'

I had the attention of all around me. 'This is insane. All of us sitting here surrounded by beautiful women in bikinis, and instead of all having fun on this 80-degree sunny day, we are studying the twelve steps and downing mineral water.'

One of my 'inmates' sat bolt upright and looked around him as if seeing the scenario for the first time. 'D'you know what, Kenny? You're right, mate. I knew something didn't feel right. I keep expecting Hugh Heffner to pop in any minute.'

In that moment I sat back and relaxed on my sun lounger and convinced myself I'd worked out the meaning of insanity – but it was early days and I was still mucking about.

It had been several weeks now since I'd had a drink, and the weight was dropping off me. When I looked in the mirror I saw something of the old me returning. The bloated, sweaty face I'd been wearing of late had all but gone.

People had been going on about how much weight I had put on since retiring from top-flight football and, although I'd made light of it, I had secretly loathed the teasing. So, I'd gained a few pounds. Wasn't that what happened during midlife?

I began to challenge my lifelong beliefs. Something was changing about the way I was thinking. Joining the dogmatic voice that had always urged me on, there was a new one quietly mumbling away in an attempt to join the conversation.

I took a seat by the window next to the large indoor swimming pool, where I had just worn myself out doing more lengths than I'd done in years. Everything outside was so green, and the blue of the sky seemed brighter. It was time to think some more.

I can't say all this was easy, but it certainly wasn't as difficult as I'd imagined. Had my fear of confronting my addictions actually been harder than simply *doing* it? If so, I may just be onto a winner.

I don't know how long I sat there in that space by the window, but by the time I took myself off to the next group therapy session a few clouds had appeared in the sky – it reminded me of the opening scene of *The Simpsons*. I was feeling lighter than I'd felt for many years, probably because *I was* lighter – in more ways than one.

I was early for group therapy, which was good news – being late for therapy is not a good idea. Stealing another man's time is frowned upon – and quite rightly so.

The others tripped in one by one, all nodding friendly hellos. There wasn't much time left as we were on Day 25, and I wondered if, like me, the others were feeling a bit edgy about going back to the outside world. I wanted to go home more than anything but, if I'm honest, I was also nervous. This was a whole new ball game. Then I opened my mouth and said, 'Hi, I'm Kenny, and I'm an alcoholic.'

I felt proud.

CHAPTER TWENTY-ONE
GOING HOME

Elaine arrived to collect me. As we drove back out of that winding road my eyes once again fell on the white ghostly figures roaming the grounds and I did not feel afraid. These were new spirits – the others had moved on.

Now I had a new challenge – the biggest of my life. Could I pull it off? Could I be as strong as Tony Adams and so many others who had uttered those empowering words, 'I'm an alcoholic', before me?

Once, not too long ago, Peter Kay had told me to look at my predicament as 'a problem of dependency' rather than alcoholism, and that was clever of him, as back then that was as much as I could digest. Now it was game on. I was going to leave the stench of death back in the prison where I once resided. A self-imposed prison where I was locked away from everyone I loved as well as everything I feared.

'You need a lifeboat,' Peter had told me while the piano man played in the background of the Carlton. Well the team at Sporting Chance had held the lifeboat out for me while I tentatively climbed in. And now I had to get out. The time was right.

But I was stepping into the unknown. I was going back into a familiar environment a changed man. In future, whenever I walked past a pub, I would remember the old times, and then I'd walk on by.

Elaine seemed strong but apprehensive, and I understood why – but I really wasn't ready for the honesty I was about to get from Natalie, Katie and Harry. Apparently, it was a tough call being the child of a famous footballer who gambled and drank.

THREE INNOCENT KIDS

it would appear that Natalie, Katie and Harry have had a
tough time being the offspring of a busy England and
Arsenal legend.

From the very beginning of our relationship, Elaine and I knew we wanted children. There was never any doubt, as this was the way of our parents before us and theirs before them. You married and you had kids.

Elaine and I were living in leafy Epsom when our first child, Natalie, was born. I was living the dream playing football and Elaine was the housewife with the added perks of a great social life. Having two more children, another daughter and a son, was a natural progression.

I don't care what anyone says, life is not quite the same when you are famous. Too many outside influences get in the way.

Having choices in life is a blessing, but having too many can lead to heartache. I simply went along with the high levels of activity and, unfortunately, there was little time left for basic everyday normalities that other families routinely get on with without questioning. I'm not saying being famous makes someone *better* than the next person – but it sets us apart and gives us a unique set of problems as well as perks.

It seems, with hindsight, and only because they have told me so of late, that our fast lifestyle wasn't necessarily conducive to making everything in our garden rosy.

Natalie, Katie and Harry have had a tough time being the offspring of an England and Arsenal footballer. For a very long time, I was oblivious of this truth. When I was young I was caught up in the wonderful world of top-class football – and so was Elaine. Inseparable from early teens, we wanted to do everything together – so we did. She came to most matches and, well, you've already read about our great social life.

As our firstborn, Natalie, grew older, she too would often come along. Dressed in her cute clothes, wearing her even cuter face, she was a regular at Highbury to watch her daddy play. Of course, she was too young to know what was going on, and at times the crowds may have been a bit overwhelming. She was, after all, a toddler in a grown-up world.

When Katie came along – if my memory serves me right – family life went on in a similar privileged fashion; and by the time Harry joined the family on Boxing Day 1987 we were really flying high and living the dream.

The champagne flowed and laughter and music filled the air, with barbecues in the summer, and late-night winter warmers through the darker months.

The children had great fun during the day and were then tucked up in bed just as all good healthy kids should be. Evenings were the time for grown-ups.

People talk about the swinging sixties, but the seventies, eighties and nineties have hardly been dull. Parents have learned how to take 'me time'. Whether it's going out for a meal or nightclubbing, theatregoing or cinemagoing, or holidays abroad – adults have learned how to enjoy themselves. Did we take it too far? I don't know. I'm just asking. Still learning.

When we were babies our older brothers and sisters babysat us and when we were teens we babysat the children of our older siblings. Now we were dressing up and going out to have fun while our children were looked after by trusted family members and friends. But, as I said, often the 'party' was at ours, so the children were tucked up under our roof with us not too far away. We did all we could to provide a safe environment and give our children a sense of roots.

Kenny Sansom and his family were, to all intents and purposes, the same as any other family who moved in the celebrity circle. Saturday night, after a match either at Highbury or away at somewhere like Chelsea or West Ham, I'd be in one corner of the nightclub chatting to Georgie Best, while Elaine was across the room laughing away with another footballer's wife or dancing with some other Arsenal legend. That was our life.

Sunday morning was a lie-in to sleep off a heavy night, followed by a traditional lunch, either at home or out somewhere – with or without the children. We had those endless choices. Life was good.

In recent times, while in rehab and then the days, weeks and months following all the treatment and therapy, I have had little choice but to think more deeply about our family life as the children were growing up.

I didn't know how they felt. I assumed I was the daddy they loved unconditionally – because that's how Elaine and I loved them. They alternated between being adorable and a pain in the backside when they were little, and now as young adults they were no different.

Natalie started her own family while still in her teens, and by the time she was in her mid-twenties she had twin boys, another son, and a darling daughter. She had (still has) her hands full, but she's a mum and that was her dream – a home with a good man and a brood of little ones. Well done, Natalie.

Katie also began motherhood early. Unsure of what she really wanted from life, she had a tough time deciding whether to go ahead with the pregnancy, but eventually, with guaranteed support from the baby's father and both families, she went through with it, and her daughter, Ella, is a blessing to us all.

Harry still lives at home. He has his struggles. *We* have our struggles. Our father–son relationship is fraught. The triangle that is Elaine, Harry and I is complex, but not exactly out of the ordinary. It's actually pretty normal – whatever normal is.

When I was drinking I just bumbled through this difficulty with my son. I'm sad about that now. It wasn't fair on Harry – but being drunk all through his teens meant *I* was in denial and blind to his needs, and *he* was growing more and more confused – and angry.

During rehab we had a family meeting. I wasn't nervous about my kids talking about 'what it's like being the child of a famous footballer'. Surely they were proud, weren't they? Yes, I had been drinking and gambling far too hard, for far too long, but kids were resilient – weren't they? I was their dad. I loved them – adored them. There was no problem. But there was. There was an awful problem that needed to be aired and addressed – *now*.

Any denial about being an alcoholic would have to be faced full on – or... or what? I was white with shock. I had hurt my children far more than I could have ever imagined. By living in my bubble of oblivion and drinking myself into a stupor virtually 24/7 I had come dangerously close to losing the respect of my treasured offspring. It was time to stop being a fool. It was a do or die moment.

This is what I *can* change.

To open up and share with you, the reader, the devastation of facing up to my shortfalls is going to be painful. But it has to be done. My Natalie, Katie and Harry deserve to know I now understand so much more than ever before. If there is any man reading this who can relate to any of my 'shortfalls', he will understand. If he doesn't understand yet, hopefully, one day, he will.

Natalie is 27 now and, despite the fact she is a mother of four, she is still very much the archetypal blonde, blue-eyed beauty who was – and still is – a 'daddy's girl'.

When we had the family meeting at Sporting Chance she was unable to attend because of her commitments to her four children. They needed taking and fetching to and from their different schools and playgroups, and geographically it was impossible – and Natalie is not the type of mum to shirk her responsibilities where her babies are concerned.

I don't know how I felt when she didn't come as I was still pretty numb. I was just going along with the treatment plan, knowing I had come to a crisis point and my choices had run out.

But to think Natalie has had her heart broken by my behaviour over the past few years is something I can no longer hide away from. I have to be as brave and grown up as she has been all her life.

Natalie is a kind soul, and of my three children she instinctively knows when someone is hurting. She is empathic and able to see all sides of the story. A natural-born carer, she doesn't like to see people hurt – let alone those closest to her. In sobriety I would never, in my wildest dreams, hurt Natalie. Drunk, I did. When I went on one of my 'benders' – when I disappeared without leaving a trace – I was abandoning not only my wife, but also the mother of my kids.

Natalie told me recently, 'One night when you'd gone missing and Mum was in bits, I wrapped little Maria up and pushed her buggy through town searching for you. I knew where to go. It wasn't difficult, because I knew you'd be in one of the pubs. I pushed the door open and there you were – just like I knew you'd be, alone with a bottle of wine. "What do you think you're doing? Mummy's in a terrible state. Come home – please, daddy."'

How about that? But there was more:

'You just disappeared, Dad, and no one knew where you were. Christmas had been horrible, especially for Harry, what with it being his birthday on Boxing Day. He'd begged you not to drink on his special day, but you couldn't hear him. Then you just walked out the door to go to the bookie's.'

Katie and Harry were different. They totally sided with their mum. They had to witness her falling apart in the knowledge that there was nothing they could do to console her. 'Don't take him back!' they screamed in fury after I'd disappeared to a hotel for several days.

I was the only one with the power to make things right. I wouldn't have blamed Elaine had she listened to their urgent cries of, 'You can't let him do this to you any more.'

KATIE AND OASIS

Katie had never fully realised how famous I was. She and Natalie had been to some of the big matches at Highbury and Wembley but all they really remembered was getting dressed up and going out with Mummy and Daddy. It was brought home to me just how little Katie knew about my life on Planet Celebrity when she was in her late teens and I had taken her to Wembley to watch England play against Italy (Zola was playing and we lost 1–0).

When we arrived at the ground and picked up our tickets we found they were not very good seats. The FA had arranged this for me – now there's a shock. I know: sarcasm is the lowest form of wit. But I'm afraid the FA are not my favourite body of people. I'll keep those reasons to myself, as I don't want to be sued.

As we walked inside Wembley I was recognised by lots of England fans who were calling out telling me what a legend I was. Now it was Katie's turn to be shocked. 'Why is everyone calling out to you, Daddy? Why is everyone asking you for your autograph?' I said, 'Well, I did play for England a few times, Katie.'

I managed to get some tickets to go into the lounge afterwards, where I introduced her to Ray Parlour and David Platt. Then, to her amazement, the Gallagher brothers, Liam and Noel, came over and started chatting to me. Katie was gobsmacked. 'How do Oasis know you, Dad? Please, Dad, please ask them if I can have my picture taken with them.'

Noel and Liam were great. They posed with her and then asked how I was doing. As we were walking away she repeated, 'But how do they know you, Dad?'

I think that was the first moment she realised I was 'famous'.

Harry probably had more to reason to be hurting than his sisters. His teens had been hell. Being Harry Sansom was not the great thing I had assumed it to be. I thought he'd be proud – but it seems he was embarrassed. In fact, when Harry admitted that he didn't tell anyone his surname at school, Natalie put her hand up: 'Me neither.' But their reasons were slightly different. Natalie found friends wanted to be around her to get closer to her dad and be given photos and autographs. But for Harry the problem ran far deeper.

Harry told me recently, 'All my teens I felt as if I had to be the man of the house. You kept telling me how lucky I was to have a father living at home – that I had a better deal than you because your dad had left home. You used to say things like, "You don't know how lucky you are being able to choose exactly how you live your life. You have freedom to do whatever you want."

'I didn't understand. Didn't you have any idea at all that it was probably worse having a drunken father who was there but not there? I don't remember a day when I came home from school and you weren't sitting in the armchair drunk. You'd been to work for an hour or two, either on the television or radio, so I guess you felt it was OK to reward yourself with a few bottles of wine.

'In the end I gave up trying to communicate and went to my room. My biggest confusion was how angry you got if Mum and I spent too much time together. I felt as if I was coming between you and you were jealous of our relationship. Can't you understand that a mother's love for a child is totally different from that of a husband and wife. There's enough of Mum to go round, you know.'

244

I was devastated by the confrontation and blown away by my son's honesty. But the confrontation had been a gift, and his honesty, although shocking to hear, was straight upfront and with no messing.

My lack of understanding and need for Elaine's love and attention had led to my acting boyishly and attacking the natural closeness my son had with his mum. I was jealous of him in a way I had never been jealous of Elaine's mothering of the girls. Harry was right. If he got more attention I got stroppy. If he could be 13 and needy, why couldn't I?

'You should think yourself lucky you've got a dad at home.' Had I really said that to my son? I couldn't remember. Was he right? Was I envious that his dad had hung around whereas mine had cleared off with another woman to another life that didn't involve me? Had my mum really managed to be mother and father to us kids? Had she been enough? Or was I angry at George Sansom for choosing the high life instead of staying put? Yes, he'd sent money; yes, he kept an eye on us from a distance – but the gulf was too wide and his love too weak.

The brutal honesty was that my dad had been selfish and abandoned his responsibilities. The harsher truth was that, although I hadn't physically left, emotionally my kids felt as abandoned and betrayed. It was a horrifying fact to face up to – but face it I would.

Then Harry confided some more: 'My anxiety about how I was going to cope in the world kept getting bigger and bigger and I was beginning to panic. When you said things to me like, "You need to sort yourself out, Harry: one day you'll marry and have children of your own and you'll need to support them," that scared me.'

That was the truth for Harry. That was how Harry experienced himself. I was mortified, and the words to Mike and the Mechanics' 'The Living Years' rang loud in my head, only now the shift had changed. I was no longer thinking about my father and me – I had moved on to thinking about my son and me.

With Natalie still championing me but feeling let down, and sensitive Harry letting me know how lost he was, I wondered about my middle child, Katie. Katie was feisty and never slow in coming forward to voice her opinion. I guess out of the three she was the best at communicating effectively, and demanding her needs to be met. I knew she was angry. Elaine knew she was angry. Everyone knew she was angry.

I thought about that fateful night many years before when I had got drunk with my father in Switzerland. In my mind's eye was the vision of many other inebriated days and nights that followed. The years of laughter and fun out on the party circuit had been great, and I honestly, hand on heart, can't say I regret those heady times in the fast lane. I had been in control of my drinking then. If I had any problem at all it was the gambling – but I enjoyed that, too.

In days gone by my blasé attitude to money had got me into hot water, such as the day when I felt terribly guilty after losing the mortgage money on a horse, but there was no way I could have stopped then.

STAYING STRONG

I became positive and stayed positive. Every morning when I woke I read my empowering 'message for the day' in my little AA promises book.

They really helped a lot to keep my spirits up. Elaine and I used to read them together in bed over a cup of tea. It was a good way to start the day.

I began to ask myself what I wanted to do with the rest of my life. It was tricky. I'd had a lifetime of thinking one way and was now having to relearn new attitudes. I needed to shake the old habits – but, as we all know, old habits die hard.

I remembered the words of Mark Twain: 'Habit is habit and not to be flung out of the window by any man, but coaxed downstairs a step at a time.'

I would do what I had to do, but would also pace myself.

Then I got a telephone call that told me destiny was sending a calling card. It was the PFA. I was being offered the job of a lifetime – in China. But it was followed swiftly by another call from my doctor.

I had become a diabetic as well as being an alcoholic. How was *that* for luck? But it wasn't about luck. It was about my excesses catching up with me. The big question loomed large – was I fit enough to travel to China for 2 months to film a new television programme called *Soccer Prince*?

They wanted me to be a coach and a judge – a mixture of Terry Venables and Simon Cowell came to mind and nearly frightened the life out of me. But I bought a new pair of high-waisted trousers and hitched them up, looked at an old photo of me and Terry and asked, 'Got anything up your sleeve for me, Tel?'

CHAPTER TWENTY-TWO

CHINA AND THE SOCCER PRINCE

I needed to find the monthly mortgage money. Harry was still living at home and the girls could always do with a few bob here and there. The grandchildren needed treats and Elaine and I were desperate for some good times. Good times that didn't involve alcohol. I became engrossed in building a new career – I was hungry again.

The first thing I did was to get some business cards printed. When I opened the packet and saw my name and contact numbers alongside the England badge and the words, 'Seventh in the country – 86 caps', the enormity of my career hit me. That was some accolade.

Some hotel employee had once asked George Best, 'Where did it all go wrong, George?' and George didn't have a clue what he was on about. As far as George was concerned, everything in his garden was rosy. He had a pocket full of cash and Miss World in his bed. Was the man in the hotel nuts?

Now I was asking myself the same question, 'Where did it all go wrong, Kenny?'

Like George, I had no concrete answers. Life isn't concrete: it's fluid, ever changing. Now my life was changing. I'd always been open to change, so I wasn't too worried. Looking at my new business cards, I knew that if I had made it once I could make it again. There had been a kind of death and now I needed some sort of rebirth. That might sound a bit soft, but it's nevertheless the truth.

I didn't have to look far. Life was once again about to present me with an opportunity – and I was going to grasp it with both hands.

The phone rang. It was the PFA and they had just the news I needed to hear – only it was better than either Elaine or I could have dreamed.

'How would you like to go to China for a couple of months to work as head coach and judge for a new television programme called *Soccer Prince*?'

Was he kidding? I couldn't believe it. What an opportunity!

I looked at Elaine and she looked at me. 'Can my wife come?' I asked.

'Of course she can,' came back the reply, and we almost packed our cases there and then. But we had to consider the family.

Katie and little Ella would have to move into our house to keep Harry and our dog Lucky company. That would be no hardship for any of them.

My sister Maureen and my mum lived just around the corner and Natalie, Mark and their children were living close by in Orpington.

There was no reason why we couldn't head off to the Far East for a new adventure.

It was all very spontaneous and so we didn't get long to prepare for the long haul and 2 months away, but wild horses wouldn't have stopped us.

We were well aware that had I not stopped drinking this opportunity wouldn't have come our way, and if it had, it would have been impossible to contemplate. But I *was* dry, and I *was* getting fitter by the day. This seemed almost like a reward – a healthy reward and not one that included a bottle of wine to fuel the euphoric feeling.

Everyone at Sporting Chance and all involved with Alcoholics Anonymous had kept telling me, 'You just see – your life will change beyond your wildest dreams when you turn away from the drink.' Perhaps this trip would prove life-changing.

A SHOT IN THE DARK

I felt just like Peter Sellers in the movie *A Shot in the Dark*. I just didn't know what to expect from the experience.

I had been told the weather was good in the region where we would be spending most of our time, so we packed mainly summer clothes. Being an original wag, Elaine packed a couple of 'dressing-up' dresses and delicate shoes with little heels.

As I was due to be on national television as one of the judges on the panel, I thought I'd better buy a pair of extra-high-waisted trousers. If it was good enough for Simon Cowell, it was good enough for King Kenny. I think Elaine was secretly hoping she was going to be a second Sharon Osborne, but in my eyes she's much better-looking.

I know Elaine was worrying about my coaching fit young boys at a high altitude. After all, not too long before I'd been a fat bastard who was drinking copious amounts of wine while sitting morosely on my ever-spreading arse watching old reruns of *Columbo*. Not attractive in any way, shape or form.

Being diagnosed with diabetes had shaken me up. This was a life-threatening illness that required my making some drastic changes in my diet. Which, apart from my new obsession with strawberry-flavoured Häagen-Dazs ice cream, was going well. (I'd done the classic thing of switching addictions.)

After an emotional farewell with our families, Elaine and I boarded the plane at Heathrow Airport full of great expectations. Having the luxury of travelling in business class, we settled ourselves down for a relaxing trip that didn't involve my getting drunk en route.

While that was definitely good, it also proved to be extremely difficult, since there was a Chinese man sitting next to me who clearly had a few problems of his own.

Tap... tap... tap... he went. He was fidgeting and sniffing and... tapping – all the way over Europe.

Elaine and I kept sharing furtive glances and shrugging our shoulders. I couldn't exactly tell him, 'Turn it in, mate,' because I didn't speak a single word of Chinese. Had I been drinking, I would have said, 'Oi, mate, give us a break. Sit still for fuck's sake.' (I'd learned in therapy that swearing now and again is good for you, as it releases tension.)

But, sober, I just put up with it, thinking to myself, 'Poor bastard – fancy not being able to sit still. He must be an OCD.' I learned all about the obsessive-compulsive disorder and I didn't think it sounded a great thing to have. Fancy having to tap, tap because you can't stop! At least Elaine and I could get away from the noise as soon as the plane landed. He had to take himself off with himself and suffer all the time. He needed help. Maybe he was simply afraid of flying.

I had been a bit anxious myself about the flight. This was the first time in years that I'd flown without the accompaniment of champagne. But I needn't have worried: it was much easier than I'd feared. In fact, apart from the tapping on our left, it was most enjoyable.

We landed in Beijing and were met by our interpreter Viola. She was delightful, which is more than I can say for the drive to our destination in Changsha.

It was unbelievable. I thought we were back in our youth at Battersea funfair on the bumper cars. There was no road rage as such – in fact the Chinese people just clutch onto their steering wheels blank-faced and stare straight ahead. If they bumped into each other they just kept going, weaving in and out of the four available lanes of the dual carriageway. Hair-raising or what? Although there was no ranting or raving with rude gestures like you get on the streets of England, they tooted their horns nonstop like the Europeans.

If there was an accident in the northbound carriageway, the drivers would join the southbound traffic, causing absolute mayhem. I am not talking about isolated incidents here – I'm talking about everyday chaos. The first time it happened to us (thank goodness we had our own driver), we couldn't believe what we were witnessing. Can you imagine that happening on the M25? It would make headline news. Actually it reminds me of a joke.

Tracy was driving down the A12 in Essex when her mobile rang and it was her boyfriend Darren. 'Babe,' he cried with some urgency. 'Don't go on the A12 – there's some dozy bugger driving the wrong way.'

Tracy squealed back to him, 'Darren, that's nothing, there's loads of 'em driving the wrong way and I'm in the middle of it.'

There are no roundabouts as such – it's simply a free-for-all. Nuts.

Our hotel, the Sheraton, was fabulous, and it was a relief to make it there in one piece. I threw my weary body on the bed, but was able to rest for only a few minutes before I had to go to report for my first job of the project. If I thought I was going to have a break before knuckling down to work, I was mistaken.

KENNY 'CHAIRMAN MAO' SANSOM

While Elaine got over the trauma of the bumper-car ride and settled in, I was taken to the Changsha Stadium where I was introduced to the fourteen boys who had been selected from the thousands who had originally applied with high hopes of becoming the Chinese Football Idol.

The boys were bright-eyed and eager, and welcomed me with such enthusiasm that I was really moved. I smiled and held my hand out to each of them in turn as Viola busily interpreted our messages of greeting.

I had made some good-luck cards and written a poem inside that I had thought up myself all about being positive and 'going for it'.

They looked a little confused and it took me a while to realise it wasn't customary for the 'teacher' to hand over a gift, but as the weeks went on, and we all began to understand each other better, they indicated to me they now understood, which was nice.

In return they all gave me a gift. It was totally unexpected, but as I grew to understand the culture of the Chinese people I realised this was common practice. One by one I was handed delightful gifts such as a statue of the Changsha Tower, some chiming relaxation balls, a pack of playing cards and some delicious cakes that apparently had no sugar in them – so I devoured them. Elaine didn't even get a look-in.

Next I was shown where the boys were sleeping, and I must say it was a bit of a shock. They were actually staying in the executive boxes, which had been made into crude makeshift rooms. The rooms slept three, although one had to accommodate four.

'Now you must inspect rooms,' I was told in broken Chinese.

'Pardon?'

'You must inspect and punish one boy.'

'Punish?'

'Yes, the boy with dirtiest room must be punished.'

Crikey! Off with his head, Chairman Mao style?

All the boys stood by their beds as in turn I had to inspect their own personal areas. It was horrible. What was their punishment to be?

In the end I realised there was no getting out of this – I simply had to choose. When I nodded to the boy whose bed was most untidy, he simply smiled. There was no trace of fear.

'Now you punish,' I was ordered.

And there was I thinking the establishment at Arsenal had been rigid.

I thought back to my young days at Crystal Palace. Were we ever punished? How on earth do you punish a Chinese boy? Then it came to me. 'OK, I'm going to take away your chop-sticks.'

You should have seen the expression on the interpreter's face. It was a picture. It also told me this was not appropriate. She'd missed the joke. No surprise there, then.

Next I tried, 'You must clean all your teammates' boots after training.'

I could see by the relief flooding over the faces of the staff on the programme that I'd said the right thing this time, and was mightily relieved I didn't have to flog the boys.

They have this word they use all the time in China: 'tic'. Everything is 'tic' this and 'tic' that. It means 'you don't know what's going to happen from one minute to the next'. You can say that again. I wished we'd been forewarned about this customary belief before we'd tackled the traffic.

Realising this was to be run like a military regime, I quickly adapted to what was expected of me. I was reminded of how much we had been disciplined when I was a young lad – painting dressing rooms, scrubbing boots and shovelling snow off the pitch during the cold winter months. None of the above had done me or the others any harm.

The following day the coaching began in earnest.

I heaved yet another great sigh about stopping drinking and losing some weight. Once I was there, the feeling that I would never have been able to take on this demanding job had I not cleaned up my act came to me even stronger.

The first 3 days were interesting. I studied the boys closely, and I liked what I saw. They were all talented boys, which wasn't surprising, as they'd been chosen from so many hopefuls all over China – youngsters keen to make the best of their lives. Each and every one was an only child, as men and women are still allowed to have only one child under China's population-control law.

THE SOCCER PRINCE

The boys didn't have a clue who I was or what I had achieved in my career. I wasn't King Kenny of the Arsenal to them. Instead, I was just this bloke who they'd been told was able to help them realise their dreams. Someone who would be coaching, mentoring and judging their performances, before helping to choose which two would win the prizes of going to England and joining Everton and Bolton. What was kept from them was the fact that *all three* finalists would be going to England – the boy in third place was going to Nottingham Forest.

The final contenders were all unique and individual, and all had great attitude. There were no shirkers among this lot.

I can't say I had favourites. As far as personalities went, they were all good kids. But there were a few that gripped my heart more.

One such player was the littlest of the boys who just so happened to play at left-back. His name was Wang Yu, but we referred to him as 'Little Kenny'. He was never going to win the competition, and I think that was another reason he endeared himself to Elaine and me.

Halfway though the contest our team played the Korean boys. It was a tight match and all the boys played well. When we lost 7–5 there were tears all round. Little Kenny came over and we hugged – his expression said it all.

I was reminded of days gone by, when winning meant everything. The day he was eliminated was really sad. I know it sounds daft, but he cried so hard that Elaine and I were compelled to join him in a three-way cuddle.

Another player, Jiang Ding Hui, who came to be known to us as 'Drogba', was one of my favourites at the beginning, but, as time went on, it became clear that he was physically too tall and stocky to become the first-class striker he dreamed of becoming. When he was eliminated he held his head up high and showed great humility. Drogba the Brave just kept on bowing and thanking me for all the skills I'd taught him. I have no doubt this boy will succeed in life – he's far too special not to.

It was in this moment I began to think really hard about where I wanted my future to lie in the game I'd been associated with all my life. I'd surprised myself how much I enjoyed passing on all the skills that Terry Venables taught me. Everything he'd said to me, all the one-to-one exercises he'd worked on with me in training came back in insightful flashes. It was quite extraordinary really.

When Drogba went out of the competition he was accompanied by Xiao Wei – another disappointed contestant. The day these two boys went home was another tearful day, and we all cuddled for ages. All these 'feelings' just keep on washing over me – often at unexpected times. But I don't mind. I'm glad I'm not afraid to cry.

We nicknamed another lad 'Sunny' – not surprisingly because of his sunny disposition. The upbeat attitude of all the finalists was fantastic, and a real eye opener.

The number one player was clear to me after just 3 days. The boys who would come in second and third also stood out as extra special.

Jin Hui was the outstanding boy I predicted to be voted the Soccer Prince. I nicknamed him Tony Adams. Jin Hui possessed all the qualities that had taken Tony to the top. The boy had a great presence and superb leadership skills. Whenever they were asked to split into two groups and play against each other, whichever team Jin Hui captained won. As well as reading the game beautifully he possessed the power of Bruce Lee and his skinny legs that ran with the speed of wind. Most of all he hated losing. He was going places – of that I was certain. Number two on my list was Song Yang, a lad with a great personality and a shock of dyed red hair. He reminded me of Arsenal's Cesc Fàbregas, with similar flair and energy and terrific passing skills.

Coming in at number three in my book was Zhao Zhihao. What a mouthful and far too difficult for me to remember, so I nicknamed him 'Smiler'. What a great kid, and what a great attitude. If he were to come third he'd get to join Nottingham Forest. In a sense, if he was to win third place, Smiler would be getting the best deal. Even though he would not be going to a Premiership club, at the age of 17 years he'd no doubt go straight into the first team and receive invaluable match experience. The Academy at Nottingham Forest has a fine reputation.

These young stars of the future spoke no English and, apart from being able to say 'hello' in their language, all we could do was improvise, but improvise we did, and communicate we did – both on and off the pitch.

The TV programme was aired at 9.30 every Friday evening. At first the ratings were average, but as the weeks went by it began to climb – it reached 30 million and kept climbing at an astonishing rate, reaching in excess of 40 million. It seems this show had everything the Chinese loved in entertainment – football, reality, uncertainty and watching eager young talent following their dreams. Being part of *Soccer Prince* was a real privilege and honour.

Over the 8 weeks the boys were given many other challenges, such as ballet dancing and ice skating to improve balance and movement, juggling in a real circus, and visiting an army camp to observe the discipline and regimentation. They were expected to do a bungee jump and most of them went for it. Song Yang ('Fàbregas') was terrified, and it showed. Eventually he said, 'I'm sorry, Kenny, can't do it.'

Through our interpreter Viola, I said, 'Song Yang, it is sometimes just as brave to admit you can't do something. It's natural to feel scared sometimes. You are being honest to yourself.'

He didn't look convinced, but maybe some time in his future when faced with another impossible moment he'll remember my words of wisdom.

It all made for great television. And remember, we are talking about Chinese television here, where anything goes. Jim Hui (alias 'Tony Adams') made for hilarious viewing when he paraded around at the ballet school in white tights that barely concealed his Spiderman pants. I think we need to watch out for the release of this piece of footage one day when he is at the top of his career.

The host was a very good-looking 20-year-old called Alan, who had found fame in the Chinese Pop Idol, where he had been runner-up. There was a bit of a hiccup halfway through the series when the ambitious young lad was offered a part in Shakespeare in Beijing and took it. There can be no passing over of opportunity in China, that's for sure.

Football in China is definitely on the rise. Serbian Red Star icon Vladimir Petrović is now in charge of the Chinese national team. He has always been considered an intelligent footballer. It has been reported that his knowledge of the game is second to none and a coaching book highlighting all his skills would be a bestseller: it would include skills, technique, flair, creativity, stylish moves and dribbles – not to mention his instinct for scoring goals. For many years he was hidden away behind a curtain of secrecy and mystery in his homeland. The executive body of the Yugoslavian Football Association had stringent rules about waiting 6 months refused to allow Petrović to come to Arsenal in 1982 on a transfer fee of £750,000. By the time the deal was finally completed his value had dropped from by £700,000 and he was with us for only 6 months. Obviously, I got to know him well. When he arrived there was this kind of hero-worshipping going on among some of the players, but in all honesty his type of game didn't fit at Highbury and soon he was off to Paris.

Now here I was meeting up with him all these years later, all these thousands of miles away. Two people in two different situations meeting up again to ask, 'How's it going?'

It was a bit like meeting up with the man I'd bumped into while in rehab. There we were, two strangers working hard on getting well, when we realised we both knew an old England schoolboy teammate of mine.

Both then and now it was pure serendipity – we'd made fortunate discoveries by accident. One was a reunion and the other a new friend. I now believe there is no such thing as a coincidence and there is a force out there far bigger than we are.

ELAINE GETS A BUZZ

All in all, my 'China experience' was great. The unfamiliar and therefore strange foods we were given with love by our generous hosts shocked us at times. Elaine didn't find the chicken's head in her soup very appetising. 'Elaine,' I said kindly, 'you've just got to get your head around this.'

The local tofu delicacy wasn't up our street, either, and I can't tell you how distressed Elaine became when she asked for some ordinary rice, only to learn that you eat rice only at the end of a meal as a 'filler'. They kept thinking she was still hungry and filling her plate with more deep-fried worms and crispy wasps. She had a right old buzz on that night.

To balance our Eastern culinary experience we ate delicious pun-cane (pumpkin) soup, tasty sweetcorn nests (honey, sweetcorn and pastry), and prawns wrapped in chicken. I know, I know, I'd been diagnosed with diabetes, but most of the time I behaved myself; and the combination of training and not drinking meant the weight was dropping off me – so that was good.

My days were filled with football, but Elaine had quite a bit of time on her hands. At first she relished the idea of exploring the shopping centres, but soon realised this was to be no ordinary excursion.

Being blonde and blue-eyed, she was something of a phenomenon for the Chinese people. Although only 5 foot high, she has all the curves of a Western woman, making her different from every other female on the street. As everyone knows, the ladies from the East tend to be very close to the bone. She was fine with the small shoe sizes, but trying to find clothing that was bigger than size zero proved impossible. I'm sure any Western women reading this will sympathise with my wife's dilemma.

Elaine also found herself the centre of much attention, which she has never liked very much. She could hear people calling her 'round eyes'. They were pointing and chattering away in their language, which was very unnerving and made staying in the hotel a great alternative.

On more than one occasion Elaine declared she was going home. Sometimes she said it half-heartedly, but other times she really meant it. Seven weeks was a long time to be away from the family. She missed the girls and the grandchildren and also worried that Harry was home alone for too long. But there was more to the tension between us than our family ties.

Being alone together in a faraway land with me sober was going to test our relationship. Without the drink blurring the edges of the reality of my life, I was able to think things through more clearly. As the fog lifted I could no longer deny the murmuring in my head that my marriage may be coming to an end. It was a devastating concept – unthinkable. I had to think about it. I *couldn't* think about it. The dilemma sent me to the hotel bar and I drank. I thought I could drown myself in denial all over again, but I was wrong.

I was also *in* the wrong as well. Elaine was angry with me and I don't blame her. Call me mad; call me weak – you would be right. Call me terribly unhappy and you would also be right. So now we had Elaine with the hump and me numb – back to that old chestnut. But not for long. I was not going to relapse – well not for any longer than a day or two. I had to stay on track. Had to keep coaching and judging and being a mentor for these boys with a dream. Had to be true to myself as by now there was too much I wanted to do with my life.

Then my mum showed up and we were no longer alone.

KENNY SANSOM

MUM SEEKS ANOTHER CHINAMAN

Yes, my mum, at the age of eighty-something, had flown to the other side of world to see how we were getting on. My sister Maureen and her two girls had joined her, and so we had a fun few family days.

Mum is very fragile nowadays. A couple of years ago she was knocked down by a car and injured badly. It was touch and go whether she would pull through – but it's good old Louise Sansom we're talking about here. She was broken physically, and confused mentally. In a sense a part of her was lost. She became disoriented and her sharpness was dimmed. But that shining personality still beamed through.

It was nothing short of a miracle that she made a full physical recovery, and for me to see her walking towards me with open arms was a special sight. 'Hello, 100 per cent son,' she said, smiling. 'Are they looking after you all right? Have you still got your diabetes or are you better now? You look better.'

The only problem she had was with the food, but, to be honest, she'd been fussy for a long time – refusing to eat chicken was a weird one but all of a sudden it was a case of, 'I don't like chicken.' We didn't dare tell her the meat in front of her was crocodile.

Only joking – I think.

The different cuisine may have been lost on her, but her sense of humour was still very much intact. When the boys had to learn the *haka* dance, which was demonstrated by some New Zealand Maoris, good old Mum joined in. She stood up and began to copy the dancers, slapping her legs and laughing just like the old Mum of years gone by.

At one point she grinned across at Little Chinese Kenny and spoke to him just as she had done to me all those years before. 'You make sure you win, son,' she told him.

We joked around with her about the Chinese man who had fallen for her when we were in Mexico for the 1986 World Cup.

'I bet you've come here to find your old flame, haven't you, Mum?' I joked.

'He's not here, Kenny.' She gave me a gentle shove in the arm. 'He's in Mexico and that's miles away.'

How do you respond to an answer like that? You say, 'Of course. How silly of me, Mum.'

THE FINAL OF *SOCCER PRINCE*

In the end it came down to three boys who had, for me, shone the most. But who would actually be crowned the Soccer Prince? There were just a hundred people in the studio audience, but many hundreds of thousands were watching on nationwide television.

The parents of the three boys were sitting in the studio and the nerves were palpable. As far as the audience and the boys themselves were concerned, only two of the three boys were to win places in English teams. Two would travel across the globe to realise their dreams, while one would be bitterly disappointed. It sounds cruel, but that's entertainment for you, and I think I'm right in saying Chinese television pushes its boundaries much further than its European counterpart. They also laugh at everything – absolutely everything – and I found that a bit strange. But that is their culture; it's as simple as that. I'm sure there are things we do that they consider weird.

So the stage was set. There were three podiums in the middle of the stage and on the podiums were three boxes. One box contained the first prize, which was an Everton shirt telling the boy he was off to Goodison Park to join the Everton squad. He held it proudly aloft and the crowd cheered noisily. The second box had a Bolton shirt in it, and that's where the boy who came second would be going. The third box contained nothing. The boy we'd nicknames Fàbregas was called first and sent to open box No. 2. He pulled out a Bolton shirt and was delighted to learn he'd come second. Next it was Jin Hui who was guided to box No. 1, which was in the centre of the stage, and when he held the Everton shirt up triumphantly we all knew he'd won, that he was the Soccer Prince. That left just Smiler, who wasn't smiling, as this meant he was third, and, sure enough, when he opened his box there was nothing in it. Devastated, he burst into tears, tugging at the heartstrings of us, the audience and almost the entire Chinese population watching from their homes. But the drama wasn't over.

Suddenly, a man in the audience stood up and approached the stage. There was a surprise in store for Smiler. The man was Brandon Furse, the representative from Nottingham Forest FC. He walked over to Smiler and asked him, 'How do you feel about going to Nottingham for a year?'

Smiler's tears of despair turned to tears of joy. He looked over at me and beamed. I was crying. Everyone was crying. The programme should have been sponsored by Kleenex. As Smiler held up is red Nottingham Forest shirt the cameras clicked away and he became the centre of attention. I wondered how he was going to deal with the massive changes in his life. Hopefully, England was going to be offering these boys a life-changing opportunity. I for one would be watching their progress with great interest. I have heard the programme was so successful that it is to be repeated. If it's ever aired over here, don't miss it.

As for me, I can look back and say that I am so blessed to have been involved in such a brilliant show and of doing something I never imagined I would do. If I hadn't given up the drink this would never have happened.

When I'd first arrived in China I was filled with so many mixed emotions. I wanted to drink socially, but knew it was too dangerous. I loved losing weight and feeling fitter than I had in years, but I was also fed up to have been diagnosed with diabetes. I was enjoying the Chinese food, but the spices and rich food in general had triggered an extremely painful toe that at first I thought was broken, but eventually, while in a strange situation in a hospital in Changsha, I was told was gout. What the hell was going on? They had told me in rehab that my new life without alcohol would see me realise life beyond my wildest dreams. First diabetes and then gout – fabulous.

BALANCING ACT

Judging a television show in China was what the PFA had asked me to do – but the experience had been so much more.

I had spent 2 months with young eager boys who loved football and wanted to make this great sport the centre of their universe – just as I had 35 years before them. It had been a privilege as well as a trip down memory lane, and so much more than I had expected it to be – far more than just a job. My fire for the game was reignited.

Here were boys chasing their dreams and here was I realising mine.

As the plane took off from Beijing taking Elaine and me back to our family, we sat back and relaxed. Thankfully, there was no one tapping or sniffing next to us and we had an opportunity to reflect on the past few months – and years.

I began to write and it seemed as if my pen was running away with me. What happened next astonished me. I was thinking about my children and was feeling very emotional, so I wrote it all down on any scraps of paper I could find – an in-flight menu, a piece of card with a blank section, and then there was a paper bag, which I ripped into two. On these random pieces of paper I wrote individual poems for my family. I would give them to them when we got back home. I will tell you them now, as I want them recorded in this book to remind them for ever of what their dad thinks about them.

First I wrote this first poem on the back of *le plat du jour* menu. When I'd finished the first one I just kept on writing.

KENNY SANSOM

On the Plane

On the plane I crossed my leg, felt like a snob because I was
    in Business Class and not economy instead.
It's funny how you think when you're sitting alone, it's hard
    to leave the drink alone.
Pen and paper I have found, does lend me a helping hand.
I write some shit but it's good for me
Pick up a pen and paper and you will see.

To Natalie

Money could not buy a girl like you.
You're so easy to love, because of the things you do.
You are so much like me.
We go with the flow – it's easy.
Billy, Charlie, Michael, Maria, and Mark
Are the lucky ones.
You love me so much
It's something I can't touch
You are warm and kind
To find another child like you would be impossible.
To Katie
You are the middle one and given us some fun
There has been some trouble with men, and cars are just a few
As well as hopping off of school.
But that's not all there is to you – the good and the bad.
I know life is not all good – and it makes you feel sad.
I also know you don't feel strong for me but
There was something you did
Made me proud you're my kid.
Your eyes are not blue
But for me they are true. Don't worry, be happy. XX Love daddy
p.s. sorry about the lost one.

CHINA AND THE SOCCER PRINCE

To Harry

To Harry, love your dad.
Harry is my son
I'm happy to have him as one
His magic little smile
To see I'd travel many a mile.
He is twenty-one this year
He will want some expensive gear
But he has a small chance
If you give my bank balance a glance
I will do my best, my very special son
Even if the present is a little one!

Then I wrote a message for Elaine. It went like this:

Hi Darling, I wanted to put this into writing so you could read
it now and again.

When we met I knew you were the one for me. I did not
know what love was then, maybe I don't know now. One
thing is for sure: Elaine Gristwood meant the world to me. A
song comes to mind, 'To hold you to touch you to feel you to
kiss you' makes me think of those days when your smile was
great and when we kept trying to break our own record for
long kisses. I did not worry about anything else. The song,
'The breaking up was not hard to do'. It was fun to do, not the
breaking, but the making up. When we chased each other I
always wanted to slow down so you could catch me. I can
still see your beautiful young face (it has not changed). I have
always known that you are an incredible person. PS: This is
not long – it's not a poem – it's just my feelings for YOU –
from Young Ken.

I didn't realise at the time that some of the message was written in the past tense. It was some weeks after we'd returned home that the enormity of my changing feelings hit me. Not that I would ever stop loving or honouring Elaine; ever. But Denise was becoming more and more important to me and I could no longer deny this either.

When we touched down at Heathrow we were secretly hoping for a big welcome party, but with our grandchildren in school we knew it would be difficult, especially for Natalie with her four children. Then we saw Katie. Our beautiful dark-haired Katie was sobbing.

Elaine was in tears and all the time I tried to be the strong daddy. It didn't work and my lip wobbled, making me look like one of the comedians I loved to impersonate.

On the drive home Katie tried to be ever so casual about what was going to happen next. 'Everyone's busy,' she said. 'Harry's at home looking after Ella, but Natalie's chasing around after the twins and Maria and Michael.'

But as we turned the corner into our road we could see the big 'welcome home' banner hanging from the upstairs window. The sight of the grandchildren jumping up and down in excitement among the balloons sent my heart racing.

When I had been the same age as little Michael I had loved to head balloons over the washing line – perhaps it was time I taught my youngest grandson this skill. I wondered if he would find walking on fences easy. Could he balance like his granddad?

I had proudly represented my country playing football. Now I was being congratulated by the PFA for a great job done in China. 'That'll do me for now,' I thought. But this is just the beginning of a new chapter.

I had a fantastic football career and lifestyle to match. My mum ensured I had the best childhood a youngster could wish for. My marriage to Elaine stood the test of time for more than three decades, which was quite something given that so many couples fall apart while their children are still little. We both consider bringing up Natalie, Katie and Harry to be our best achievement and we love them dearly. The grandchildren are the golden ticket.

Yet after 37 years of being everything to each other we both knew in our hearts our marriage was over. Problems had been left festering for too long, but we were afraid to take our heads out of the sand and therefore lost sight of options and choices. One of us had to bite the bullet. One of us had to say 'enough', and that person was me. I think I had been changing for some years, because once in rehab I was ready to listen and learn. Twenty-eight days may not sound long enough to realise you can turn your life around, but sometimes it just takes one light-bulb moment of understanding. What I now understood was that we were all hurting and it had to stop.

While in Sporting Chance I had the very first opportunity to think things through without being smothered by negative criticism. There were no judgements and demands in there. No worries about my next job (or lack of it) or how I was going to pay the mortgage. Of course, I knew these things would come back at me but, instead of feeling inadequate, I wanted to be able to cope next time round, and – dare I say? – be happy.

In rehab I got a chance to hear 'my' voice – the voice that had got lost underneath everybody else's for so long that at first there was no voice to be heard. It was terrifying. How could I speak on radio and TV and have all the football fans think they know me when I didn't know myself? This was crazy. But slowly I began to hear my voice – not Columbo's or Norman Wisdom's, but Kenny Sansom's.

One morning when I was in China I got up and walked into the bathroom. Then a weird thing happened. I gazed into the mirror and couldn't see myself. Instead, I came face to face with this distorted image of a stranger. I closed my eyes and held my breath for a moment. Then I opened them and blinked for a second or two as I tried to refocus. Still nothing.

KENNY SANSOM

The experts would say I was 'fragmented'. That I had fallen apart and was now a blank canvas ready to become whole again. It was all a new language to me, I can tell you.

I felt as if I were in no-man's-land. I couldn't go back to being how I was before – that way was not working. When I was little I used to jump across rooftops and there would be this moment between leaving one building and reaching the next when I was suspended in midair, and that's how I felt now. I suppose you could say I'd done a 'Johnnie Laws' (my childhood mate who used to jump across roofs with me but never quite made it to the other side) and crashed into the wall like Roadrunner, but I wanted to land safely on the other side, just as I used to as a kid.

It was time for me to make some radical changes. It was time for me to be honest – about bloody time. Elaine and I were so unhappy with each other – the rows, the shouting each other down and saying horrible things to each other we didn't really mean. All of it had to become a thing of the past. If I was on my last legs, so was my wife and therefore our marriage.

During the summer of 2007, after my spell in rehab, I began to rebuild my career. Football was what I knew and football was what made me happy. I belonged and functioned in this world. Being a footballer was what had defined me all my life. Here I felt a sense of belonging. Fit and raring to go after my China experience, where my fitness and confidence levels had grown, I began to fill my diary with work. The mirror on the wall had shocked me into action. If I chose to remain in denial about who I was and what I wanted for the rest of my life I would be a dead man – my liver results a few months before had confirmed this scary fact.

I left home. I didn't want to go but one morning I just went. The pendulum that had been frantically swinging in my head, screaming 'for' and 'against', had finally silenced – but not before this huge dilemma had tested my ability to stay sober. I'm sorry to say I began to drink again. Not in the way I'd drunk before, and by no means in the volumes previously consumed. But I was searching for that old comfort blanket – the oblivion. I'd relapsed, as they say in AA. Perhaps I'd relapse many times, or maybe I'd be able to control my drinking now my circumstances had changed. Questions I can't answer right now.

I was loath to go straight into the arms of another woman. It upsets and disappoints me that I couldn't stand alone for a while. But the truth is I wanted to be with me *and* I wanted to be with her.

Denise loves me but she also 'likes' me. This is the real revelation. Elaine and I had long since lost our 'liking' for each other and this, I believe, is what eroded our love of a lifetime. In her eyes I was a failure and I could do nothing right. In my eyes this wasn't exactly true. I was doing my best, but my best was not good enough. I was damned if I did and damned if I didn't.

There are mornings in my new home when I wake up and don't feel so good – but I'm genuinely surprised by how few. Denise is a great listener and somewhere along the way she has filled my emptiness with words of wisdom and genuine care. She hasn't had the best time lately – being 'the other woman' is not the easiest of labels to live with. But our channels of communication are open – I hear her and she hears me. Now when I look in the mirror I see a man in transition. My biggest regret will always be that first drink I took in my twenties, because it really is the first drink that steals your control over life – and I allowed that to happen.

I know that in order to have my new beginning – for Elaine and our children to have their new beginnings – I have had to be the one to force the ending. It's probably the bravest thing I've ever done in my life, but I certainly don't deserve any medals or caps. I'm no hero on the home-front. Ironic, isn't it? Eighty-six caps defending my country and yet so many years of being clueless as to how to defend myself in the big wide world.

Today I have lost my home and much of all I hold dear to me. I guess I deserve it. But I hope to God I can one day win it back.

For now I will continue to build my new career in the game I love and the game that seems to love me. The Beautiful Game. I enjoy sharing my views and expertise and I really enjoyed coaching the boys in China – perhaps I can do more of that with our British boys. You could say the world's my lobster. But all I really want is to be happy and try to help those I love to find happiness.

Now that *would* cap it all.

APPENDIX A

MY CAPS

Listed below – in date order – are my record-breaking eighty-six caps.

1. Under-21s match.
2. 23 May 1979, my England debut – England v Wales, Home Championship at Wembley, drew 0–0.
3. 12 June 1979, England B in Austria.
4. 22 November 1979, England v Bulgaria, European Championship, won 2–0.
5. 6 February 1980, England v Republic of Ireland, European Championship qualifier at Wembley, won 2–0. The goal-scoring power of Kevin Keegan was clear. It was the debut of Bryan Robson. I was playing against David O'Leary, Liam Brady and Frank Stapleton – two of my soon-to-be teammates. Unfortunately, Brady left Arsenal just months before I joined.
6. 13 May 1980, England v Argentina at Wembley, won 3–1. I was 21 years old and playing against the 17-year-old Maradona. It was a phenomenal match. Maradona did not make a single mistake – just brilliant. A real battle and an amazing experience.

7. 17 May 1980, England v Wales, lost 4–0. I came on as a sub for Phil Neal. The match was played at the Racecourse Ground at Wrexham. It's after this match I became established as England's number one left-back.

8. 20 May 1980, England v Ireland, at Wembley, drew 1–1.

9. 24 May 1980, England v Scotland at Hampden Park, Glasgow, won 2–0.

10. 12 June 1980, England v Belgium at Studio Communale, Turin, Italy, drew 1–1.

11. 15 June 1980, England v Italy at Communale, Turin, Italy, lost 1–0.

    (All of *the above were played while I was still at Palace*)

12. 15 October 1980, England v Romania in the 23 August Stadium, Bucharest. (World Cup qualifier). Hard for England's defence to cope, lost 2–1.

13. 19 November 1980, England v Switzerland at Wembley, won 2–1.

14. 25 March 1981, England v Spain (friendly) at Wembley, lost 1–2.

15. 29 April 1981, England v Romania (World Cup qualifier) at Wembley, drew 0–0.

16. 12 May 1981, England v Brazil (friendly) at Wembley, lost 1–0.

17. 20 May 1981, England v Wales (Home Championship) at Wembley, drew 0–0.

18. 23 May 1981, England v Scotland (Home Championship) at Wembley, lost 1–0.

19. 30 May 1981, England v Switzerland at St Jakob Stadium, Basle, lost 2–0.

20. 9 September 1981, Norway v England in Oslo, lost 2–1.

21. 23 February 1982, England v Northern Ireland at Wembley, won 4–0.

22. 27 April 1982, England v Wales at Cardiff, won 1–0.

23. 25 May 1982, England v Holland at Wembley, won 2–0.

24. 29 May 1982, England v Scotland at Hampden Park, won 1–0.

25. 3 June 1982, England v Finland at Helsinki in the Olympic Stadium, won 4–1.

26. 16 June 1982, World Cup finals, Group Phase One, England v France in Bilbao, won 3–1.

27. 20 June 1982, World Cup finals. Group Phase One. England v Czechoslovakia in the San Mamés Stadium, Bilbao, won 2–0.

28. 29 June 1982, World Cup finals, Group Phase One, England v West Germany at the Bernabéu Stadium, Madrid, drew 0–0.

29. 5 July 1982, World Cup finals, Group B Phase Two, England v Spain at the Bernabéu Stadium, Madrid, drew 0–0.

30. 22 September 1982, England v Denmark (European Championship qualifier) in Copenhagen, drew 2–2.

31. 13 October 1982, England v W Germany at Wembley, lost 2–1.

32. 17 November 1982, England v Greece at the Kaftanzoglio Stadium in Thessaloniki, won 3–0.

33. 15 December 1982, England v Luxembourg at Wembley, 9–0.

34. 30 March 1983, England v Greece (European Championship qualifier) at Wembley, drew 0–0.

35. 27 April 1983, England v Hungary (European Championship qualifier) at Wembley, won 2–0.

36. 28 May 1983, England v N Ireland (Home Championship) at Windsor Park, Belfast, drew 0–0.

37. 1 June 1983, England v Scotland (Home Championship) at Wembley, won 2–0.

38. 21 September 1983, England v Denmark (European Championship qualifier) at Wembley, lost 1–0.

39. 16 November 1983, Luxembourg v England in the City Stadium in Luxembourg, won 4–1.

40. 29 February 1983, France v England at the Parc des Princes Stadium, Paris, lost 2–0.

41. 26 May 1984, England v Scotland (Home Championship) at Hampden Park, Glasgow, drew 1–1.

42. 2 June 1984, England v USSR at Wembley, lost 2–0.

43. 10 June 1984, Brazil v England in the Americana Stadium in Rio de Janeiro, won 2–0. During this friendly Renato gave me a hard time, but we played well and deserved the victory.

44. 13 June 1984, Uruguay v England (friendly) at the Centenary Stadium in Montevideo, lost 2–0.

45. 17 June 1984, Chile v England (friendly) at the National Stadium, Santiago, drew 0–0.

46. 12 September 1984, England v E Germany (friendly) at Wembley, won 1–0.

47. 17 October 1984 England v Finland (World Cup qualifier) at Wembley, won 5–0.

48. 14 November 1984, Turkey v England (World Cup qualifier) at the Inönü Stadium, Istanbul, won 8–0.

49. 27 February 1985, N Ireland v England (World Cup qualifier) at Windsor Park, Belfast, won 1–0.

50. 26 March 1985, England v Republic of Ireland (friendly) at Wembley, won 2–1.

51. 1 May 1985, Romania v England (World Cup qualifier) at the 23 August Stadium, Bucharest, drew 0–0.

52. 22 May 1985, Finland v England (World Cup qualifier) at the Olympic Stadium in Helsinki, drew 1–1.

53. 25 May 1985, Scotland v England (Rous Cup) at Hampden Park, Glasgow, lost 1–0.

54. 6 June 1985, Italy v England (Aztec 2000: three-team tournament) in Azteca Stadium, Mexico City, lost 2–1.

55. 9 June 1985, Mexico v England (tournament as above) in the Azteca Stadium, lost 1–0.

56. 12 June 1985, West Germany v England (friendly) at the Azteca Stadium, won 3–0.

57. 16 June 1985, USA v England (friendly) in the Coliseum Stadium in Los Angeles, won 5–0.

58. 11 September 1985, England v Romania (World Cup qualifier) at Wembley, drew 1–1.

59. 16 October 1985, England v Turkey (World Cup qualifier) at Wembley, won 5–0.

60. 13 November 1985, England v N Ireland (World Cup qualifier) at Wembley, drew 0–0.

61. 29 January 1986, England v Egypt (friendly) in the Nasser Stadium, Cairo, won 4–0.

62. 26 February 1986, Israel v England (friendly) at the Ramat Gan Stadium, Tel Aviv, won 2–1.

63. 26 March 1986, USSR v England (friendly) at the Dinamo Stadium, Tbilisi, won 1–0.

64. 23 April 1986, England v Scotland (Rous Cup) at Wembley Stadium, won 2–1.

65. 17 May 1986, Mexico v England (friendly) at the Coliseum Stadium in Los Angeles, won 3–0.

66. 24 May 1986, Canada v England (friendly) at the Swangard Stadium, Vancouver, won 1–0.

67. 3 June 1986, Portugal v England (World Cup Group F, Mexico) in the Tecnológico Stadium, Monterrey, lost 1–0.

68. 6 June 1986, Morocco v England (World Cup Group F, Mexico) in the Tecnológico Stadium, Monterrey, drew 0–0.

69. 11 June 1986, England v Poland (World Cup Group F, Mexico) at the Universitario Stadium, Monterrey, won 3–0.

70. 18 June 1986, Paraguay v England (World Cup second round) at the Azteca Stadium, Mexico City, won 3–1.

71. 22 June 1986, Argentina v England (World Cup quarterfinal) in the Azteca Stadium, Mexico City, lost 2–1.

72. 10 September 1986, England v Sweden (friendly) at Söderstadion, Stockholm, lost 1–0.

73. 15 October 1986, England v N Ireland (European Championships qualifier) at Wembley, won 3–0.

74. 12 November 1986, England v Yugoslavia (European Championships qualifier) at Wembley, won 2–0.

75. 18 February 1987, Spain v England (friendly) at Bernabéu Stadium, Madrid, won 4–2.

76. 1 April 1987, N Ireland v England (European Championships qualifier) at Windsor Park, Belfast, won 2–0.

77. 29 April 1987, Turkey v England (European Championships qualifier) at Ataturk Stadium, Izmir, drew 0–0.

78. 9 December 1987, West Germany v England (friendly) at the Rhein Stadium, Düsseldorf, lost 3–1.

79. 14 October 1987, England v Turkey (European Championships qualifier) at Wembley, won 8–0. The poor old Turks had already been beaten 8–0 at their own stadium 3 years earlier.

80. 11 November 1987, Yugoslavia v England (European Championships qualifier) in Belgrade, won 4–1.

81. 23 March 1988, England v Holland (friendly) at Wembley, drew 2–2.

82. 21 May 1988, England v Scotland (Rous Cup) at Wembley, won 1–0.

83. 24 May 1988, England v Columbia (friendly) at Wembley, drew 1–1.

84. 28 May 1988, Switzerland v England (friendly) at the Slade Olympique, Lausanne, won 1–0.

85. 12 June 1988, Republic of Ireland v England (Euro 88) at the Neckar Stadium, Stuttgart, West Germany, lost 1–0.

86. 18 June 1988, USSR v England (Euro 88) in the Wald Stadium, Frankfurt, lost 3–1.

Nobody is indispensable. All players, whether mediocre, great or exceptional, find themselves surplus to requirements some day. That day, for me, came on 18 June 1988.

I would have liked to have gone out on a high, but the reality of anyone's career, whether in sport or not, is that one day it will come to an end.

Now I am left with some medals in my cabinet and some photographs on my walls, but most importantly a heart full of terrific memories of when I played for England. I am grateful, honoured, and very, very lucky.

APPENDIX B

INFORMATION FOR ADDICTS

A common thread lies behind all addictions. It is the mindset of the addict that needs to change to allow them to move away from rigid thinking patterns that keep them stuck in destructive behaviour.

Below are some helpful tips to beat the demons.

Habits: These begin way back in our early childhood – understanding the reasons behind habitual behaviour breaks down harmful repetition. But habits need to be respected and cannot be thrown out of the window, but coaxed slowly down the stairs and shown the door.

Repeating patterns: these are extremely powerful. Once you understand this truth and become more self-aware you can choose to stop living in the past. Change is not as difficult as you think – not if you have a new way of 'being' waiting in the wings.

Defensive obstacles: These can and must be understood and removed. We continually put up obstacles (reasons) for not moving forward (procrastination). Once the negative reasons have been pushed out of our path, we have a clearing through which we can walk forward into positivity.

Attitude: Life is all about attitude, and life is difficult. Get your head around that and you can achieve anything you want. Remember: you need tools in your emotional toolbox to help you cope with whatever life throws at you. Contrary to popular belief, the more times you try to stop, the more likely you are to succeed. If you think about it, this makes sense. Remember: the difference between success and failure is this – you can fall down time and time again, but you must get up again and again. Failure is about staying down and success about getting up. So *get up*. Giving up your addiction is much easier than you ever imagined, and life free from addiction is like being a millionaire.

Willpower: Some people naturally have lots while others have very little. Most people fall in the space between. Tell yourself you have more willpower and it will happen.

Frustration: There is a state of mind called LFT – low frustration tolerance. The aim is to gain more control over your tolerance levels. This is a skill that takes some time to acquire and is a useful tool in helping to lower and manage one's anger levels.

Satisfaction: To sit for a while with the sense of satisfaction of a job well done is often overlooked, especially by people who are hard on themselves and expect ridiculous levels of perfection. Perfection is unattainable.

Midas touch: Addictions derive from a natural phenomenon. We instinctively seek or crave 'natural highs' – often chasing natural highs like those we experienced during childhood: the thrill of winning a running race at school; the euphoria of falling in love for the very first time; the ecstatic feeling of belonging in a team; or the buzz from winning a place in the football (or other) team. This natural high is very addictive and we fear losing it. We are living in an era where 'instant gratification' is expected. We don't seem to be able to wait for our needs to be satisfied, but LFT clicks in and we want everything *now*. Addiction is the quick fix. We win the instant high – but the price to be paid is higher. We *can't* have it all, and this is the biggest myth of all time.

Addiction: Don't misunderstand your addiction. It is easier to give up than you imagine. Human beings are supposed to survive. Physical withdrawal is not as unbearable as we imagine – the difficult part is getting our mind around the fact that we *can* cope with difficult life situations. Don't misunderstand your imagination – the part of your mindset that creates (or keeps you stuck in) your suffering. Don't underestimate 'addiction' – it thinks it is as clever as you are, especially if you hand over the control. You cannot outthink addiction, but there *are* successful ways of beating it. Addiction may feel like your friend, but it's really your enemy. *Is the price of addiction higher than you want to pay?* I think so.

Kenny in the Mirror, by Anna Wright

APPENDIX C

IN PRAISE OF KENNY

GEORGE GRAHAM: 'At times, Kenny could barely stand on his right foot. But his left foot was a different matter. He was, quite simply, a left-footed, left-back genius. When I look back at my time managing the Arsenal in the eighties I wonder how much more we could have achieved had my team not been boozing so much. Don't get me wrong – they gave their all: Kenny, Tony Adams, Paul Merson and the others – but their activities off the pitch *must* have had a detrimental effect on their overall performances. Tony and Paul have spoken about their battles with addictions – now it's Kenny's turn to tell his story. Well done, Kenny.'

TONY ADAMS, summer 2007: 'A few months ago I saw Kenny talking on Sky, and I felt sad. As a pundit he said all the right things. He knows his stuff and, being sharp and funny, he has the personality to deliver. But I was also acutely aware of how lonely he looked. I know about that lonely place. In "life" terms, Kenny and I were similar. I grew from boy to man in my forties. Now it's Kenny's time. I am relieved he eventually came into treatment. I just hope he doesn't relapse.'

PETER KAY, chief executive, Sporting Chance Clinic: 'Never a month went by without Tony [Adams] asking, "Has Kenny Sansom called yet?" When he called in the spring of 2007 there was a huge sense of relief. Yet we were also nervous about his ability to stay sober and stop gambling. It's not easy to give up habits of a lifetime. It takes courage. But if Kenny can put as much hard work and determination into his recovery as he did playing football for England and Arsenal he will be a winner all over again. He has proved he has great leadership skills; now he has to take charge of his life.'

TERRY VENABLES: 'I advised Kenny, "If you're writing your book, do the second half first." If only we could live the second half of our lives before we had to tackle the first 30 tricky years. I have no doubt whatsoever that he has the second half of his career ahead of him.

He has the knowledge and skills to coach or manage top-flight teams, and the personality to work in the media. The world's your lobster, Ken, so, in the words of Del Boy, El Tel says, "Bonnet de douche, King Kenny."'

PETER TAYLOR, former England Under-21 manager, caretaker manager of the full squad (where he gave David Beckham his first cap) and Crystal Palace player and manager, now at Stevenage: 'Being 5 years older than Kenny, I was a senior player when he joined Palace as a young boy. I was immediately struck by his tremendous talent and it was clear from day one he was going to be special. Kenny joined us back in the late seventies when "The Eagles", under the management of Malcolm Allison, were referred to as the "Golden Boys". In a sense, Kenny was too good for our team – he was out of his league. Consequently, we began to rely heavily on him – rather as the recent Arsenal team began to rely on Thierry Henry. Terry Venables was right to sell him to one of the massive clubs. It was where he belonged.'

IN PRAISE OF KENNY

TOM WATT, actor, author and BBC broadcaster: 'Kenny Sansom is a class act. As an ardent Arsenal and England fan, I have followed the career of this great left-back for many years. I always loved the way he just nicked the ball and sprinted off in attack, leaving his bewildered opponents standing. His defensive skills ensured clean team sheets and pristine white shorts. He never got down and dirty – he didn't need to. I believe he was the greatest Arsenal left-back *ever*. Nowadays, I love his work as a pundit. He has never lost his love of football, and this comes across.'

KARL HOWMAN, actor, director and TV personality: 'After watching Kenny's skills on the pitch for many a year, I was delighted when we became personal friends. Both family men, we have had some hilarious times, along with my other great pal, Ray Winstone. I'm sure Kenny will recount these stories in what I'm certain will be a fantastic autobiography. I, for one, can't wait to read it.'